# THE POWER OF PLAY

For over twenty-five years the Caplans have been pioneers in the field of educational playthings. They have introduced play sculpture to the American playground movement, initiated lab learning in mathematics and science, and simulation game play in social studies and geography.

FRANK CAPLAN is a graduate of the College of the City of New York. He holds a master's degree in philosophy of education from Teacher's College, Columbia University.

THERESA CAPLAN, a collector of folk toys of the world, is presently engaged in cataloging books and toys for inclusion in Museum of Fantasy and Play.

# THE
# POWER
# OF
# *PLAY*

BY
FRANK AND THERESA
CAPLAN

ANCHOR BOOKS
Anchor Press/Doubleday
Garden City, New York

*The Power of Play* was published in a hardcover edition by Anchor Press/Doubleday in 1973.
Anchor Books Edition: 1974

Portions of Lawrence K. Frank's article "Play Is Valid" appeared in *Childhood Education* magazine in March 1968 and are reprinted courtesy of *Childhood Education*, Journal of the Association for Childhood Education.

Selections on "What Is a Toy?" appeared in *Play Orbit*, published by Studio International of New York and London and are reprinted courtesy of the publisher.

The authors also gratefully acknowledge permission to use photographs supplied by the following:

Childcraft Equipment Company of New York City for photos 16 and 21.

Community Playthings of Rifton, New York, for photos 18, 19, 22, and 30.

Edcom Systems, Inc. of Princeton, New Jersey, for photos 5, 6, 8–13, and 32–36.

Bill Housell for photo 24.

Elaine Miller for photo 31.

Questor Education Products Company, Bronx, New York, for photo 7.

Ullie Steltzer for photos 1–4, 14, 15, 17, 20, 23, and 25–29.

155, 4
C244p
1974

Many of our insights were garnered from diverse experiences with sensitive people who shared their scholarly wisdom on play and learning with us, from correspondence with countless "Creative Playthings" parents who encouraged our pioneering efforts in playthings and play, and from warm association with playful industrial designers and concerned toy manufacturers who translated exciting play concepts into tangible toys and equipment.

We are especially grateful to that hardy band of preschool and nursery educators who, over the past fifty years, guarded the autonomy and play of young children and built support for the use of play as a powerful growing and learning technique.

Our sincere thanks go to Loretta Barrett, our editor at Anchor Press, for suggesting that we write our book.

We are obliged, too, to copy editor Georgiana Remer for her painstaking work on our manuscript and to the many other Doubleday & Company staff members who helped see it through to completion.

*Frank* AND *Theresa Caplan*

*November* 1972

# Contents

ILLUSTRATED

# Introduction

## The Extraordinary Power of Play

We aim to present a hypothesis of such far-reaching implications that no parent, pediatrician, educator, sociologist, or politician can afford to ignore it. It is our intention to present data that will substantiate our premise that the power of play is all-pervasive. We invite our readers to examine the power of play with us so that we might garner for child play the prestige and wholehearted public support it deserves and must have.

We will set forth how play serves children, and even adults; how it can help to strengthen personality, encourage interpersonal relations, further creativity and the joy of living, and advance learning. We will trace the nature of play and playthings; how one can set the stage for creative play; how play is used to help the emotionally disturbed child; how it reveals the strengths and weaknesses of a child as well as his desires and satisfactions. Although we run the risk of taxing our readers with repetition, we must take them afresh through the various ages and stages of development in order adequately to illustrate the many basic facets of growing, learning, and living inherent in the play process.

We will also explore the ideas of some of the early pioneers of play who used play as a dynamic tool in child development and education and in play therapy. Imbued as we are with the vitality and validity of play, we will ourselves play with some bold ideas by presenting some of our own notions about how the power of play might change the drive, initiative, and goals even of nations.

*We believe the power of play to be extraordinary and supremely serious.* Play is a child's way of life practically from infancy to his eighth year. The young child plays from early morning until he goes to sleep at night. It is the most natural way for a child to use his capacities, to grow, and to learn many skills. What is it that gives play its exceptional power?

*Playtime aids growth.* It takes time to grow, a childtime to experience the magic of one's own growth and development. A child needs sufficient time to find his place in the culture. In time, he learns the rudiments of control and responsibility and forms useful habits. Through his play a child gains the time he needs to gratify his basic needs. Our society is tender with the young child and gives him the playtime to imitate, to explore, to find himself, and to test his ideas.

An important by-product of play is the feeling of strength it gives a child, a relief from the sense of powerlessness that many children experience as junior members of a well-ordered adult society. In play, children are afforded opportunities to counteract this helplessness to some extent. Like nothing else, play gives every child a chance to lay plans, to judge what is best in each play situation, and to create and control the sequence of events.

*Play is a voluntary activity.* It is intensely personal. Self-powered, it embodies a high degree of motivation and achievement. It is a happy activity which begins in delight and ends in wisdom. The child puts his ideas and feelings into action as he plays. Play is an autonomous pursuit through which each child assimilates the outside world to the support of his ego. Because of the self-choice inherent in play, each child builds confidence in his own powers. Feelings of autonomy and competency help a child function effectively as an active agent in his environment, not merely a reacting one.

In his play world, the young child is the decision-maker and the play-master. There are no superimposed directions to follow, no rigid rules to which to adhere. In the academic environment, a child is usually called upon to perform according to set patterns. The teacher does the directing, and the child has no choice but to follow. In the play world, on the other hand, the sensitive adult intervenes tactfully, if at all.

The more thoughtfully and flexibly organized the play environment, the more confident the child becomes. His outgrowth of drive and self-esteem is the result of years of engrossing, satisfying play in home and preschool. Like nothing else, play develops a child's ego as it builds his will power.

*Play offers a child freedom of action.* Play is always free in the sense that the child wants to perform each act for its own sake and for its immediate results. In his play world, the child can carry on trial-and-error activities without fear of ridicule or failing. Free from restrictive adult interference, he can pretend and role-play any adult or animal character, any real or imagined thing or situation.

Play and fantasy are a vital need of childhood for which opportunities need to be provided if a child is to be healthy and happy. In play, there are two forms of the will to power: that which consists of learning to do things and that which comprises fantasy. Every normal child likes to pretend to be a giant, a lion, or a train. In his make-believe, he inspires terror and gains a sense of power. However, his pretending does not keep the child's play from proceeding with the utmost seriousness. The contrast between his make-believe and earnestness is so fluid that a child considers play a real-life experience.

*Play provides an imaginary world a child can master.* Every child is born with the desire to affect his environment. In a well-planned play world in which the real world has been brought down to manageable size, the child can manipulate and maneuver it to suit his own whims. He can try his talents for structuring life. He can take glorious flights into the wide, wonderful realm of his imagination. Play is a voluntary system that admits both reality and fantasy. The child is in full control! Play gives a child the feeling of his own power, of "being ten feet tall."

In the ideal play setting, a child can initiate an action or oppose it. He can be the subject or the object. Wherever his play impulse leads him, that is the way to go. There is freedom of choice and action and an absence of boundaries and restrictions that we cannot grant him in the adult world.

*Play has elements of adventure in it.* It has uncertainty and challenge which activate exploratory examination and a child's spontaneous sense of wonder. A child exults in surrounding his play with an air of secrecy. In his play, the ordinary laws of life do not count; his play is larger than life. A child will frequently reverse the normal state of affairs. There are new combinations and new procedures that sometimes are irrelevant to the end result. This making of an image of something different is an exercise in imagination and creativity.

*Play provides a base for language building.* The earliest years are non-verbal years. Words come only from a foundation of play experiences, from encounters with people, objects, and events which make up our world. Sensory play experiences are required to permit a child to make perceptual discoveries of long and short, loud and faint, high and low, round and square, hard and soft, and smooth and rough. The concept of the sequence of sizes comes from play with color cones and other fitting toys and from handling assorted pots, pans, and utensils. Multiple images provide an inner schema and help words come into use. Then vocabulary grows. Play nourishes reflective thinking, associative memory, and the naming and labeling necessary for the eventual mastery of reading.

*Play has unique power for building interpersonal relations.* Play provides contacts with others without demanding inappropriate adjustments. Play also promotes the formation of special social groupings, each with their attendant ceremonies to highlight differences from everyday happenings. Play is the most pliant medium for feeling one's way, for understanding one's environment.

Not all play, however, is directed to exploring the physical world or practicing new skills. Much of it is social in direction and permits the child to fit himself into his social world. All the important people in a child's world figure in his play. He imitates, symbolizes, and becomes. Pushing a boat around lets the child play the role of the captain as well as of the boat. A doll, to a little child, can become a mother, a nurse, or a witch. By acting out the happenings in his life, frustrations are often brought out into the open, and even unpleasant experiences can be reduced to controllable size. The arrival of a new baby, the death of someone close, a hospital experience—all call for materials for dramatic play to enable a child to give expression to his feelings as a preliminary to his mastering them.

Play fosters group life since it often requires more than one child to re-enact home and community life situations. Through such play, a child practices interpersonal relationships with his equals and learns consideration as well as techniques of leadership.

Spontaneous dramatization, role-playing, doll play, and disguises enable a child to work out interpersonal relations, personality difficulties, and emotional disturbances. It takes years of play with its varied interpersonal relationships to make a child a social being.

*Play offers opportunities for mastery of the physical self.* Preschool children relish play that gives them facility in locomotion and permits the maximum use of energy. They learn bodily control through active physical play: running, jumping, skipping, pushing, pulling, hopping, climbing, balancing, throwing, and keeping up with one's own age group. Fun and exhilaration are components of physical play, and coordination and agility which are necessary to the learning process are enhanced. The discovery of spatial relations, the many patterns in space made by a moving body, is a fundamental concept. Laterality and directionality—left and right, up and down, and behind and in front relationships—are incorporated in every physical play program. There is in physical play activity for its own sake, as well as opportunity for self-validation of one's skills.

*Play furthers interest and concentration.* A child is his own agent for learning as he plays. His power of concentration and his sharp interest in the here-and-now world give evidence that play builds and expands will power and attention span.

In play, children have a natural urge to explore and discover. They find pleasure in this and, therefore, it is self-perpetuating. A child can play for hours with his building blocks and repeat building experiences without obvious incentives. He will become totally involved and find it difficult to tear himself away. No one has to be forced to play!

Watch a five-year-old learn a new language while in a new country. If he is sent to a formal school, presented a few new words at a time, drilled in pronunciation, taught grammar, given homework, and tested periodically, the learning is painful and slow, and interest wanes. Now allow the same child to play freely with the neighborhood children, without formal language instruction, and see how he learns the new language in two or three months. In play there are no inhibitions, no self-consciousness, and no rigidity. Play creates complete involvement. It carries the child along, letting him respond and communicate freely.

*Play is the way children investigate the material world.* From infancy, children reconcile their inner lives with the external realities of the world. Their interest in the material elements may not always be scientific, but the desire to understand and control leads them to much investigation, invention, and creation. Whether they tear down or build up, they still learn about the properties of things and thus formulate rudimentary concepts of weight, height, volume, texture, et cetera. Such elemental materials as sand, water, clay, and wood are especially attractive to young children, and their manipulation results in a concentration and inventiveness few adults can match. Manufactured materials of varied shapes, colors, and textures also evoke imaginative creating and learning.

*Play is a way of learning adult roles.* In early imitative play children re-create the behavior, attitudes, and language of the important adults in their lives. Play may be considered a rehearsal for adult roles and anticipatory to adult life. Boys and girls play out community worker roles and enact housekeeping and mothering chores. As they play out these adult roles, they are applauded by adults. After many years of free play, more mature expectations and performance are demanded. After adult forms of behavior are mastered, the child is considered to be ready to take his place in grown-up society.

*Play is always a dynamic way of learning.* The layers of meaning implanted by play often include conscious organization of the environment, exploration of physical and social relationships, and deep levels of fantasy. A young child's perceptions of reality often grow out of his fantasy play. Self-activity and experiencing are still a young child's best means of learning and acquiring facts. Facts are best maintained when they are understood and used. Much verbal learning bewilders young children because it usually outruns their experience.

*Play refines a child's judgments.* It is the very young child's only way to exercise his innermost feelings and thoughts. The young child lacks sufficient imagery or words, as well as experiences to clarify his thoughts or to reason abstractly. He needs countless and varied "doing" experiences—handling, classifying, ordering, patterning, matching, measuring—to illuminate and enrich his thinking about the attributes of objects and his world. Through his play, he analyzes how things work and what they can be made to do.

*Academics can be structured into play.* Mathematics, science, geography, foreign languages, et cetera—all can be integrated into play so that a child can grasp and use concepts. The energy a child expends in his play far surpasses that which he gives to formal learning. Actually, learning has always been closer to play than to work. It is closer to the pursuit of knowledge for its own sake than to required reading or study. In essence, play is a lifelong education.

*Play is vitalizing.* The act of play has important neurophysiological effects on children, as well as adults. Play is a diversion from routines, from cultural demands and pursuits. It transcends ordinary behavior. For a period of time, play permits one to reverse one's behavior and do the opposite of what one has been doing. It is an "upside-downing of behavior," as Professor Edward Norbeck of Rice University terms it, "during which the social hierarchy is inverted and customary rules of conduct are suspended." These rites of reversal turn out to be important safety valves for the release of feelings of aggression, disapproval of authority, and resolving other conflicts. With social approval, they can become opportunities for aesthetic expression and invention, as in art, the dance, festivals, and so forth.

Play is essential to the survival of humans. It deserves a place of honor in our scheme of things and should be put to broad social use.

*If play has such positive power, why is it not valued in today's life schema?* In the United States, as well as elsewhere, puritanical influence has dictated that play and learning are not synonymous. Play is placed at one end of the value scale, with learning and work at the other. Play and playthings have been called "the companions of a lonely childhood," "a way of keeping a child out of mischief," "the discharge of a superabundance of vital energy," "the imitative instinct," "the outlet for harmful impulses," and so on, in the same general vein.

We have been conditioned to think of play and seriousness as antitheses. Most educators make a sharp distinction between academic work and play. They relegate all play to the preschool period and all work to the primary and secondary school years. Few educators, even today, readily consider play as the art of learning. A sharp line is drawn between the kindergarten and first grade. The formalization that enters upon the scene removes all semblance of free choice, self-direction, exploration, and self-discovery. The rigidity of the set curriculum demands that autonomy and decision making be turned over to the authority of the teacher. Teaching replaces self-discovery, hatred of school replaces love of learning. The school supplants the environment of preschool play—which the child can manipulate and affect—with a setting he can no longer control. School bells restrict personal research; stationary desks prevent gross motor exercise; large classes curtail freedom. Mastery of overwhelming and often unrelated subject matter replaces insightful experimenting. The reading of texts and recording of the conclusions of others are emphasized to the detriment of self-learning. The child who feels that he can no longer influence his environment soon loses interest. He ceases to be responsive to academic learning. As a result, he may often require expensive, intensive remedial attention.

Formal education, as practiced today, will have nothing to do with the advocacy of the tremendous learning power of play. Since Sputnik I, the so-called educational reformers have offered only "the grim certainty that we play at our own peril; that the Russian students don't play around, and neither should we!" Yet circumscribed curriculums have not succeeded in winning children over to a love of learning nor to excitement for the mathematics, science, and other subject fields so essential to our dizzily changing and advancing technology.

Recent studies by eminent psychologists and educational researchers indicate that by eight years of age—the end of the most intense period of play—a child's personality, character, creativity, and academic motivation are 80 per cent accomplished, that the subsequent years enlarge the content but often do little to increase personal commitment or interest in learning. The research of Dr. Benjamin S. Bloom of the University of Chicago has established the validity of the proposition that the period of the most rapid growth in learning achievement and growth in certain personality traits occur during the age span encompassed by infancy, toddlerdom, the nursery school, and the kindergarten—when children are apt to be playing, not studying. By the time a child goes to grade school, some of the most important things that ever happen to him are already behind him.

There are those scholars who question the power of play because there is as yet no definitive research on the effects of play on the educative process. Although there is ample research on the influence of play on monkeys, rodents, and dogs, the researchers maintain that this has no direct bearing on human learning. We say that play cannot be discounted until research ascertains its powers. It is timely that we give new meaning to play, not only in childhood but in adulthood as well. It is time to study as thoroughly the tools of play as we research the tools of learning. It takes a skilled hand to set the stage for spontaneous play and to know how to guide it unobtrusively.

Take any book on the philosophy of education and check the index to see if it contains the word "play." You may find "Plato," but rarely "play." Many philosophers have assumed that man's ability to survive has been a tenacious contest. Actually, man has prevailed because he was more playful and steadfast than other creatures. In an article that appeared in the 1967 issue of *Think*, Eric Hoffer had this to say: "Whenever you trace the origin of a skill or practices which played a crucial role in the ascent of man, we usually reach the realm of play." Every utilitarian device, according to Mr. Hoffer, has evolved from some non-utilitarian pursuit or the pastime of play. For example, the wheel, the sail, and the brick were probably invented in the course of play, and although the Aztecs did not have the wheel, their playthings had rollers for movement. Thus play has been man's most useful preoccupation. Man as an artist is infinitely more ancient than man as worker. Man has made his greatest progress when not grubbing for necessities, when nature was so bountiful that he had the leisure to play and the inclination to tinker. It is the child in man that is the source of his creativeness.

We have tried to make clear throughout this book that we are discussing play and education as we know it in the United States and are addressing ourselves to all those parents and professionals who have some awareness of the power of play. It is our hope that our presentation will arouse interest in others. So little research on the subject of play is available that it has not been possible for us to document each one of our propositions. Had we waited for such research, this book never would have been written.

# THE POWER OF *PLAY*

# CHAPTER ONE

# The Body-Building
# Power of Play

*Physical activity is a prime aspect of play.* Children use their bodies when they follow their natural impulses to run and shout, skip and hop, jump and climb, and so on. The more a child uses all his muscles, the greater will be his physical and emotional release and his growth and enjoyment of life. Physical play frees children to practice their motor skills and test their derring-do. It enables them to discover their physical selves and their power to affect the world in which they live.

All play is active and, in most instances, is associated with bodily activity. It can be unco-ordinated, as in the haphazard (sideswiping) movements of an infant. Most psychologists define this as an early form of play and the practice of infantile sensori-motor powers. An infant enjoys trying out his capacities and gets great joy from repeating physical movements until he masters them. Associated with such physical activity is vocal expression. At first, however, the infant's sounds are unco-ordinated. Children of all ages shout with glee at some physical (or other) accomplishment. There are those who term this "letting off steam"; we call it the child's way of expressing pure delight in his bodily power to achieve.

Physical activity is used, too, to express exasperation and even rage. A child who kicks at a stone or brandishes a bat in the air finds relief in the use of his body. Some children use sports, or hammering, or beating a drum to assuage tension or release excess energy. Children also use rhythms and experiment with bodily motions and musical sounds to express themselves. Rhythm and music can be a direct play way to give form to shapeless emotions.

There is natural individual progression in maturation. If suitable environmental stimuli are provided exactly when the child's powers are ready for them, the learning is more intense and inclusive than when each one is offered at a later time. Thus we say there are sensitive periods during which greater plasticity for gaining control of one's body and learning are in operation. The periods actually begin at birth. Parental intervention and play stimulation can encourage advancement in bodily growth, sensory awareness, and intellectual growth. Each physical maturation level brings out a different set of bodily skills that each child appears to have an innate need to practice. The number of environmental inputs that can influence these skills can be infinite since the general capacity of each child is unknown. Because physical changes come more often in the earliest years, flexibility in mastering skills is greatest then.

*Many bodily conditions must be right so a child can play and learn.* Good health and nutrition and physical maturing are basic to the mental, emotional, and social development of a child and set the stages and limits of his activities. Sheer physical energy and exuberance must be nurtured if a child is to be able to do what is before him day by day. To increase his physical aptitudes, a child requires an orderly sequence of play experiences appropriate to his advancing size, strength, and skills. Parents need to provide fully for their children's complete development in the first years before they are subject to the restrictions and coercions of formal schooling.

All this entails a wide variety of physical and sensory experiences, visual and auditory as well as tactile. A child needs to have increasing muscular dexterity so he can relate directly to his own body and also cope with the physical dimensions of the world in which he lives. He has to have an acceptable image of his own body so he can feel at ease in his own skin. His good control of his body is one important way he can feel good about himself and about life. The more adept he becomes at controlling his body, the more a child feels a full and satisfying sense of his autonomy. Much play is sheer physical activity. A child experiences total enjoyment as he learns and practices mastery over his own movements.

*Mothering is the best first plaything the newborn can have.* Dr. Margaret Mead, world-renowned anthropologist and teacher, in her fascinating book *Family,* presents this succinctly: "There is no substitute for the mothering relationship . . . During the long months of infancy, while the child's tie to the mother is a bodily one, the child learns through his own body what the world is like, and what it is to be a person. As the mother feeds the child when he is hungry, the child learns that the world can be trusted to provide the things he needs. As the mother senses her child's sleepiness and lulls him to sleep, the child learns to fit together feeling and action . . . As the mother smiles when her child smiles . . . and clucks in response to his first playful babbling, the child learns that the world is a place in which people can reciprocate moods and meaning."

The mother brings new sensory experiences to her baby. She provides the encouragement in caresses and words that allow her infant to explore his body, crib, and bath and the sights and sounds of his room. She puts her finger into his closed fist to open and grasp and exercises his arms, hands, legs, and feet lovingly. His ears, eyes, and nose are touched gently. He is carefully and playfully given his bath and his hair is patted and brushed softly. All these stimuli promote a baby's discovery of his physical self. Harmonious interactions of mother and baby produce the ego power that will lead him to continue exploring and extending his body skills and, at the same time, lay the

foundation of his will to master his environment. Self-discovery
and playfulness are thwarted when will power is lacking, and
all learning will suffer when a child feels his physical self to
be inadequate. We believe that babies are "ornery" and physically fearful when they are permitted to feel unloved and unwanted.

There is much research evidence that frustrating infant-
mother relationships, in which the baby is convinced that he
cannot affect his world or in which his needs and actions are
not met and rewarded by understanding and approbation, result inevitably in gnawing longings, hatred, and even withdrawal from the world of play and people. This is disastrous for
the child and for society. Therefore, early parent education is
called for, in which all professionals concerned with early childhood will join forces and become personally involved.

However, parental "smothering" can also hinder an infant's
self-image and achievements. Many mothers interpret the desires of their babies in ways that inhibit their physical development. The baby who seeks to move or change his position and
fusses while trying, although he may well achieve success after
some effort on his part, often causes his parent to anticipate his
needs by turning him over or changing his position too quickly.
Such an infant soon realizes that he does not have to exert
physical effort, that a little fuming will get him to the place or
into the position he wants. If a mother is constantly attentive
and "reads him" every time he cries, her infant may never learn
to crawl or go through the natural progressions of physical
activity that pediatricians believe to be necessary for every
child.

There are sequences in each child's physical action system
that he has to pass through by himself. Right from the start, he
sucks, tastes, sees, moves his hands and arms, grasps, fingers,
hears, supports his head, moves his feet. Control of the eyes
antecedes that of the fingers, head balance that of body balance,
grasping with the palm of the hand that of digital retention,
willful grasp that of voluntary release, banging that of poking,
vertical and horizontal hand movements that of the circular and

oblique, crawling usually that of creeping, pulling oneself up that of standing, and creeping usually that of upright walking. Large body movements develop first, more refined physical control comes later; for instance, the shoulder, hip, and knee move before the wrist and ankle. In this regard, it is important that little children be given appropriate toys and things to play with. They should be asked to do only what conforms to this growth pattern. In addition, gestures come before words, gibberish before speech, solitary before social play, perception before abstraction, and practical before conceptual judgment. It takes time to grow, and no one can rush growth—one can only stimulate it. Suitable toys, presented at just the right time, can play a vital part in reinforcing every healthy infant's innate push toward growth completion. Proper playthings can help the infant practice his newly discovered physical and sensory skills.

*The sensori-motor years.* Dr. Jean Piaget, professor of child psychology at the University of Geneva, describes the period from birth to two years as the "sensori-motor period." The infant moves from being a "reflexive organism" that responds in an undifferentiated way to his environment to a "relatively coherent organization of sensori-motor actions" to master and affect his immediate environment. He uses external stimulation —parents and play—and his inherent reflexes in an unreflective manner. An infant's movements lack precision. His activities, like his attention, are dominated by external stimuli.

John H. Flavell, professor of psychology at the University of Rochester, has also studied these earliest years. He points out that a child goes through six distinct maturation stages. The first lasts about a month during which the infant shows little but reflexive behavior. During the second stage, from one to four months, varied reflex activities are modified by touch, taste, and auditory experiences that co-ordinate with one another. Infants at about three months look at objects from which sounds are coming—human beings and their voices, for example—and seem to realize that they belong together. In the third stage, four to eight months, the baby begins to act toward objects and events outside his body as though they had permanency. He begins to engage in purposive activity.

Writes M. D. Vernon, professor of psychology at the University of Reading, in his book *The Psychology of Perception*, "During the fifth month, the infant flings out his hands towards an object dangling in front of him, and if it touches one of his hands, the hand may close on it. Presently, he deliberately reaches out and grasps it, and if he can, pulls it towards him and puts it in his mouth. These actions indicate that the baby is beginning to realize that if he sees something, he can also reach out and touch it; that he can move it about and try to taste it. He is learning that certain visual and touch impressions may belong together; and that by his own actions he can investigate how this happens—how something with a particular visual appearance will feel when he touches, handles, and mouths it. This is the real beginning of all the experimentation and observation which children carry out to find out what the world, and the objects in it are like." The foregoing is the start of investigative play which needs full encouragement with a proper environment and suitable tools of play.

In stage four, between eight and twelve months, the child tends to use what he has already learned in searching for objects and repeating patterns of behavior. By twelve to eighteen months, stage five, he begins to experiment. He seeks new ways to solve problems. In stage six, at eighteen months to about two years, the toddler shows the ability to grasp primitive symbol relations. He is beginning to invent solutions mentally rather than by trial and error only. Most of his intellectual development comes because he has learned to co-ordinate physically, which enables him to actively respond to his environment. Each child is dominated by the physical attributes of his environment. If parents provide propitious physical challenges and opportunities at each stage of development, they help augment their child's physical growth. Piaget calls these major learnings "schema," each scheme being an organization of interrelated actions.

Sensory powers of seeing, sucking, and smelling are present

at birth. Dr. Lewis P. Lipsitt, director of the Child Study Center at Brown University, has for some years been researching the learning capacities of neonates, using the few well-organized behaviors available to them: sucking, smelling, head turning, and blinking. He has been discovering some amazing facts. Babies with as little as fifty-five hours of experience on this earth can differentiate smells. A baby alerts to a new smell, becomes used to it, and even grows bored with some smells. The ability to smell is just one of the inborn sensory discriminations. A baby can taste at birth and has taste preferences; for example, a neonate will suck sweeter solutions faster than others and spit out bitter or sour ones. Just as with adults, taste is related to smell. Dr. Lipsitt states, "The newborn is remarkably sensitive to events in his environment, particularly those related to food intake and stimulation of the mouth." He believes that the environment and training can slow or speed a baby's development. Thus, Dr. Lipsitt manipulates the features of the environment in his research work in order to study behavioral differences in newborns. In one experiment, he found how babies learned that their sucking could make a mobile turn. In another he found that infants at six weeks could be taught to blink to a musical tone. In still another he found that rocking a baby *when he is quiet* instead of crying, forestalls crying. The traditional approach of rocking a baby only when he is cranky merely reinforces his fussing. These fascinating findings are fast demolishing the image of the "mindless" human newborn as being engulfed in a blur of impressions.

Current research indicates that an infant differentiates visually before he is six weeks old. He shows preference for particular visual patterns, fixating longer on horizontal stripes than on concentric circles. Infants also respond selectively to movement and sound. Some research findings imply that the pattern preference of the infant is for complexity and that such discrimination can occur as early as age three weeks. Children can discern colors early. They are able to do this before they can name the colors. More two-year-olds can match colors than name them. The ability to match and name colors simultaneously comes later. Infant researchers are inferring from the data collected that the human brain has built-in preference and capacity for dealing with form and pattern and that early visual stimulation is pertinent to the development of the perceptual acuity that is needed for later word learning and reading. What is highly significant is that while infants at three months or so can learn complex patterns easily, too many children above six have difficulty recognizing shapes and making word distinctions.

*Twelve to twenty-four months: the walking-talking stage.* Pediatricians and child psychologists know that the average twelve-month-old can walk with some assistance. He can lower himself from a standing to a sitting position. He can hold a pencil well enough to scribble. If a brightly colored object tied to a string is placed out of his reach but with the string near him, he will pull the string to get the object. Often he says two words in addition to "Mama" and "Dada." He understands many more words, however, as proved by his doing things he is told to do, for example, clap his hands, play "peek-a-boo" and wave "bye-bye." He can put a wooden cube into a cup if asked to do so, without any gesture being made for him to imitate. He can hold a cup to drink from. He will help to get himself dressed by holding his arms or legs appropriately. He will inhibit simple acts when so instructed, for example, when asked not to touch something specific. If he does something that makes people near him laugh, he will repeat the action to make them laugh again.

Most fifteen-month-olds can stand and walk alone. He can build a tower of two blocks. If he has two cubes in his hand and a third is placed in front of him, he will reach and grasp the third one without dropping the other two. At a younger age he usually would drop one of the first two in order to pick up the third. Some fifteen-month-olds now say three or four words and others talk expressively in a sort of jibberish. Some begin to use a spoon fairly well. Others co-operate quite effectively in being dressed.

At eighteen months he can climb onto a chair or up a flight

of not too steep stairs. He can throw a ball into a box and build a tower of three or more blocks. He can take four or more cubes without dropping those he already has. Many eighteen-month-olds scribble freely with pencil on paper or chalk on a board. When asked, he will point to his eyes, nose, or hair, which indicates that he understands what those words mean. Most eighteen-month-olds now use five or more words. He can use a spoon well to feed himself. He turns the pages of a book and looks at the pictures. He imitates the dramatic gestures of other people in his play with pleasure and laughter.

The twenty-one-month-old can walk alone for considerable distances. He can walk backward and forward, which indicates improvement in balance and the control of his limbs. If you build a tower and a bridge next to each other with his blocks, he will show that he knows the difference between them, even though he cannot yet build the bridge imitatively. He can name pictures of a common object and use two-word sentences. He verbally asks for things he wants at the table or in the bathroom. His bowel control is normally established around this time.

At twenty-four months the toddler does many more things. He not only walks, he runs! He can build a tower of six blocks. He is able to put blocks in a row to make a "choo-choo" and play with them as if they were a train. He can name at least three familiar objects and point to about five simple pictures of familiar objects when asked to do so by name. If he is of average language development, he uses many simple sentences. He enjoys listening to very short stories and nursery rhymes. He will tell others what he has seen. He delights in playing with sand and can play easy catch and toss with a ball. He can maneuver a kiddie car. The control of his bladder is now fairly constant.

Fingering, handling, and manipulating. To recapitulate, the first is one of the most rapid physical growth. The infant normally doubles his birth weight in his first five months and adds about four inches in length. By the end of his first month he can hold up his head and look straight ahead. Dr.

Arnold Gesell noted that "vision is so fundamental in the growth of the mind that the baby takes hold of the physical world with his eyes long before he takes hold with his hands. The eyes assume the lead in the patterning of behavior. But he cannot attain full acquaintance with things through his eyes alone; he must touch them with his hands as well. He must feel their impact in his palm, and move his fingers over their surfaces and edges. Movement is an essential part of sense perception."

After an infant is able to bring his thumb and other fingers together, he can grab a proffered finger and then a rattle. By the second to third month his whole body goes into action. He will reach for a rattle or teether with jerks of his legs and movements of his whole body. Soon he is able to grip the rings and shaped stems of teethers and rattles. This is when an infant should be introduced to solid forms that fit his hand and fingers and subsequently to other kinds of manageable shapes and varied textures. Such physical experiences give a baby the feel of the world. All the physical experiences he engages in give him feelings of increasing mastery and nourish his curiosity.

What kinds of things should an infant handle? Fingering and tasting go together for the baby. Thus the discovery of hardness and softness and smoothness and roughness is as much a tasting as it is a handling operation. For this reason, conscientious toy manufacturers "play it safe" and use non-toxic plastics and paints in the infant toys they produce. At the same time, parents must be careful that everything a baby handles is of such shape and material that it will not get lodged in his throat. When fingering shapes and squeezing toys result in sounds or motion, there is a feedback to the infant that brings him the satisfactions of accomplishment and power. Parents often find the sounds from rubber animals and toys disagreeable. The sounds do not have to be harsh; they can be pleasant chords or music-box melodies. The feedback can take the form of seeing the displacement of bubbles of air or colored liquids from one squeeze bulb to another. It can be the pleasing rattle sounds of smooth, round, colored plastic discs on a safe metal chain, as in Plakies. Toy manufacturers have not yet begun to experiment fully enough with the kind of educational chain reaction the fingering of playthings can afford the infant.

There are those psychologists who would program the infant's desire to touch, finger, and taste more effectively than has been possible heretofore. They are building electronic "memory boards," with which an infant can learn that touching the correct button will set lights into action. Some creative toy companies are experimenting with rolls of assorted cloth and fur textures and transparent plastic strips embedded with things for the infant to see, to touch, and to squeeze which can be snapped securely between the bars of the crib to allow a baby to finger-explore all kinds of textures and physical actions.

The infant's reflexive period is followed by directive behavior. Some of his purely physical movements may produce pleasure; others may be unpleasant. Thus begins a whole program of learning to adapt to the environment, combined with constant touch and movement experiences, as the baby explores everything in a room with his hands, mouth, and feet. Picking things up, examining them, and then releasing them to hear them fall with a thud becomes a deliberate activity to be repeated again and again. When the child has a parent retrieve things for him, his feeling of control over the action of another being is so satisfying that a conscious game of retrieval usually ensues. This type of play is also prompting new exploration by toy manufacturers of retrieval toys. Unfortunately, they will leave out the best part of the game—dear Mother!

*Oral gratification is essential to physical growth.* A hungry child is too preoccupied with his need for nourishment to be free for the satisfactions of playing and learning. Psychologists and psychoanalysts have long stressed that the gratification or frustration of this oral need can affect the personality of an infant in a variety of ways. An orally gratified infancy is said to be conducive to "oral optimism," that is, to generosity, sociability, receptivity to new ideas, and a positive outlook on life. The lack of oral gratification is said to lead to "oral pessimism," that is, to anxiety and insecurity, the need for constant reassurance, selfishness, aggressiveness, and impatience. There seems to be a significant correlation between infantile oral gratification and the coping capacity and behavior of the preschool child. Adequate coping includes a feeling of self-esteem, resistance to fatigue, and emotional control.

The fundamental coping capacity of the ego seems to be laid down in the first six months of life when the desire to suck and bite appear to be strongest. One cannot afford to ignore this meaningful psychological insight. Urged on by psychologists and pediatricians, progressive toymakers have begun to explore the creation of playthings that gratify the oral needs of infants—things to suck and bite on which are being produced in all shapes and sizes in rubber, plastic, and wood. What kind of sucking and biting toy would be acceptable to an adult who frowns on this normal infant activity? This is a crucial question because a whole generation of present-day parents was not allowed to have a pacifier by its parents. Today's grandparents view the use of pacifiers with alarm, which shows up as tension between newer and older child-rearing methods. We may have to devise abstract rubber figures with "multiple nipples" (there is already a rubber porcupine on the market which is very popular), or multiple protrusions on wooden or rubber toys (in the form of a giant jackstone, for example), or carved wood abstract forms that go easily from hand into mouth. It might be a good idea to incorporate sucking possibilities into the shape discovery of spheres, cubes, ellipses, or other geometric forms.

Biting usually comes with teething, between six and ten months, at which time a baby will bite on anything that comes his way. Wooden rattles, wooden spoons, and interlocking wooden rings, like the space teether, are excellent for this purpose.

*Hearing is a considerably developed sense at birth.* The infant's first responses are only to sudden, violent noises which may shock him into twitching his face and body and even screaming. From the sixth week onward, other sounds begin to engage his attention, and he will turn his head to listen. After this the hearing faculty develops rapidly, and the baby soon comes to know such everyday sounds as the bath, the voice of his mother, and even her footsteps. Between the second and fourth months the infant becomes very sensitive to different tones of voice. He can distinguish encouraging voices, mild scoldings, sounds of affection, or the angry banging of doors. There is evidence that a child's hearing becomes used to regularity of street sounds. An infant actually will stop crying to listen to the daily arrival of the postman, the garbage removal man, or others who break into his routine.

Before long the baby begins to use his own sounds, imitating them at first, then repeating them over and over again, and slowly mastering them. He learns that cries will bring his mother to him, that his cooing and gurgling will make her smile responsively. Ultimately he uses sounds to express his desires and feelings and to control the people around him. Slowness in talking sometimes results when a child is seldom talked to or because all his needs are anticipated and he does not have to talk. There is also such a thing as too much coaching and too much correction. Definite harm may come from trying to force a child into perfect speech before he is ready for it. Almost all young children go through an ungrammatical stage. In the early stages of speech, there is a great deal of repeating, pausing, and prolonging. This is the time for great tolerance on the part of parents and other listeners. The child who misses early hearing and sound experiences has difficulties later on with language and the abstract skill of reading. For these reasons, educators are working today with toy manufacturers in this area of learning. Music boxes in stuffed toys, musical crib and carriage toys, and turntables will provide early listening experiences. Making sounds with squeeze toys and turnabout cylinders gives infants a sense of control, at the same time introducing them to new sound effects. There still is limited research in ascertaining the sounds to which infants listen and respond. With the miniaturization of circuits and the introduction of cartridge sound and sight systems, it should be possible to automate a crib safely so the baby can control, select, and manipulate his own sound environment.

*Providing visual experience.* The infant's eyes focus better day by day. Soon he is able to see all the objects in his field of vision. Large red balloons and colorful mobiles floating gently in the air will excite his response. The movement of live fish in a plastic tank securely attached to one side of his crib will have the infant spellbound for long periods as an exciting, perpetually moving "nature mobile." Wind chimes made of wooden beads and brass bell-shells combine interesting motion and pleasing tinkling sounds. A movable, color-changing projection on ceiling, wall, or screen will be intently observed. Battery-operated, revolving transparent plastic balls, wind- or spring-operated bird mobiles, with or without music boxes, keep eyes alert and sharply focused. Research reveals that infants see almost at birth and that they early develop preferences for certain shapes (first, straight bold lines, triangles, and bull's-eyes) and colors (bright red, yellow, blue). Because of parental hovering over the crib, the baby seems to respond to two-eyed figures, whatever form they may take—an animal, a doll, or a "faces" mobile. After his mother's, the face that most attracts the infant is his own. Ways should be found to include in the sides of the crib or even in the top of the crib mattress strips of safe, unbreakable mirrors so the baby can freely view himself.

*Mastering movement, practicing crawling and walking.* The drive to overcome helplessness is strong in the healthy baby. An infant is happier when placed on a firm surface, such as a rigid foam-rubber mattress or a rug on the floor, on which he can give full sway to his body movements, than on soft, yielding cushions that impede such adventuring. A baby's mobility begins seriously when he can turn himself over, usually around five months. Mother can no longer leave him alone unless he is safely placed for now he can "go places." This is one of the major forward thrusts in an infant's physical maturation for which most homes are not prepared.

Some toy companies are experimenting with molded environments and contoured playscapes that permit an infant all the exploring he desires without parental anxiety or the need for caution. On one side of a mattress or rug or molded in a "blow-up" playpen there are incorporated, by an embedding process, things to see, shapes to feel, small "mountains" to scale, a slide to roll down, and corners in which to hide. Protective clear plastic bolsters around the sides of a crib offer the infant see-through patterns to explore visually.

At three months the infant's neck muscles are strong enough so he can hold up his head. While this is an important forward thrust, it is only at the fifth or sixth month that he makes the spectacular advance in body control whereby he can stay put in a sitting position. Now that he is able to see his world, his mother should allow him ample time for absorbing sight-and-sound experiences by placing him in a slanting webbed chair or a baby's car seat. The more a child sees, the more he wants to see. Psychologists and anthropologists studying the strapped-on-the-mother's-back infants of the Hopi Indians have discovered amazing alertness on the part of these babies at the end of their first year. Obviously varying an infant's visual and aural experiences by changing his position, by taking him on tours around the house, and by letting him in on the action in the kitchen will spur his active interest in seeing.

Just past the fifth month or around the sixth month, most infants attempt the difficult feat of crawling. It may take them up to the eighth month, or fortieth week, to master the process. Parents can lend encouragement and opportunity by getting their infant out of the crib when he is three months old and giving him the freedom of clean, hard surfaces and providing an infant crawler. An infant crawler, which is on casters, will extend an infant's horizons to include any object or piece of furniture on or near the floor of any room. After the mother places her baby on this safe device, the chance movement of his hands will start the casters moving. Ultimately, using his hands and feet in unison will lead to self-steering and maneuvering ability not heretofore conceived possible by the adult. Crawling opens up a fabulous new world for the infant to see, touch, explore, and manipulate. A great surge of physical activity ensues. Soon the baby learns to pull himself up. After sufficient practice, he walks, hanging onto the sides of his crib or playpen or the arm of a sofa or upholstered chair. When he can stand unaided, he is ready to take his first wonderful step. Some time between his first birthday and his sixteenth month, he usually walks alone. Normal children do not have to be taught to walk and run, jump and climb, hop and balance; they do these things naturally with vigor and pleasure—if provided enough space and unlimited opportunities for free physical play.

One of the early pioneers in research in the physical maturation of infants, Dr. Myrtle McGraw, retired professor of psychology at Briarcliff College and originally director of its Baby Teaching Laboratory, has shown concretely that when physical dexterity is present, external environmental stimulation can make babies use their sensori-motor powers to walk and talk sooner and more efficiently. Unlike most other psychologists of her time, Dr. McGraw was one of the few who recommended the challenge and practice of the sensory and physical powers of infants. To her, one of the most critical features of human growth is "learning readiness." Behaviors appear at certain opportune time periods at which, with the utmost energy expended by the child and the least amount by the mother—and the least distractions from other learnings —a baby will most quickly and easily learn a particular physical skill.

An opportune time to teach a baby to roller skate, according to Dr. McGraw, is *before* he is learning actually to walk. In two months' time, she taught a twelve-month-old to start, stop, start again, and whip around corners on roller skates. At twenty-two months, his brother had difficulty learning how to skate. Dr. McGraw caught the former infant before he had learned a specific way to displace his body weight forward but after he had learned to balance his whole body. After a child has learned to walk well, his tendency to lift his feet interferes with his learning to "roll" his feet for skating.

Using the opportune-period approach, Dr. McGraw also taught infants at ten months to swim and, before twelve months, to climb vertical inclines and to push boxes of varying heights into positions so that the infants could achieve the exhilarating position of "being at the top." Equally important to a child's sense of accomplishment is his interaction with supportive adults who understand him. Says Dr. McGraw, "If a child of a year or two gains confidence in handling his body, then it is reasonable to assume that confidence will subsequently serve him well in other areas."

Growth is not a straight onward-and-upward process; rather, it is a jagged procedure of spurts forward and regressions. "Older" does not always mean more advanced. In comparison to a fifteen-month-old who can feed himself, a three-year-old may want to be fed because he is preoccupied with learning other things. A baby who can balance very well while standing may constantly lose his balance when he starts to walk. The newborn has reflex swimming movements, but in five months this ability is lost, only to reappear at twelve months. The single-minded devotion of an infant to each new learning task at hand—maneuvering upright or walking, for instance— will cause him to forget that he has crawling ability that he could use to get under a bar. Thus old skills are constantly realigned with new awareness.

Parents and preschool teachers need to learn to observe, interpret, and nurture with a stimulating environment the signs and qualities of physical growth. Dr. McGraw feels that a baby should be exercised after his earliest signal of readiness. As long as he has not mastered a physical task, he will work very hard to accomplish it. This may explain the infant's endless, repetitive practice of each one of his incipient motion skills: crawling, balancing, walking up and down, and so forth.

Little children become physically adept by moving and doing. They learn to climb by climbing, to balance by balancing, and to swim by swimming. In her book *The Nursery Years*, Dr. Susan Isaacs succinctly expresses the value of movement thus: "Walking and running are enjoyed not only for the pleasure of actual movement, but also for the new discoveries of space they bring. For the knowledge of space relations grows by the fusion of what is seen and touched with the feelings of one's own movements in stretching or walking through the space seen."

Some psychologists say that missing any physical developmental stage may lead to deficiencies in spatial perception, in left-right relationships, and even to ultimate difficulties in picture and word understanding. There is need to make special play provisions for the crawling, standing, and walking stages of maturation. Cribs are necessarily confining, and a short walk around it seems to give an infant little gratification. We need to provide stable pipe rails that "go places," with a reward at the end of the line. While a home may not be able to afford such a rail system, the child development center or pediatricians' offices would do well to provide this infant aid. Stable walkers with flat, transparent, colorful, resounding rollers can enhance beginning walking. Sturdy push trucks and flatbed trucks with heavy hollow blocks can also give toddlers confidence and walking enjoyment.

Walking opens up fresh vistas. The toddler is in everything, and always on the go. He has attained mobile use of his whole body and is determined to exploit his power to the fullest. He has reached the full-bodied age of wonderful toddlerdom and savors to the full his growing sense of independence. To the toddler, everything is physical. Perpetually in motion, he lugs, tugs, pulls, pushes, dumps, drags, and pounds. He tries to maneuver anything and everything within his reach—a chair, table, lamp—even if his strength is not up to it. He will carry a package, open a door, try to button up his coat. This is the "me-do-it" age which requires infinite patience and tact on the part of the parent.

How to provide challenging, satisfying, but reasonable activities and play equipment for these dynamos is the test of a good toymaker, and some of the best of them have been working at it a lifetime. However, most toy manufacturers have missed the potentials of playthings for the busy, insatiable, indefatigable walker-runner. He needs playthings and equipment that are engineered to his size and current capabilities so that instead of feeling more helpless, he gets to be more and more independent. Small wonder the toys children this age most enjoy are those which add to their feelings of bigness and independence. Playthings that make big noises, like drums or pounding benches, rank high because noise making is one way for little children to feel strong and powerful. Hammering is also a test of strength, and getting the wooden pegs banged down is a real physical accomplishment. Dr. James L. Hymes, Jr., retired professor of childhood education at the University of Maryland, puts it this way: "Often we buy toys to show love. This doesn't work. But toys that are right for one-to-two-year-olds stand a chance of giving a child a sense of power. The youngster learning to walk is the world's most eager 'pusher.' A baby carriage, a toy lawn mower, anything on wheels that he can hold on to for support means both good walking and good feeling. A little later the slightly more skilled walker is the world's most eager 'puller.' He toddles along pulling his wagon, sometimes empty or sometimes loaded . . . but feeling as big as all-get-out."

*Preschoolers live dangerously in their press for bigness.* Therefore parents and toy manufacturers need to guard against providing them with playground equipment they cannot reasonably manage. Slides should not be too high because great heights do not deter the toddler and they can be dangerous. Children will even slide down head first! Playground equipment must be well designed, well constructed, and suitably scaled to the abilities and limitations of their users. Some concerned toy manufacturers are now producing sturdy, safe, toddler versions of large outdoor equipment in the form of a rocky boat, climb-around, jungle gym, low slide, et cetera. These items look so much like the older children's models that two- and three-year-olds conceive of them as being equal to what the "big boys" and "big girls" use. The rocky boat, long-time nursery school favorite, provides rocking motion to enthrall one to four small children when turned on one of its sides;

turned on its other side, a small child can run up the stairs to a raised platform and then scamper down.

As soon as he is able to climb stairs, a child enjoys sliding down a stairway slide. The toddler's gym has steps, a slide, and a hiding area under its platform. Toddlers express their burgeoning bigness by driving large ride'em trucks, trains, oversized furry animals, and carriages on free-wheeling casters. Casters are most successful because toddlers can make them go where they want them to. As they scoot about on these, foot and leg muscles are being exercised and strengthened. Two-to-four-year-olds adore a kiddy car, a pedal car, and later the ever-favorite tricycle. Seeing how fast he can go, how sharply he can turn, how to bring his trike to an abrupt halt— these are some of the exciting physical activities every toddler wants and needs. Each age level needs to have its appropriate physical equipment and challenges so children can affirm their confidence in themselves while fully developing all their body skills.

When they get to the stage of dramatic play, from four to eight years, it takes more than bodily challenge to engage the physical involvement of children. Early childhood educators, Caroline Pratt among them, knew this. Miss Pratt set about providing for three-to-six-year-olds a climbing-carrying-pulling-pushing environment with limitless city and country building and dramatization possibilities. From the carpenter she borrowed the sawhorse; from the painter, the ladder and walking board, as well as wide water brushes, pails, and rope; from the bricklayer she adapted large hollow blocks for building houses, stores, forts, et cetera. From the cement worker she took the single-wheel barrow and made it into a two-wheel barrow for greater stability. From the longshoreman she adapted the huge, open packing box, barrel, and crate. Out of all of these she created a mobile play environment that could start physical activity and imaginative play working overtime. Lifting the heavy but portable hardwood hollow blocks activates the back muscles. Maneuvering a packing crate and building a house or a boat require the strength and co-operation of a group of children. The walking board calls for physical co-ordination and a keen sense of balance. This type of outdoor play equipment is preferred by preschools and kindergartens today because it has inherent in it creative physical activity and, equally important, it offers learning lessons in how communities are built and how the workmen in them function. Here are physical play and community worker role playing at their very best!

Three-to-six-year-olds have greater large-muscle control. They enjoy a swing, slide, jungle gym, tricycle, and later a bicycle, a sled, a board on which to balance, and enough space in which to run and jump freely. A group of small children will play happily for long periods of time on a jungle gym, climbing up and down, stretching their arms and legs, and hanging on in all positions. On the playground children develop physical skill and courage. They learn, too, the social values of fairness and, to some extent, the rights of others.

Only through movement can children learn to conquer height. There must be a wide variety of equipment to provoke bodily and space experimentation: the three-way wood ladder, Fireman's Gym, climbing rope and ladder, hollow blocks and walking boards, a steel or wood wagon, scooter, porter's hand truck, wheelbarrow, and so on. The role of the parents and teachers is also very important at this time. Overanxious adults who are fearful that the children will hurt either themselves or each other and who find it necessary to interfere with the play at frequent intervals inhibit learning and delight. They may even communicate their fears to such an extent that the children become timid in their approach to the equipment.

Each child finds his own way to build the strengths he needs. Each time he mounts the parallel bars, for instance, in a different way, attempts to climb a little higher on the climbing rope, or balances himself on the next rung of the jungle gym, he enjoys again what he has already learned to do. This readies him to forge ahead to his next physical accomplishment. It feels great to be the master of one's self, no matter what one's age happens to be. As they grow older, children look for increased challenges to expand their vaulting body and muscle control. Three-year-olds can throw, dodge, stop-go, and turn sharp corners on their tricycles. They want to walk across a long, shaky balance board. Four-year-olds hop, skip, jump, climb, and race. They will climb to the top of a playhouse and daringly survey the world from this thrilling vantage point. Five-year-olds are also fond of climbing and all kinds of gross motor activity. They love riding their bicycles and show a marked interest in roller skating and stilt walking, but often there is more excitement than real accomplishment. Sixes generally want other children to share their physical play. Boys and girls like to play tag and hide-and-seek. Both like to rollerskate, swing, swim, and do stunts on parallel bars. Girls more than boys bounce a ball and jump rope. This preference may well be the outcome of cultural imposition and community notions of what activities are suitable for each sex. Increasingly today females are engaging in athletic sports that used to be the sole domain of their male counterparts. Seven-year-olds show a new awareness of heights and are cautious in climbing. They bicycle well and are beginning to really enjoy skating and even skiing. Boys favor marbles and tops, while girls continue to jump rope and play hop scotch. Action and daring characterize the play of eight-year-olds, who continue to run, jump, and chase. Boys more than girls add wrestling to their physical repertoire. Both boys and girls like to play baseball and are eager to learn new sports techniques.

*Feeling adequate in the active world of childhood requires body control.* It means gaining poise and co-ordination—learning physical movement skills—handling play equipment competently—performing athletic feats—participating in group games. Few public playgrounds are equipped with the very young child in mind. Increasingly parents are joining together to get cities to build more usable and dramatic playgrounds. Given suitable equipment, space, and freedom, children can gain comfortable mastery of heights, rocking, swinging and sliding motions, resiliency in falling, balancing, and climbing. Children find new ways of using their bodies when exposed to new pieces of outdoor equipment. Other important elements in a child's ability to control his body are parents and teachers whose attitudes toward children and outdoor equipment make it possible for him to be courageous and experimental.

Young children also use their bodies as "vehicles of expression." They express their feelings and ideas through their body movements. Their bodies "talk" about how animals move, how a plane takes flight, about a day at the circus, et cetera. Even the mood of a word will be translated into body action. Children role-play actively—"You be the Indian and I'll be the cowboy"—and they will chase after one another endlessly. They use their bodies in gymnastic ways as well and will endure even uncomfortable positions for the sheer emotional satisfaction their postures express. Physical play also promotes the discovery of spatial relations: right-left motions; circular, clockwise, and counterclockwise movements; the varied shapes the body can assume; and the patterns in space made by a moving body. Walking and running are relished not only for the release of energy and pleasure they afford, but also for the new discoveries of space that they provide. All are part of the symbolism in learning that becomes useful later on in such disciplines as geometry, astronomy, art, and so on.

As healthy children grow, they use their bodies with increasing dexterity, assurance, and satisfaction. But to perform any physical act well, a child must first get the hang of it. The child throwing a ball has to learn how to accent his swing just so far in order to make the ball reach the catcher. Active physical learning takes place best on the playground or the ball field. Functional movement is always incorporated in the performance of a physical feat and has in it an element of time—quick, slow, sudden, or sustained. To encourage sustained movements, parents and teachers may introduce a skipping rope, hoop, ball, as well as percussion instruments to work out fast or slow movements. The mastery of functional movements is aided by climbing equipment like arched climbers and three-way ladders, as well as tumbling mats and obstacle-course equipment.

Older children seek to use their bodies under more controlled conditions. Although organized athletic games have an important place in the outdoor play of older children, there are a few drawbacks in competitive sports as far as the young child is concerned. Most young children lack the physical skills or emotional set needed for the intense body control and inevitable rivalry inherent in such activities. Today there are Little League baseball teams, formal tennis matches, football games, swimming meets, and basketball, each with their rules, prizes, cups, and esteem. Thus free physical play is exchanged for the high pitch of organization, rigid rules, and tense competition. A trial of strength and speed is the essence of the athletic contest, whether it be running and skating races, weight lifting, swimming, or diving. Organized sports increase regimentation and systematization to the detriment of spontaneity and casualness. Linked to every competitive athletic game is the prime goal of winning, and winning always means that someone has to prove himself superior. Ego for a few may grow out of this type of competition, but we are afraid that many of those who are less skilled players become "turned off" to athletic activities of any kind.

We should like to see children use their physical powers with confidence and pleasure according to their age levels and individual capacities. Below the competitive "professional" level, it might be better to provide children with athletic games played co-operatively for sheer love of a particular sport.

There is increasing research evidence that difficulties in academic learning are often attributable to failure in the mastery of early body-space relationship learning. In 1967, for example, in Dearborn, Michigan, a physical education teacher at the Oxford Elementary School, with the support of its principal, decided to develop a gross motor program for "today's TV-age kids who have missed out on physical development that would help them learn to read." The school's seventy-seven six-year-olds were divided into three groups, with only one group participating in the experiment. The teacher's physical activity program was devised to give each child a sense of *laterality* (this term relates to one's internal awareness of the right and left sides of one's body and also entails the ability to use different parts of one's body at will without engaging the rest of the body) and *directionality* (a sense of what is up, down, behind, in front, et cetera). A child must be able to use his eyes without the rest of his body to follow left to right directions, as needed in reading and writing. To try to make up for missed physical experiences, the test group walked and balanced on two-by-four beams set narrow side up on the floor of the gym to make the exercises really challenging. The children also did special exercises on tumbling mats and trampolines. Another exercise was a large clock face drawn on the blackboard in the classroom, and each child asked to face it standing perfectly still, moving only each of his hands to point to the teacher-requested "o'clocks." On the theory that physical activities skipped in the earliest years, including creeping and crawling, can keep the upper levels of the brain from functioning fully, the principal of the Salina School, also in Dearborn, in 1962 set up a remedial program of creeping and crawling in the gym for its kindergartners. Reports from both schools indicate that vast progress in academic learning and physical poise has been made in the children of both experimental groups.

Physical activity can also get its stimuli from challenges in nature: rocks to scale, hills and trees to climb, rivers to swim, ledges on which to balance, and caves to explore. Unfortunately these are not readily available to most children. In our urban and suburban cities and towns, therefore, man-made environments and physical play equipment must provide the necessary challenges. The home, the school, and the community have an important role to play in providing young children with a wide range of opportunity and equipment for physical activity. This often requires tremendous ingenuity, and even some sacrifice. Parents may have to surrender the big bedroom. Climbing platforms may have to be built in the upper air space of the playroom to free the floor for ride'em activity. A climbing rope and swing may have to be hung from the ceiling and a chinning bar fastened to a doorway. Garages may have to be emptied and transformed into gyms. Playhouses may have to be built in trees or on top of garden tool storage houses.

No parent who has gone through a severe winter or given a toddler freedom of the house will question the premise that the physical maturation level of each age must be adequately provided with suitable space and play equipment to insure normal physical development of a child. All schools know that a well-planned, well-equipped environment is even more important when large groups of children go out to play. The variety and flexibility of use of the equipment and the range of play activities possible determine the extent to which children build body power.

# CHAPTER TWO

# The Personality-Building Power of Play

Play has the power to deeply influence a child's personality development. It incorporates a child's self-initiated efforts toward adjustment to and control of himself and his environment. Every time his efforts are successful, they give rise to feelings of self-worth. A strong ego permits a child to accept the consequences of his behavior and, when he is old enough, to admit his mistakes and tolerate justified criticism. The child who handles play and real-life situations positively develops the confidence to accept new challenges as they come along. As each new stage in his development is reached, the effects of the child's achievements and frustrations are consolidated in his total personality.

Each child's unique pattern for personality development is affected by the physical qualifications of his birth, his singular temperament, the kind of mothering (and fathering) he receives during his earliest years, and the flexibility of the world of things which he can manipulate to satisfy his ego. Also important are his interpersonal relations with adults and his peers, with whom he can establish social rapport and become valued. The child's play life, all his physical, emotional, social, and intellectual experiences during his crucial early childhood, and the freedom he is given to be at one with himself have great influence on the kind of personality he will build.

The Mid-Century White House Conference on Children and Youth reported in 1950: "All who have had the opportunity of watching children of like ages have been impressed with the high degree of individuality which each one shows. Even as newborn infants they differ not only in such physical characteristics as weight and height, but also in the manner in which they react to events."

Yes, each infant is a distinct, dynamic, growing, reacting organism, and all his efforts toward self-realization must never be overpowered, ignored, nor minimized. The integration of a child's personality is a gradual, complex process. It is the end-product of all his play and living experiences, and there is little doubt that much of the framework for his life career as an "organism-personality" is set in his very early years.

*Interaction with parents profoundly influences personality.* Every child needs parental love. He needs opportunities to test himself. He will benefit from the freedom to make mistakes and, above all, chances to succeed. The mother plays a major role in establishing comfort, security, and love and in providing appropriate and sufficient sensory stimuli in her dependent infant's immediate world. A baby's sense of identity is closely linked to his mother's ability to communicate her love to him. As she feeds him, cradles him in her arms, changes his diapers, bathes him, and sees that his sleep is comfortable, the mother is also conveying her regard for him as a valued individual in her life. Her wholehearted responsiveness, care, and understanding are basic to his structuring a sense of security. The loved, well-nourished, and well-cared-for infant can move more freely from one stage of his development to the next by virtue of his confidence in himself and his assurance of responsiveness to his accomplishments. If his nurture is salutary, he will trust himself and others. If his emotional experiences are affirmative, he will possess a deep sense of harmony with himself and the world.

In addition to good mothering, fathering is an important element in a child's personality development. Margaret Mead neatly assesses the father's role in the early stages of a child's responses in *Family*, to which we referred in our preceding chapter. She writes, in part, "As the child lets go of his mother's hand, sure that he can return to be fed . . . and comforted, the father reaches out his hand. As another person, he helps the child to establish his own sense of identity as a member of society . . . The father can give his son a sense of triumph that stands him in good stead all his life. But the father who rubs his unshaven cheek too hard against the child's, the father who tosses the child higher and higher, not noticing how the first screams of delight have changed to screams of pure terror, robs him of the ability to take the risks on which a boy tries out his maleness."

"The child's play begins with and centers on his own body," Erik H. Erikson, psychoanalyst and professor of developmental psychology at Harvard University, writes in his book *Childhood and Society*. He goes on to say, "It begins before we notice it as play, and consists at first in the exploration by repetition of sensual perceptions of kinesthetic sensations, of vocalizations, etc. Next, the child plays with available persons and things. He may playfully cry to see what wave length would serve best to make the mother reappear, or he may indulge in experimental excursions on her body and . . . face. This is the child's first geography, and the basic maps acquired in such interplay with the mother no doubt remain guides for the ego's first orientation in the world." An infant must feel that he is playing an active part in getting his needs satisfied. He proves repeatedly in his behavior and play that he is a distinct individual with wants and a will of his own. He continually tries to feel, select, and order everything that touches him and his life.

Every baby experiences many limitations. He cannot reach

the toy he has dropped. He stumbles when he first tries to walk. He is not allowed to touch many intriguing objects. There are many necessary but perhaps too many needless limitations in a child's world. Frustration rouses resentful feelings. How much hostility a child feels depends somewhat on whether the adults in his world help to minimize the inevitable frustrations or aggravate and increase them by a mistaken idea of disciplining him. If necessary restraints are administered with gentleness by a loving, reliable person, they will not create too much resentment. If they are set by someone who is struggling with his own hostile feelings, they will stir a great deal of negative feeling in the child so that he will want to hurt in return. Aggressive, hostile feelings will spill out against anyone who interferes with a hurt or angry child. A child will find it easier to accept restriction and face frustration if he feels affection and understanding in the person who limits him.

There are few objective facts in the earliest years of a child, only subjective ones. Reason may be present, but behavior is governed mainly by the child's own wishes, impulses, fears, delights, and fantasies. The feelings of other people do not count. Little happens in the young child's life which he does not subvert to his own feelings and needs. As the toddler meets some of the unavoidable disappointments of daily living, he is challenged by the rude discovery that the world is not in fact always his for the asking. Every child encounters difficulties in the course of growing up, just as adults do in the course of living. If the child has a healthy personality, he learns that his efforts can be effective. Therefore, each child needs to learn early that he has to exert effort in order to attain a goal. Alert parents and teachers make sure that the goal is not so difficult and remote that a child's efforts are not successful because persistent failure prevents the forming of autonomous responses.

Parent-child relationships determine to a large measure the early patterning of a child's personality. Competent parents provide their children with a home atmosphere of "relaxed concern." They communicate their feelings and standards directly and clearly, and what they impart is appropriate to each situation, to the child's stage of maturation, and to his temperament. Effective parents are consistent in their demands from and responses to their children. They express displeasure when poor behavior and disobedience are intentional, but they never humiliate their children. They react with approval to their children's efforts to learn and show appreciation for accomplishment and consideration. Parents who enjoy their children can be sure that their children are also thriving.

Sound mental health is a basic component of a healthy personality, in connection with which Ernest R. Groves and Phyllis Blanchard wrote, in their *Introduction to Mental Hygiene:* "It is evident that the mental hygiene of childhood is essentially a problem of efficient parenthood. Parents who understand the emotional needs of their children are in a position to guarantee their young a well-rounded development . . . The adult who is still infantile in life attitude cannot hope to raise self-reliant children." The too-sheltered child is usually fearful. He rarely is able to build confidence, initiative, and drive. The child who has inadequate family affection, protection, and encouragement is often deeply insecure. He cannot shape a well-integrated personality.

Responsiveness from the environment also affects personality. While love and competent mothering and fathering are essential to a child's well-being, they are not enough. Beyond this is the challenging world of manipulative and kinesthetic tasks, athletic skills, group games, and all kinds of learning experiences waiting to be discovered, tackled, controlled, and even remade through play and work. The 1966 Yearbook of the Association for Supervision and Curriculum Development, entitled *Learning and Mental Health in the School,* indicates that "Emotional support or love, in its pure sense, could not by itself produce the happy, productive child unless such support or love were hinged onto the learning of significant . . . developmental tasks. A healthy emotional relationship between a child and a parent would supply the basic harmony and orchestration to the main theme of development which involves a child learning competence in and about his environment."

If a child's environment gives him nothing to challenge his increasing physical powers, if his environment is barren of things that excite intellectual curiosity and academic learning, then the child is liable to give up trying. Often he will retreat into himself, and his personality development suffers. Adverse environmental conditions in home or school, and the length of such deprivation, can decisively damage the emotional accretion of any child.

The child's curiosity about the world of things prompts him to explore his world, to play freely, to plan and try to carry out his ideas, as well as to imitate, dramatize, and personify. Edwin A. Kirkpatrick wrote in his book *Fundamentals of Child Study*, "Curiosity may be described as an appetite for new experiences. In infancy everything is new, hence everything is interesting . . . By means of curiosity, a child is brought into intimate relation with various phases of his environment, instead of simply those that minister to his existence. Everything around him is made a part of himself . . . The greater the knowledge of environment gained through curiosity, the greater the possibility of adaptation to environment as occasions arise involving applications of knowledge that have hitherto been useless."

Child play is an ongoing active, personal research activity. As the child plays the part of other people and experiments with various ways of behaving, he is learning to understand and organize his feelings and to appreciate the feelings of others. From infancy, the child collects knowledge about himself and his surroundings and learns how to handle changes in himself and his ever-widening horizons.

*Personality gets imprinted very early.* Personality develops as early as three months, parents tell us. They see the forming of a definite personality: sluggish or responsive, uninterested or enthusiastic, quiet or aggressive, et cetera. Most parents regard these first three months as a passive growing period and usually come to the false conclusion that the child was born with such traits. Obviously certain physical traits—obesity or frailness, for example—can affect the behavior of a child. However, the personalities of most infants are the culmination of countless interactions, play or otherwise, with people and things.

Even so seemingly passive an activity as breast feeding is an active, reaching out process whereby, according to Dr. Bruno Bettelheim, professor of education at the University of Chicago, the infant is not only "tackling a mountain, but sucking it dry." A baby's eating behavior is one indicator of his responses to the outside world. The healthy, happy infant feeds well. If he is on an even keel physically and emotionally, it makes no difference if he is fed on a strict schedule or on self-demand, whether by breast or by bottle.

For well-integrated development, if infants are to learn new skills, they need to have stimulating things done to them during their first year of life, as well as opportunities to do things themselves that produce provocative results. A baby needs incentives to perform intentional, repeated efforts that result in needed learning. Many child psychologists now believe that even babies need a chance to produce dramatic effects on their environment. This is where cause-and-effect toys come in. A baby wants to see everything that is going on around him. He usually discovers his hands as early as two months of age and he will try to reach an object held up above him. He needs ample time and experience to learn to reach and grasp objects because he keeps his hands closefisted in the beginning. Contrary to what some psychologists believe, it is hard to overwhelm an infant because he will not pay attention to what is overly stimulating. There is today little question that an environment enriched with discriminative stimulation will forward the development of the ego of an infant and that the more information he takes in, the greater will be his intellectual growth.

Actually, every waking hour of infancy is devoted to taking in thousands of images, sounds, touches, and tastes and relating them one to the other. With a receptive parent, with proper handling and love, a child is encouraged to try and to adventure. With an environment full of new play challenges, curiosity and a spirit of adventure are fueled, and with each success, a baby's self-confidence flourishes. Curiosity and self-image are not always spontaneous in infants. Sometimes they have to be fired by discretional stimulations in the environment. These can be play challenges provided at sensitive stages in the infant's development.

When an infant has the physical ability to reach out, grasp, and hold, the parent needs to provide a wide array of things to reach for, finger, handle, pull, feel, and cuddle. In selecting first toys, the mother should seek out those that do not limit her baby's range of exposure to new experiences. Playthings that encourage relationship thinking, even in the early months, are preferred items: a pull of a ball on a cord that sets bells into motion and sound; roll-down beads in a cage that creates beguiling sound effects; sucking that sets a light blinking; the random push of an arm that starts the four-month-old moving along the floor on a Dolphin Crawler.

The environment of the eight-month-old should provide unlimited albeit safe opportunities for exploration: balls with different textures, finger holes, or sounds; tough toys that can take being dropped repeatedly; assorted shapes and textures to finger; objects to grasp; bowls and boxes to handle and nest. The beginning crawler needs things that make him want to crawl; mirrors placed on the floor in safe corners of a room for him in which he can see and approve of himself; balls and musical rollers to chase after and retrieve; small cars to push about. The desire to walk can be facilitated with handrails, wherever practicable, to allow the pretoddler to improve his growing power of locomotion; a nursery school-type wood doll carriage to push is welcomed by novice walkers.

*Walking expands opportunities for personality development.* With locomotion comes a need to communicate verbally with new adults and children. If parents do not allow normally for this interpersonal activity, there is little reason for a child to express himself verbally. With the ability to locomote also comes the child's need to test out his newly found physical skill. Parents need to offer the toddler unlimited walking and then running and climbing opportunities. Indeed, with locomotion and verbality whole new areas of exploration and accomplishment present themselves. The toddler must try every closet door, explore every drawer, pry open every available container. Every chair or sofa becomes an inviting mountain to clamber. Every person on the street or in a shop is to be engaged in lively conversation. The imitation of people and events becomes a part of his vocalizations and play life. He personifies and tries out different personalities—their ways of walking, talking, and behaving. He enjoys playing with sounds and words, as well as with chants and rhyming. The people and experiences he dramatizes become part of his imaginary play life and a real factor in his later social functioning and acceptance. We may say that each positive play experience adds to the molding of a child's character, his personality, his image of himself, and his understanding of what he can or cannot do. Selfhood begins in earnest unbelievably early.

*Social acceptance in family and peer group builds self-image.* A child's ego power is initiated and encouraged by positive, responsive interpersonal relations between parents and siblings in the first year of life. It continues to grow as he is accepted and needed by members of his family and then by a social group of his peers and other adults. An infant responds with well-being and enthusiasm to his parents' approval of his physical and play accomplishments. As the infant enters toddlerdom, he increases the number of people he must relate to and from whom he requires response. Then, unless the preschooler feels wanted by a larger circle—members of a play group or the nursery school—he can lose his sense of worth. At the same time he needs to master the play skills necessary for group participation—building with blocks, painting, dancing, singing, et cetera—or he will develop a feeling of inadequacy about himself and his powers. Nursery school educators are aware of the need to help each young child find his place in the group. Likewise, if the school-age child feels that group or community acceptance will not necessarily come from his tackling an academic problem, he often will not settle down to the task of scholastic learning. This appears to be especially true of the emotionally or culturally deprived child who, because of his negative environmental experiences, feels that he cannot get parental or school approbation no matter what he does, that there will be no reward for study, and that good work is of no consequence to him. This may account for many of today's school dropouts.

Essential to ego building is the establishment of individual and group norms that take into account family and environmental factors. Failure of a community to accept a child as a racial or economic equal also deters personal drive and can drive him to subvert his need to build a sense of worth and accomplishment. There is no community segregation or discrimination in the free play of children unless superimposed from without. A play group is more tolerant and accepting than a bigoted society. In play, a child can build individual ego and social poise. There is little possibility of personal failure in play because there is no right or wrong way to play!

"Children reveal themselves most transparently in their play life," wrote Arnold Gesell and Frances L. Ilg, one-time research pediatricians at Yale University, in their important child-rearing book, *The Child from Five to Ten.* "They play . . . from inner necessity . . . It is a natural, enjoyable exercise of growing powers. No one needs to teach a child to play . . . Nature plants strong play propensities in every normal child to make sure that certain basic needs of development will be satisfied. . . . A child puts forth his most strenuous energies in moments of play. He concentrates with his whole being and acquires emotional satisfactions which he cannot get from other forms of activity."

*Building self-confidence and will power through play.* The late Lawrence Kelso Frank, at one time director of the Caroline Zachry Institute of Human Development in New York City, wrote in the July 1955 issue of the *American Journal of Orthopsychiatry:* "Play is the finest form of education because it is essentially personality development, whereby the individual organism becomes a human being willing to live in a social order and in a symbolic cultural world."

A child's total personality includes his physical characteristics, mentality, habits and attitudes (his "character"), his emotional reactions, ability to get along with other people, and the impression he makes on others. In brief, his personality includes his social reactions to his environment. The child who has a sense of personal worth feels free to explore, to test, and to attempt more than he has heretofore. The more a child succeeds, the more he builds self-confidence. The better he feels about himself, the people close to him, and his universe, the more he builds a healthy personality. Play frees a child to attain his potentialities at his own rate of progression. A child feels powerful each time he handles a situation well, whether at play or in a concrete life experience. He feels effective each time he comes to apprehend the many forces acting upon him. He wants to come to grips with his world, not merely exist in it. Play, like nothing else, affords the child a sense of real freedom, control, and mastery. A child's ability to do things independently may well impinge upon all his early personality building and play experiences. Professor Jerome S. Bruner of the Harvard Center for Cognitive Studies believes that the prevention of living and learning difficulties depends on a child's sense of personal identification, his play life, and his freedom from anxiety and excessive drive.

The most uninhibited period in a child's life, during which he can build his ego, is the two- to four-year age level. For this age group, play is the only means of building self-image. The child has to be the center of every play situation. He wants to play the mother, father or the baby. He is not yet ready to allow dolls or play people to be the characters. He has to embody each role himself. Sometime during his second year he begins to get a conception of himself as a person. Parents can be sure of this when their two-year-old calls himself by his name or says "me" or "I." The two-to-four-year-old is completely egoistic. He is unable to take the point of view of others. He does everything in his play schemas to build his self-image and to prove and show off his own powers. One may well shudder to think what would happen if there were no time for this basic egocentric play. We are convinced that if children did not have this period of ego play, drive and will power would be adversely affected in their adulthood.

Research studies indicate increasingly that deprivation in the early years may cause permanent living difficulties. The affective growth of an individual is thwarted without adequate environmental stimulation. In a symposium on sensory deprivation held at the Harvard Medical School in 1961, Dr. Bruner said: "Not only does early deprivation rob the organism of the opportunity of constructing models of the environment, it also prevents the development of efficient strategies for evaluating information . . . Ego processes which have low differentiating abilities . . . are often the result of a lack . . . of representational symbols by which objects can be named, events mediated into experiences, and individuals related to as persons . . . Where there are marked degrees of deprivation of sensory experiences because of a child's environment or constitution, the results can be devastating on the organism."

Healthy personality development is tied to each child's own biological time clock, to his endowment, and his very early life experiences. In an article in the Sunday, February 12, 1967, issue of the New York *Times Magazine,* entitled "Where Self Begins," Dr. Bettelheim wrote about his twenty years of study and work with autistic children in Chicago. (The autistic child is an emotionally sick child who rigidly rejects people and the world.) The research at the Orthogenic School of the University of Chicago indicates that this kind of child has failed to develop a personality. He does not have an ego-sense that can operate in relation to real-life experiences. Unlike a feebleminded child, however, the autistic child may often possess potential for good or even superior intelligence. His emotional defenses, which range from muteness to complicated rituals for the most elementary bodily functions, can be reached only through psychoanalytic skill, empathy, and patience. The hatreds and longings of such a severely damaged child seem to stem from extreme frustrations in the mother-infant relationship, the result of which is the infant's crippling conviction that he can have no effect upon his environment.

In the New York *Times Magazine* article Dr. Bettelheim also noted that ". . . personality depends on the child's own spontaneous reaction to the conditions of his life . . . Our experience suggests that most critical of all conditions are those that affect the ability to act . . . If a normal child is to develop initiative and have it take root, he must be given the chance to test out for himself that taking action really gets him what he wants . . . The decisive factor . . . is whether or not the infant is encouraged to act on his own to reach a goal—and how much so. It is for this reason that time-clock feedings are so potentially destructive . . . they rob the infant of the conviction that it was his own wail that resulted in filling his stomach when his own hunger timed it. By the same token, if his earliest signals, his cry or his smile, bring no results, that discourages him from trying to refine his efforts at communicating his needs. In time he loses the impulse to develop those mental and emotional structures through which we deal with the environment. He is discouraged from forming a personality . . . If . . . the infant is stymied in his threshold efforts to do things for himself . . . retardation of personality sets in."

When people fail a child, play may be his only salvation. Play remains one of the most reliable factors in personality building and self-education during a child's earliest years. Through his play, a child lays the base for his development of a wholesome personality and the ability to function satisfactorily in the world in which he lives.

*A child can affect his environment by manipulating it.* The two-to-seven-year-old lacks fully developed logical thought processes and other skills needed for coping with the demands of everyday life. He deliberately creates a make-believe play world for himself because he finds he cannot yet affect the real world. In his play, he subjugates all the elements of his reality—his parents, other children and adults, things, and events—to his desires and drives. He employs make-believe because this permits the sense of mastery he can feel only in his illusory play world. His ego nudges him to escape the demands and restraints of the real world. As he maneuvers people and events in his play, he is fortifying his inner feelings about his own powers.

The child from four through seven years of age is very conscious of the fact that he is creating an unreal world in his play. He revels in using toys and objects to impersonate people and happenings in his imaginative play. He often retreats to this play world when he feels unable to control his external circumstances and feels truly masterful when he is able to shut the demands and controls of adults and reality out of his play life. Hence, when he plays, he enjoys an internal reality of his very own choosing and making. If his ego development is progressing well, he discerns reality from illusion and transfers with conscious ease from one realm to the other. When he has developed the ability to think logically and is secure, he gives up his make-believe kingdom and begins operating on the real world. At this point we say that the child is growing; he is ready to take his place in the world of adults and work.

The play materials that most readily permit a child to affect his environment by free manipulation are the nursery school-type unit building blocks and large hollow blocks fabricated of natural hardwood. They not only offer immediate and easy escape from the limitations and frustrations of being little, they afford children a deep sense of power, achievement, and pleasure. With large blocks, a child can build a "big world" in a relatively short time. Buildings that are bigger than the child can go up fast and be torn down or crashed without fear of breakage. At the same time, their non-restrictive form enables children to create imaginatively and purposefully. Among many others, Ruth E. Hartley, Lawrence K. Frank, and Robert M. Goldenson laud building blocks for children. In *Understanding Children's Play* they write: "When they build airports, skyscrapers, etc., they are not merely reproducing objects —they are, at least in fantasy, gaining control over things that ordinarily dwarf them. But their very real and apparent satisfaction in building these models probably has a further source. Gigantic structures symbolize release from a physical world that is cramping them more and more as they grow, as well as escape from an interpersonal world of parents' and teachers' demands that becomes more confining as their psychic horizons expand . . ." In other words, blocks serve as an effective link between the observed dynamism of the external world and the wishful magic of their own fantasies and desires.

We live in the most mobile of all ages. With all our systems of rapid transportation, it is inevitable that much of children's play will center on planes and trains, cars and trucks, buses and boats. Transportation toys give the child more of the means of "being in the driver's seat." Children feel masterful when they play the pilot of an airplane, captain of a boat, driver of a car or bus, astronaut in a space capsule, garageman or mechanic. They feel titanic as they cause harmless head-on collisions of their toy vehicles on their building-block superhighways. Racing a toy fire engine to a make-believe fire helps a child bridge the gap between his relative helplessness and the possession of adult skills and power for which he yearns. When a child knocks down his block structure, he merely is asserting his right to destroy his own product—in short, to control a self-created element in his play environment. He feels best and learns best when he is in complete charge.

Every child who is not handicapped or defective will attain the size, the weight, and the capacities for living and producing that are solely his own. Hastening or delaying his development usually imposes physiological and psychological handicaps that impair his strength and drive for achieving self-fulfillment. Chronological age norms are not valid because each child has his own built-in timetable of maturation. The child learns and unlearns many things in the course of his successive growth stages. He often returns to earlier experiences because he seemingly needs endless repetition of activities he has enjoyed or because he is trying to acquire elusive skills.

"Development is a continuing process with overtones of the past continually seeping into the present," write Drs. Berthold Eric Schwarz and Bartholomew A. Ruggieri in their book *Parent-Child Tensions*. "These processes of fixation at or regression to earlier stages of development are seldom complete.

They are a patchwork of variable changes. The feelings of both the earlier and the later stages of development are inextricably mixed together, and determine the child's feelings and modes of behavior, as well as his ways of obtaining pleasure."

Like no other device, play allows a child to return temporarily to an earlier stage of his development without necessarily evoking adult dismay or disapproval, or peer rejection or ridicule. If he feels unwanted or neglected because of the arrival of a new baby, he can act out his situation, play the baby, drink from a bottle, and get tucked into a wood doll bed by his partners in play. Temporary retrogression is good release for a child. It permits him to give expression to pent-up feelings of hostility, rejection, and frustration. Big, tough, inflatable figures to punch or a punching bag on which to vent aggressive feelings may avert many a flare-up, in addition to being thoroughly enjoyable. The kindergartner will spend countless hours wondering at the magic of a kaleidoscope, creating myriad patterns with a magic designer, constructing simple models with wood and metal construction sets, and delighting in the movement and fusion of hues of a color top. Making a top spin makes a child feel masterful.

Appropriate play facilities and encouragement are long-mileage components along each child's pathway to competence. Independence and a creative spirit are spiked when the child is spurred on to make or do something according to his personal preference. Awareness, flexibility, will power, versatility and eagerness for learning are the outgrowth of rich sensory play. What the child learns before he is six becomes the basis of his whole structuring.

*Ego-building power in play and play materials.* Jean Piaget points out that play allows a child to enjoy a "private reality of his own." It is the function of play to protect each child's egocentric world against forced accommodation to everyday reality. Parents who understand the ego needs of their children know that their emotional health can also be promoted through play. They provide their children with suitable and sufficient play materials, adequate play space, full opportunity for play, and the approbation and backing all human beings thrive on. Some play materials are better for a child's emotional well-being than others. Unstructured playthings lend themselves to the full expression of a child's imagination. Invariably they are more easily manipulated. They require no blueprints and little or no parent participation. They stimulate the dramatic acting out of a child's troublesome emotional situations. Above all, they tend to strengthen a child's need to feel generally capable.

The selection of play materials should never be haphazard nor casual. A good toy leaves room for the free exercise of a child's imagination. It can be used in different ways. It is handsome in shape and color and is good to touch, beautiful in line, and interesting in texture. It is sturdy and will take heavy use. A good toy can fit into varied play settings as dictated by a child's fancies. It quickens curiosity and invention as it lets the child find things out for himself. A balanced assortment of good playthings and play equipment should be chosen for the sensory experiences they can provide for manipulative and constructive purposes—unstructured materials for creative expression, equipment for homemaking play, dramatic play, and outdoor physical activity. Mechanical toys should be avoided for preschoolers because they are destructive of play; the toy does everything while the child sits passively by. All too often the fragile wind-up toys break in a youngster's hands. This is not only frustrating; it fills him with a sense of wrongdoing. We especially like the way Joseph Lee put it in his book *Play in Education*: "Toys, not fiz-jigs; it is the child's own achievement, not that of the clever man who made the toy, that counts. A toy with very small children is chiefly a peg to hang imagination on. It is the child's alter ego, to whom he assigns the parts that he cannot conveniently assume himself. And literal resemblance to their originals is the last thing he requires in his subordinates. An oblong block will be successively a cow, a sofa, a railway train, and will discharge each part with perfect satisfaction to its impresario. Too much realism is indeed a disadvantage."

The young child leans heavily on first-hand sensory contacts to explore the unknown and refine that which has become

familiar to him. The broader the sensory challenges and accomplishments he has in his earliest years, the greater will be
his creation of an acceptable image of himself. In addition,
the more ways a child can use a toy, the longer it will interest
him, the more pleasure he will have, and the more he will
learn.

An infant likes to feel, squeeze, poke, and handle things.
He responds actively to the colors and patterning of a texture
ball. Wood rattles in varied shapes and a space teether will
satisfy his need to suck, to chew, to finger. There is the added
delight of pleasant sounds in rattles and safe squeeze toys.
When he knocks a roly-poly over and it bounds back to him, he
is indeed the manipulator. A "baby-see" mirror helps him reinforce his image of himself. The cradle gym and infant
hand-and-foot twirler offer him beginning exercises in eye-
hand co-ordination. A music box safely embedded in a stuffed
animal heightens a baby's aural awareness and pleasure. Preschoolers develop confidence and competence as they create
patterns with colorful design cubes and play with nested boxes
and dolls, geometric insets, and assorted dressing frames.

We cannot overemphasize that building blocks are the finest
home and school play material for children from two up to even
ten and twelve years of age. Hardwood unit building blocks are
sturdy and stable, and offer a great variety of play possibilities
and values. Children who have been made fearful by parental
goading to be overly careful with things are not afraid to play
with blocks. Block play helps children believe in themselves.
It bolsters their self-image because they can control the structures they create. Two-year-olds carry blocks at first and then
stack them or lay them out on the floor. They enjoy knocking
down their simple piling of blocks. Experienced three- and
four-year-old block builders erect detailed structures. Fives start
reproducing the world and bring their constructions to life with
such supplementary materials as cars, boats, trains, planes, toy
people, and play animals in appropriate scale. Sixes and sevens
build even more complicated layouts. They use their building as

a background for the lessons they learn about community living and for imaginative play about interpersonal situations in home and school. The motivation to build comes from within the child. Because blocks can be used in countless ways, the child's interest usually remains keen and active over a long period of time.

Young children play best when materials are scaled to their size, neither too small nor fragile for still uncertain manipulative skills nor too large for comfortable handling. Child-sized equipment is especially needed in the housekeeping play corner where children enthusiastically imitate real home life situations. Housekeeping is a natural play activity, and both little boys and girls relish house play. They take turns being the mother or father, the baby, nurse, or visitor. They cook food and care for their babies. They clean the house and wash and iron the doll clothes. Domestic play activity provides children with socially accepted outlets for "letting off steam," for expressing their aggressive feelings. A child in a housekeeping game can punish other children in a manner that would not be tolerated outside the play setting. The play stove, sink, cupboard, pots and pans, tea set, cutlery, laundry equipment, carpet sweeper, broom, mop, dust pan, iron and ironing board are perfect play tools for children with which to practice and test their relationships with their peers.

*Manipulative toys forward manual dexterity while reinforcing self-image.* The nursery school child has fairly good control of his large muscles. As he learns to control his small muscles, he likes to test his developing dexterity with large Masonite sewing cards, wood and metal nut and bolt construction sets, a lacing boot, postal station, large beads to string, a landscape peg board, color cone, parquetry blocks, Tinker Toy, snap blocks, jigsaw puzzles, and a woodworking bench and good tools. Manipulation, experimentation, and functional construction are the stages through which most children pass when handling wood and nails. Imaginative ideas and paper, cloth, wood and metal collage materials motivate creative construction projects. Besides a finished product, an acute sense of achievement results, and the feeling of personal worth is strengthened.

*Water play has irresistible fascination for young children.* Water is one of the few natural substances still available for exploration by city children. Water permits a great variety of activities and experimentation: immersing objects in water, pouring, blowing bubbles, splashing water to produce movement, et cetera. The home, the nursery school, and the kindergarten should make greater and more frequent provision for free play with water. In addition to the sensory delight and learning experiences it offers, water is a basic material with which a child can readily realize fun and accomplishment. For some children, particularly those who are not well adjusted emotionally and those who have innumerable restrictions imposed on them by adults, the primary satisfaction in water play seems to be connected with their personal control of a fluid, non-threatening substance. A large metal or plastic tub serves these play purposes well, as do pails, washbowls, or basins. Soap, bubble bath, and other foam-producing agents are excellent play enriching accessories, as are assorted containers for holding, pouring, and measuring water, sponges, floating toys, funnels, strainers, small rubber balls, rubber gloves, plastic dishes, doll clothes, straws, bubble pipes, and suitable housekeeping utensils.

Sand is another basic material all children, and especially the emotionally disturbed, deeply enjoy. Cups and spoons of various sizes, sieves and sifters, and molds of all kinds heighten the play and pleasure. A child at the beach will play contentedly for hours. Why? Because sand and water are natural substances with which a child can do anything his imagination and desire dictate. Most children are completely at ease in a sand-and-water milieu. Child psychologists make use of both to soothe disturbed children during play therapy sessions.

*Doll play encourages role playing and brings understanding of others.* Doll play goes back to the beginning of recorded history. An eighteen-month-old may grab a doll by one leg, drag it along the floor for a short distance, hug the doll, and then summarily drop it on the floor and leave it there. The two-year-old will pick up a doll with more care. He may put the doll in a doll bed and cover it to keep it warm. The three-year-old may dress and undress the doll and even talk to it. The four-year-old begins playing with the doll dramatically, calling a doctor to the bedside, and taking the doll's temperature. The five-year-old's doll play can be an involved play project carried over imaginatively from one day to the next.

According to Jean Piaget, doll play not only shows the maternal attitudes of the child, but also serves as an opportunity for the child to relive his own life symbolically in order to more easily assimilate its various aspects, to resolve conflicts, and to try to realize unsatisfied desires. Happy or unpleasant events in a child's life are often exposed in his doll play, just as they are revealed in his homemaking and dramatic play. Doll play also reflects the child's family life experiences and so is related to the whole life of the child. Children long to do what their parents and other adults do. Little boys and girls enjoy pushing doll carriages in the nursery school. Caring for a baby doll satisfies acting out the mother and father roles. For this primeval and imaginative play there are all kinds of sturdy and appealing dolls, doll carriages, high chairs, cradles and beds, rockers, as well as houses with their attendant furnishings.

*All children need assorted art materials so they may express themselves freely.* Painting is a prime medium whereby a child's imagination is permitted full sway. The years between two and four, when a child's painting is least representational and most directly reflects his playful responses to the raw art materials, are especially appropriate for painting as a purely expressive medium. Painting appears to have its greatest significance for supporting self-image when the child's products seem to have their least apparent meaning. The child should always paint for the fun of it, rather than to please others. It is much more important for the young child to enjoy painting than to learn its techniques in the very beginning or to have to adhere rigidly to rules about cleanliness and order. The mother and then the teacher need to value his efforts and show their sincere appreciation for his finished paintings.

Young children use paints and crayons to communicate the experiences and preoccupations they are unable to express in words. When a child first attempts to draw, he goes through an exploratory stage. Then as he acquires some manual control, he attempts to make designs. At about three and a half to four, he begins to make representative drawings. The younger the child, the more spontaneous and direct is his art work. It is as natural for children to paint and draw as it is for them to talk. Non-verbal children especially express their innermost feelings in their paintings and drawings, which are more elemental than spoken or written words because they are more immediate and straightforward.

The response to finger paints also follows a general sequence, starting with pleasure in feeling the substance, in smearing and being messy, and in indiscriminate color mixing. Then comes experimentation with patterns and, finally, full use of all the potentials of the material. Perhaps the chief virtue of finger painting is that it quickly frees the inhibited child for greater spontaneity.

An adjustable easel, good poster paints, assorted long-handled flat bristle brushes, large sheets of paper, a smock, finger paint materials, paste, scissors, construction paper, and large crayons are a child's surest passport to the fascinating world of free art expression. A wall board on which his finished paintings and drawings can be displayed enables the parent and teacher to tell the child concretely that his efforts and products are appreciated. Parents and teachers need to steer clear of the mistake of prizing a child's talents over the child himself!

Clay is another unstructured material that lends itself to creativity and ego building. The young child regards clay only as a means for immediate sensory investigation and fun. Gradually it becomes a raw material out of which he finds he can make something else. Nursery schools and kindergartens provide moist clay because children can work it easily. There is great satisfaction for the child (and adult) in what his hands can do with the physical world. In fact, the acquisition of manual dexterity may lay the cornerstone for a child's feeling of competency about his ability to reshape it.

*Dramatic play helps a child relive important life experiences.* Dramatic play, according to Susan Isaacs, ". . . is supremely the activity which brings psychic equilibrium in the early years. In his play activities, the child externalizes and works out to some measure of harmony the different trends of his internal psychic life." There is an element of dramatic or fantasy play in many of the preschool child's free pursuits. His experiences keep on expanding, and his powers of observation grow keener all the time. The three-to-five-year-old likes to re-enact events he has been part of or has observed. He imitates the people and things about him. In his dramatic play he reflects his interpersonal relationships, expresses pressing needs, and tries out solutions to his problems. He also releases ordinarily unacceptable impulses and often reverses his usual life role. Just as adults relive experiences in thoughts or words, children play and replay the important happenings in their lives. Children who act out a painful scene repeatedly are not doing it to preserve the pain, but to try to make it understandable and bearable. They incorporate those parts of the situation that are endurable and add others as their self-assurance and courage grow. This is one of the ways in which they bring under control the feelings and frustrations that are often experienced by children—who are dependent upon the will and love of adults.

With regard to this, Jean Piaget has said: "As to the child's relations to parents, brothers and sisters, a comparison of all the games in which they are symbolized clearly shows how revealing the detail of the symbolism is of tendencies and feelings, many of which the child is not clearly aware of because he never questions them. The first to appear are identifications with the mother . . . the father, and with older or younger brothers and sisters. Although at first sight these may seem to be merely a reproduction of the child's environment, they reveal a mass of contradictory feelings; affection or resistance, acceptance or revolt, attraction or jealousy, a desire to be grown up, to live elsewhere, etc. . . ."

The motifs most commonly delineated in dramatic play fall into the categories of protection, power, attack, and destruction. Children with serious adjustment problems are preoccupied with one motif; well-adjusted children are able to shift from one to another. Some aspects of the child and his world that are stunningly exposed in dramatic play are the specific character of the child's world, his anti-social feelings, what he thinks of himself, and his innermost concerns. Clinical evidence indicates that when children express in fantasy play the hostile emotions they feel, they siphon off their antipathy so it will not be buried to cause inner tension and possibly erupt in real-life situations. Strongly aggressive or hostile children must never be permitted to continually dominate weak and timid ones because the withdrawal of the latter from a play situation may cause further ego damage.

Young children delight in reproducing phrases, rhymes, and actions. They will represent Daddy at the office, being the doctor, going to the supermarket, helping Mommy, visiting grandparents, and other here-and-now events. Their games of pretend enable them to be more fully a part of their environment and help them overcome self-consciousness. The healthy child knows when he is pretending. Before he is six or seven, he does not fully possess a mental image until he has given it bodily form, because his logical thinking processes are as yet too weak to stand alone. He acts out in order to understand. In the realm of his imagination, his freedom is complete. Fairy tales fascinate six-year-olds and older because they playfully exercise the imagination.

Puppets and puppetry permit children to be the producers, directors, and actors in their fanciful presentations. Puppets have qualities which make them especially entrancing. Their appearance and size spell make-believe. Puppets are relatively easy to handle. Even a very young child can manage a hand puppet with sufficient skill to please himself. Finger puppets work best with the youngest child because they are the easiest to manage. Marionettes are more suitable later on because manipulating the articulated figures and keeping the strings unsnarled are tasks for dextrous fingers. Puppets, marionettes, and shadow-play figures are the child's three-dimensional storybooks with which he can breathe dramatic life into anything and everything he so desires. Puppets permit the child to express thoughts and feelings that more realistic play materials often cannot liberate, and the sharing of his feelings with a group of children can extend his understanding and social contacts.

As a child meets obstacles in his play, he employs all his capabilities to tackle them. His self-reliance comes to the fore as he tries out many ways to solve a problem. It is amazing how much patience and perseverance a young child displays when he plays. He needs unlimited opportunities to play with materials that challenge but do not defeat him. Says Ethel Kawin in *The Wise Choice of Toys*: "Children should frequently experience success, for the feeling of satisfaction which comes with a sense of achievement is a constructive factor in developing a wholesome personality, and encourages the child to go on and to attempt more difficult things. Toys which present problems completely beyond their level of development are undesirable in that they give children a sense of failure and of futility of effort. Some of the child's toys, however, should always be sufficiently difficult to challenge his best abilities."

Of course, in addition to its proper objects, play requires appropriate playmates. No adult can behave toward a child as does his age-mate. At the same time, each child needs as much playtime by himself as he wishes. Play offers more than tools for building personality and a sense of achievement. Play experiences enable a child to cope constructively with the realities of his life.

*Research in the play of animals has important meaning for humans.* In the early 1960s, the United States Government established primate centers in four locations in the country where controlled medical, mental, and psychological experiments with all species of monkeys could be conducted. In the Atlanta center in Georgia extensive experiments with play in the life of infant apes have been carried out. In one experiment, monkeys were treated as human infants. They were given the same care (diapering, powdering, hugging, et cetera) and long periods of supervised play in and out of doors with carefully selected play equipment. In other experiments, play materials were placed in the environment of the experimental group while the control group had no playthings. After considerable periods of play, the brain weight of the playing monkeys was taken and studied and compared with that of their non-playing peers. In all these experiments, the data revealed overwhelmingly that the environment of play and loving interaction with adults resulted in a more alert, socially mature, and heavier-brained monkey than was the case with the control group of "deprived" primates. The relevance of these studies for human growth in early infancy and childhood merits further serious consideration.

Despite this pointed evidence, there are many pediatricians and psychologists who complain that these studies may be correct for animals, but have no meaningful significance for humans. Too few psychologists are willing to study play and environmental effects on the human baby. Most funds from the federal government are sought for the study of interpersonal relations between mother and child. Environmental effects on child personality development are studied only in extreme cases—institutional versus home care. But the day-to-day interaction of infants with planned or prearranged play environments is seldom a subject for study.

A few years ago a well-known toy manufacturer in the United States offered for sale an "infant crawler." A three- to six-month-old infant could be placed in a safe, prone position on the scooped-out back of a plastic animal made mobile by free-wheeling casters. As a result, about eighty thousand babies became activated to explore their environments beyond the confines of their cribs some three to five months before an infant normally crawls. Despite the concern expressed by the president of this toy-manufacturing company to the research director of the National Institute of Child Health and Human Development for the need to research the effects of such intervention in the usual crawling habits of infants, the federal government saw fit not to act. To this day, countless thousands of such infant crawlers are sold annually without any research to reveal whether it is good or bad for the growth of an infant. Yet parents are delighted with the development and pleasure this product affords their babies.

An environment or interpersonal actions can have profound effects on the future personality and behavior of a child. An off-hand recommendation by a noted pediatrician will be taken seriously by parents, even when it may bring about a conditioning of infants that may have disastrous effects on their functioning when they are adults. In the late 1930s and early 1940s most pediatricians advocated a rigid schedule of feedings four times a day. They recommended that parents let their infants cry long periods, as much as twenty minutes or more, before they picked them up and fed or cuddled them. Mothers and fathers were usually at their wits' ends watching the clock so they could do something to stop the wailing—either with food or fondling. Most parents had the good sense to ignore the pediatricians' dictum with their second babies, resorting to demand feeding and picking their babies up whenever they seemed fretful or bored. We believe that this measuring out of food and comforting by the clock brought forth a generation of middle-class young adults who continued to "cry out for love." Many turned out to be socially immature, despite their intellectual superiority. Many married early and inadvisably, divorced early, and are still searching for self-identity and wholehearted affection not metered out by a clock.

*Play therapy for severely disturbed children.* Childhood appears to be a trial run when children are given the time they need to find out about themselves, other people, and the world in which they live. In the course of growing up some children develop different kinds of emotional problems (fears of many kinds, feelings of hostility, aggressive behaviors, lack of self-esteem, anxieties, poor social adjustment, intense jealousy, shyness, showing off, and withdrawal being most prominent among them). A disturbed child also usually suffers from unconscious feelings of guilt. Since it is impossible to determine exactly what goes on in a child's mind or to get children to talk like adults, specialists who work with distressed children have found that much can be learned about them from watching them at play during which most children are able to reveal both their imaginary and real life. Because play is the most natural form of expression of the young child, it can also reveal his inner conflicts and his immaturity.

One of the most striking characteristics of an anxious child is a strong inhibition of play activity. Often such a child is not able to play at all. When in a well-equipped nursery school, he may remain tense and incapable of doing anything with any of the playthings. Other traits of the neurotic child are his lack of constructiveness and an overpowering, persistent impulse to destroy. The disturbed child (whether emotionally ill or mentally retarded) when he does play acts as if he were younger than his chronological years. If a child of six with an enriched environmental background were to spend a whole hour just filling a box with sand and emptying it endlessly, it would signify, needless to say, some immaturity worthy of further investigation. Constant reversion to an earlier level and the compulsion to use materials that are charged with symbolic significance (sand, water, or fire) might well signify some early, unresolved conflict or overly strict home training. A child who has been rebuked or punished in his very early years regarding his toilet training may busy himself only with sand and water during his hour in a psychiatric clinic, evincing no interest in the many toys available to him.

The nature of a child's play can also indicate the type of disturbance that underlies it. Children who are meticulously clean and avoid "dirty or messy" play, who arrange toys in neat patterns only, who dislike painting and shun finger painting, whose drawings are "dominated by rulers and compasses," who play silently and alone, or keep up a constant chatter to hide their deepest feelings through their obsessional play, indicate a rigidity that can mask a serious problem. The child who aimlessly handles every toy in a playroom without playing with any one thing, who initiates half a dozen games only to drop each one moments later, such a child's conduct connotes grave instability and an acute state of anxiety. A child whose play is accompanied by explosive excitement and who loses control of whatever he may be doing (for example, throws clay about uncontrollably or destroys the constructions of his playmates) may well suffer from hyperactivity because of deeply buried inner turmoil. Such conflicts can only be uncovered by careful professional observation and analysis of the child as he is helped to play and to talk in the ameliorating atmosphere of the play therapy room or clinic.

It was Dr. Anna Freud, one of the pioneers of psychoanalysis for young children and the use of play therapy, who recognized that "the day dreams of children and activity of their fantasy in play is equivalent to the free associations of adults in analysis." She gave broad recognition to the play therapy techniques advocated by the English school (Melanie Klein, Susan Isaacs, Margaret Lowenfeld) for the analysis of little children. Anna Freud believes that play therapy as a system for child analysis is best suited to the investigation of the ego, which often is shielded by the traditional verbal method of psychoanalysis. She has pointed out that child analysts, "in their observation of affective processes, have to be largely independent of a child's voluntary co-operation and his truthfulness or untruthfulness in what he tells us."

The denial of reality is one of the particular features of play in general and especially in games of make-believe. The elements for constructing a pleasurable world of fantasy and play are readily available to the child. The task of the child analyst is to get the child to separate fantasy from fact and to help him assimilate reality into his personal scheme of things. Fantasy is the name given to a kind of day dreaming that is the opposite of controlled thought. Every small child recreates a world of fantasy for himself at some time. Some children however sink too deeply into the world of their own thoughts and feelings and so lose contact with reality. At some point the healthy child gets to grasp the difference between fantasy and reality and becomes involved in explorations of the world of real people, things, and situations. He wants to understand himself and the adult world. The disturbed child cannot make this transition.

Play therapy is a professional method of using play with non-threatening play materials to discover what is troubling a child and to help him attain better accommodation to himself and to his life. Because verbal communication with a very young emotionally disturbed or mentally retarded child is very difficult, such a child is closely watched by the therapist while he is at play. For children from three to twelve years of age, regular visits to a play therapist have proved effective in relieving them of emotional conflicts that often find expression in such manifestations as temper tantrums, bed-wetting, withdrawal, or general destructiveness. By bringing out into the open fears or anxieties that are distressing and immobilizing to a child and his sharing them with a tolerant grown-up (the play therapist), his terrors become less terrifying.

The ideal play therapy room is a fully equipped, sound-proofed large playroom. All the carefully selected play materials are displayed on open, low shelves so a child can freely choose the toys he wants to play with—without fear of interference, breakage, criticism, or soiling his clothes or the room. Water, sand, and clay are flexible materials that release most children to play. Especially useful in play therapy, these materials often can nudge fearful children to be less inhibited and help calm overexcited ones. The young child often identifies dolls with the important people in his life. When he makes dolls do what they do to one another, the child is indicating to the therapist exactly how he feels toward the members of his family and how he thinks they feel toward him and each other. A doll house can also stimulate an emotionally disturbed child to re-create situations that impinge on his daily family life. In the play therapy room there also are toys that permit a child to express his aggressive feelings, including a punching bag, large cloth dolls that look like a mother, father, et cetera. There are rubber daggers, guns with rubber darts or corks, cannons, and miniature toy soldiers. In addition to grotesque masks, there are cowboy and Indian outfits and other accouterments for dramatic play. Acts of anger and defiance are acceptable in the therapy playroom as long as they do not become dangerous or needlessly destructive.

To handle complex emotional problems, therapists often try out in their play therapy sessions special, custom-made playthings. Among some better known items in the United States there are "amputee" dolls with female or male sex characteristics that represent all the family members, with heads, hands, and feet that can be snapped off by a child. A child's hatred might be expressed not in his words but in his unconsciously but tellingly tearing the doll apart as he held it. In subsequent sessions the child might verbally air his feelings of guilt and anger, far beyond the expectations of the therapist. There also are dolls with either male or female sex features which permit a child to delve into any sexual fantasies or problems that beset him. Most play therapists spend hours searching through toy shops for play materials that might encourage a child to surface his difficulty or serve as an encounter of significance between child and object.

Play therapy usually is conducted on a one-to-one basis between disturbed child and therapist. It is a basic therapeutic technique today for helping a severely disturbed young child face and come to grips with his emotional problems. However, there are situations where a school-aged disturbed child (but one without deep-rooted inner conflicts) can profit from participating in a small planned play group. (Organizing and manipulating the play life and social activity of a carefully composed small group for the best interests of a disturbed child should not be attempted by untrained parents or teachers.) Usually there are no more than five children in such a group, one or two of whom may be timid, aggressive, anxious, or fearful. The emotionally and socially healthy children in the group are selected on the basis of their acceptability to the "exceptional" ones. The atmosphere of a special playroom needs always to be permissive in character, where spontaneity is given full reign but where exploding will not hurt anybody or anything. After a group meets for its first supervised play session, the play specialist in charge brings out carefully selected play materials that can further dramatic play and help satisfy a disturbed child's craving for group power—which he has little chance of exercising in his real life. Materials that permit individual activity are avoided in this planned play group. Included, instead, are all kinds of dress-up accouterments: handbags, shirts, jewelry, and colorful scarves, as well as a tool kit, lunch box, badges, handcuffs, rubber knives, baby nursing bottles, stethoscopes, and male and female puppets. Water is available, but clay work and painting are not included in the program.

In this setting the timid or aggressive child is encouraged to play a role completely different from the role he usually assumes in the regular classroom assemblage of his age-mates. In the controlled play group he becomes emboldened to pick up the nursing bottle and act out "the baby." A timid little girl can feel free enough to put on a badge, pick up a stethoscope and a rubber knife, approach the other children and boldly proclaim, "I will cut your stomach out, I'm the doctor!" The special play props and composition of the group make it possible for a disturbed child to assert himself by means of leadership roles in his dramatic play which he could not dare initiate elsewhere. This type of planned play group goes on for as many sessions as are required for the relaxation of a child's tensions or other anxieties. The outcome of several months of such planned group play usually shows up in positive changes in attitude toward teachers and schoolmates on the part of the helped child.

"Lack of ability to play is not natural and is not an inborn characteristic," writes Dr. Margaret Lowenfeld in her book *Play in Childhood*. "It is a neurosis and should be reckoned with as such. Children who fail in their ability to play with their fellows are children with characteristics that will make them unable to combine with their fellows in after-life." She goes on to say, "Play is an essential function of the passage from immaturity to emotional maturity. Any individual without the opportunities for adequate play in early life will go on seeking them in the stuff of adult life. Emotional satisfactions which the mind missed at the period to which they properly belong do not present themselves later in the same form. Forces unrealized in childhood become an inner drive forever seeking outlet and lead men to express them not any longer in play (since this is regarded as an activity of childhood), but in competition, anarchy, and war."

# CHAPTER THREE

# The Power of Play for Social Development

In "Social Deprivation in Monkeys," the now-classic article by Drs. Harry F. Harlow and Margaret K. Harlow published in *Scientific American* in 1962, the researchers described their experiments that revealed that baby rhesus monkeys caged with their mothers but permitted no play or social contact with other monkeys displayed gross abnormalities in their adult sexual and social roles. Young monkeys permitted daily play with their peers, even though isolated from their mothers, showed nearly normal behavior as adults. The report of the Harlows is not an isolated finding. In 1964 others reported that monkeys kept in isolation and relative darkness from infancy to three years manifested bizarre forms of behavior and activity that suggested sensory hunger: for instance, biting themselves, slapping their limbs, moving ceaselessly about the cage, and so on.

*Important animal research verifies importance of social play and enriched environment.* One of the most conclusive pieces of animal research on the values of an enriched play environment was undertaken over a period of twelve years, from 1960 to 1972, by a team of biologists and psychologists led by Dr. Mark R. Rosenzweig. As described in the February 1972 issue of *Scientific American*, he used rodents from the same litter in his work. Rodents proved convenient because they bear large litters, so litter-mates have a common genetic background and they could be sacrificed (the brain could be removed to be weighed, studied chemically, and so forth). In the experiments, rats from the same litter were placed (1) one in a cage with no playthings, (2) three in a cage without playthings, and (3) twelve in a cage with playthings that were changed every day for thirty days.

Very early in the experiment it was found that the rats that spent four to ten weeks in the enriched environment with frequent play changes differed markedly from the rodents in the impoverished milieus. For example, rats with enriched play had greater weight of the cerebral cortex, stronger nerve endings and transmitters, and greater enzyme activity. When the experiments were replicated some sixteen times with the same strain of rats, the same pattern of differences was found repeatedly. Only when the play environment was changed and new challenges were offered the rats were there any decisive anatomical and chemical changes in the brain.

To check whether brain changes were brought about by the amount of handling, stress, or maturation differences, a series of experiments were undertaken to handle one group of rats several times a day while their other litter-mates were never handled. It was found that there were no differences in brain weight or enzyme activity between the handled and the non-handled rodents.

The research indicated that two hours a day of enriched experience over a thirty-day period were sufficient to produce changes in the brain weight of the experimental rodents. Placing twelve rats in a large, plaything-free cage for two hours a day for thirty days did not bring about a change in brain weight. Placing a single rodent in a cage with an enriched play environment was not so effective because a single rat would not play. It was found that the rodent had to be stimulated to interact with the objects.

What does animal research teach us? We believe it points conclusively to the need for frequent changes in environmental challenges, especially for infants. The research thus far clearly demonstrates that single containment (in a crib or playpen) can be a disaster for an infant unless his parents intervene and encourage their infant's interaction with the elements of play in his environment.

Animal research to date appears to indicate also that learning comes more readily when animals (and young humans, we believe) are put in a responsive social setting with their peers. Peers can teach each other by their example and interactions. It is participation in family life and peer groups that provides the important one-to-one relationship that child psychologists tell us motivate early learning. Social development is an essential part of the growth process. Becoming a social animal (in good standing) is a complex learning task.

*The human infant is a "social organism" as soon as he is born.* Actually even before birth, he affects everyone who is concerned about him. While his role in social relationships is fairly passive in the beginning of his life, his responses grow increasingly more active. The brand new baby starts quickly to build and use skills for living with people. Thrust abruptly into the complicated world with its myriad social institutions, customs, values, ideas, and language, he continually struggles to find his place. For many years his immaturity keeps him within the confines and protection of his family. Then as he becomes increasingly more self-sufficient, he begins to advance beyond the limits of his home into the realm of the larger society.

Although the family remains a fundamental human institution, many of its controls seem to be waning. Nonetheless, the values and attitudes in the home and the quality of interactions within the family help shape each child's social (and other) behavior. Intentionally and otherwise, parents provide their children with awareness of social attitudes and behavior and contribute importantly to their offsprings' social precepts. Even though a child's evaluation of himself and his capabilities is formed largely by parental attitudes toward him, his experiences in the company of other children sharply color his unfolding image of himself and the social world. There is little doubt that a child's first notions of social values are formed from the ways in which he is treated and from the manner in which he sees other children and adults behave. In brief, his interpersonal experiences are vital aspects of his early living and significant forces in molding him. Fortunate indeed are the children whose parents are loving, relaxed, responsive, and understanding.

Throughout the first year of life, it is the mother who is paramount in instilling a sense of well-being and security in her charge. However, good mothering becomes even more challenging when the mother needs to cease hovering. Indeed, when her infant marks his first birthday, she must increasingly liberate the child from herself so he will be able to venture forth with assurance into a larger social circle. Children who remain bound to their mothers are rarely able to build self-reliance and comfortable sociality. A child has to learn to depend on himself if he is to become an autonomous and contributing social being.

In the beginning the infant spends most of his time sleeping, some time eating, and short periods looking, listening, and touching. Research studies indicate that under three months of age, a baby rarely smiles. Between three and six months, he will smile at any full-faced view of a human or humanlike face. It appears that at this time he regards all adults as sources of gratification of his needs for food and love. When an infant first smiles in response to the smile or voice of his mother or father, he is showing that his social awareness has begun. When he starts making noises in anticipation of being picked up and cuddled, he is indicating that his social development has taken a forward step. A baby enjoys playing with his voice. He repeats sounds endlessly, no doubt in order to master them. Later he imitates sounds made by others. He learns early that his cries will bring his mother to him, that his cooing and gurgling will evoke a smiling response. He begins to learn to use quite definite sounds to express his particular feelings and desires.

Sensory stimulation, including bodily touch, involves an infant completely. Facial and vocal responses give him the guarantee he needs to let him know that his efforts at playfulness and imitation are valued. Face-to-face rhythmic finger and body games are enjoyed not only for their repetition by the infant, but because they are played with loving, attentive parents. At the same time, such games impart some basic facts to the infant about himself and the world about him.

The game of imitating his mother's sounds that the baby plays with his mother in the sixth month is the beginning of conversation. It is an infant's intuitive social intercourse with a loved one that leads ultimately to his language learning. The game has to be played actively, for nothing stimulates a baby to turn his head, to reach, and to babble better than a feedback that he gets from his smiling mother's face and her warm, responsive voice. Some of the games babies love to play at this stage involve touching the baby's toes and other parts of the body, hand clapping, et cetera.

Making mother-baby interactions easier in the important first period of social interrelationship requires adjustment in the infant's environment as we know it today. First, an infant needs to be seen easily by his mother so their faces can interact freely with each other. This can come from the use of a baby-carrying sling which provides face-to-face "reading of each other." Sitting in a reclining seat and watching mother at work in the kitchen or another room is a tremendous advance over the old way of keeping a baby always in his crib. Cribs without bars which feature large transparent "windows" also permit easy mother-child interaction. A carriage with a transparent plastic hood will likewise allow an infant to respond to his mother's affectionate stimulation.

No child can flourish in an unresponsive environment. Healthy ego development requires stability, affection, and reliability in early family life. Friendliness and spontaneity are linked with a warm family atmosphere. Dependent behavior is heightened where a family lacks unity and parental discord or rejection are present. Every normal child has great drive for social competency unless he has been injured psychologically during the course of his growing up. Throughout his childhood a child's expenditure of energy for growing and learning is controlled by the emotional responses he experiences along the way from all the people who touch his life.

*The sixteen-week-old recognizes his mother.* He also recognizes all familiar caretakers in expectancies established through feeding, bathing, dressing, and expressions of affection. He usually smiles on familiar social approach but may keep an unsmiling face on seeing a stranger. However, the adult who bides his time will find that before too long the baby's strong social feelings will come out, and the new face will not remain rejected. Even though he cannot yet balance his head squarely, the sixteen-week-old enjoys being propped up in a sitting position because this vantage point affords him a new social vista.

*At forty weeks of age, the infant likes to have people around.* He can now play himself for a half hour or so, but he does not like to be left alone for long stretches of time. His new social responsiveness enables him to play and thoroughly enjoy "Pat-a-Cake." He will smile at his own mirror image. He may still show some reserve when greeted by a stranger, but it is fascinating to note that his reaction to strangeness is itself an indication of his increasing social sensibility.

The extended family, with grandparents, aunts, uncles, and cousins close at hand, provides, where it still exists, a natural bridge between the familiarity of life at home and subsequent coexistence with strangers in the wider world of the park, the playground, and the school. There are fewer extended families in the United States today and as a result many mothers have less relief from the care of their very young children, which does not always result in good mothering. At the same time, increasing numbers of married women with young children are at work outside the home. The result of this is the occupation of registered and unregistered child-minders. Many professional families rely on *au pair* girls or other help to look after their young children all or part of the day. Unfortunately, most child-minders are not trained to look after the young child. There is a new movement in our country to train high school seniors to become semi-professional child-care workers. Senior citizens are also being given paid assignments as child-care assistants. We believe that social relations with differing age levels is an important part of rounding out a child's experiences in social living.

*Crawling expands an infant's social horizons.* After the restricted and often sterile environments of the crib or playpen, the crawler can now encounter many more people and objects and engage in new social actions, out of all of which he must learn to make some sense. His mother begins seriously her role of sensitively guiding her infant's interaction with a broader world. She bolsters him in all his accomplishments, thus encouraging his eagerness to learn. Placing a colorful rolling toy on the floor will impel him to move toward it. Putting a favorite toy out of reach and playing hide-and-seek games with him will add to the infant's understanding of things outside of himself. Language learning takes place every moment of an infant's day, especially when there is active parent-child interplay. In the street, in the park, in the supermarket, in a ride in the car, the mother calls attention to objects and lets her infant handle them whenever possible as she labels each thing with its appropriate name.

*The one-year-old has social status in his family.* He has become an influential family member. He shows a meaningful inclination to repeat performances laughed at whereby he pleases himself as much as he does his appreciative audience. Through repeated interchanges, he starts to feel his self-identity. He resorts to vocal and other means to procure attention, another basic social reference. He is now able to connect specific sounds with specific effects and to know these sounds when others make them. He has begun to recognize more and more of the people and things around him.

*There are optimal periods for infants to build interpersonal relations.* At eighteen months, when locomotion and some language enable a child to shape his relations with others besides close relatives, he can approach or avoid individuals and actually influence them. Maturing and learning cause most of the changes that take place during a child's development. Often these changes are stages in the dynamic growth of each child. Learning to walk changes the supportive emotional and communicative relationships between the child and the meaningful people in his life. His environment is considerably enlarged and enriched because his mobility permits him contact with ever-expanding varieties of people, things, and places. He is no longer wholly dependent upon his parents.

Communicating with others besides parents and siblings is a hard task for the toddler. Heretofore his non-verbalized needs were usually properly interpreted by his family members, who perceived from his face or sounds what he wanted. When he is able to walk, he suddenly needs usable language in order to get along with others. Now he is ready for vocabulary building as never before. Especially in this period, a child's command of language grows or retards, frustrations ease or become complicated, ego grows or deflates, depending on the play settings and toys that are provided for verbal interchanges.

Placing small objects in toy containers, fitting shapes, and searching out a miniature auto and putting it in a toy garage, all at the relaxed direction of a parent, encourage sorting activity, sequence learning, and the naming of objects. Giving a toddler a favorite stuffed toy and having him do different things with it—making it sit, stand, lie down, walk—and labeling each act will greatly help vocabulary building.

*The normal toddler behaves egotistically and asocially.* He is still not experienced enough to have awareness of the feelings of others. He is interested in other children or adults chiefly as objects to touch, explore, hug, and sometimes to hit or bite.

If another child were to be in the way of a toddler pushing a carriage, the toddler would move forward as if the other child were an inanimate object. Should the other child fall over or cry, the toddler would continue along his merry, self-centered way. At this stage, a Teddy bear or other stuffed toy is a perfect playmate because one can do anything one wishes to it. The toddler also enjoys push-and-pull toys, especially those that make pleasing sounds. His stuffed animals and dolls wear out from constant lugging and hugging. The toddler is an indefatigable imitator and investigator. He delights in pretending to read a newspaper or magazine, cook, sweep the floor, or shovel snow.

*The eighteen-month-old engages in solitary or parallel play.* However, he may cry if a companion leaves or he may tag along after him. His quick changes in attention are reflected in his gross motor shifts. He moves with lightning speed from place to place and gets into everything. He is completely egocentric because he does not yet see other persons as beings like himself. While the happy eighteen-to-twenty-four-month-old will gravitate to his age-mates, he is not ready for steady play with other children, no matter what their age. He has to learn how, and social development takes much time and experimentation. Although the toddler is starting to be somewhat independent of his mother, he must keep on increasing his disengagement if he is to have a healthy image of himself.

*The two-year-old likes to be with other children even before he is prepared for co-operative play.* Normally he is affectionate and happy and laughs wholeheartedly and infectiously. He will mimic the emotional expressions of all the people in his social sphere. Two-year-old boys and girls act out the mother-baby relationship through play with their dolls and stuffed animals. They especially respond to playthings they can hug, pat, or pound. Their interest in stuffed toy animals and dolls will continue for many years. They also like to string large beads and drop them into holes on the top of a box and then dump them out. They will repeat the play interminably. Toddlers prefer having blocks in a small wagon to building with them. They have little obvious interest in what other children do or say at this stage of their upgrowth.

In time, the child who has been treated with affection and consideration will develop his own spirit of generosity. However, his unselfishness and feeling for others are limited during his first three years of life. It takes a long time for a child to learn to share and to control his negative behavior when he is frustrated. As a result, it is up to the parents to nurture good will and the spirit of co-operation in their small children.

*Much frustration among two-year-olds stems from their inability to control the adult world.* Things are too big to manage, to push around, or to make do what the toddler wishes. The beginning walker is not aware of "precious" things or fine furniture as being out of bounds. He has no notions as yet of "right" or "wrong." The toddler seeks to be in the driver's seat of every car, to push every carriage himself, and throw himself into every doll bed. The two-year-old feels he must play the dominant role in every situation, and perhaps that is his temporary right at this stage because ego building is a necessary first step to developing social competence. To assuage the inevitable frustrations every two-year-old faces, it is necessary to provide him with a planned environment of toys, equipment, and furnishings that are scaled down to his size and capabilities. Everything should be neither too small for his inexperienced hands nor too large for his not yet fully developed body to handle.

*Infant-toddler play groups.* Some mothers form infant-toddler play groups, which usually include five or six little ones who meet regularly in each other's homes to play, with each mother taking turns to supervise the activities. Such play groups are not baby-sitting arrangements; rather they are co-operative undertakings. The participating mothers plan the play sessions and provide suitable play materials and activities. Even though the infant-toddler members of the play groups do not play together, it may be that their play takes on more meaning when they are in a group. Each play session usually lasts about two hours.

Even if babies do not need or benefit from a play group, some psychologists say that it may be that their mothers do. Most young mothers, especially of first-borns, learn a great deal from watching the behavior and play of all the children in the play group, and many grow more relaxed. Even though very young children seem to learn more from older children and adults, the play group can help each co-operating mother to understand and enjoy her own child more. In addition, the organized play setting permits the children to choose from a broader variety of well-chosen playthings and activities than they may have available in their own homes.

*The three-year-old shows he is maturing by being more outgoing.* However, writes Susan Isaacs, "Storms of open defiance are very common towards the end of the second year of growth and for a year or two later, even in children who have been placid babies. They seem to be largely an early form of self-assertion that passes away as the child comes to greater skill and social ease. They are trying enough at the time, but an atmosphere of calm and firm patience and steady affection helps them to disperse."

The behavior of the three-year-old toward his peers indicates that he is now better able to identify with others. He displays increasing interest in playing with other children and is beginning to understand what it means to wait his turn, although he does not usually relish this. Sometimes he will even share his toys. The play groups of three-year-olds constantly shift in composition and activity. The children may play together for half an hour or so, but when the common objective has been achieved, the group falls apart and usually each child goes his own way.

The three-year-old delights in combining building blocks and all kinds of toy vehicles to make cities with roadways, bridges, tunnels, garages, and so forth. He enjoys playing house, flying planes, driving trains, or being fireman. Before long, he discovers that it is more fun and more interesting when a few children carry out the play together. Maneuvering wooden ride'em trucks and trains on casters works well with a few children playing together. Pushing or pulling a wagon or doll carriage in which another child sits and building co-operatively with large hollow blocks likewise contribute to the establishment of agreeable social relations. Sharing a sandbox also enhances social awareness. Thus, sometimes alone and sometimes with a few age-mates, preschoolers go about their momentous task of growing up and learning.

A *child's social growth impinges upon his ability to communicate with others.* Accordingly, the need to communicate is a great motivating force for learning language. Toy telephones elicit active talking and verbal interchange. Picture books and simple stories and poems are perfect media for language building during a child's preschool years. Children especially enjoy picture books that deal with experiences with which they are familiar. Each child identifies completely as he looks at the pictures and listens to his mother or father telling the story. He delights in naming and renaming all the objects pictured. The young child listens to phonograph records endlessly until he knows all the words of a song, and folk singers like Woody Guthrie and Pete Seeger are favored because of the word repetition and lilt of their material for children.

Many three- and four-year-olds intently watch TV programs —"Sesame Street," for one—that emphasize perception, word recognition, and language. No one works harder at learning language than the two-to-four-year-old. He repeats words and phrases over and over again until he masters them. One of the dangers of "Sesame Street"-type presentations, we believe, is that they rely primarily on pictures and words and do not encourage the viewing child to interact with the material presented by using his own body actively. Most child psychologists today agree that the handling of objects serves the preschool child as a dynamic frame of reference.

A child's spontaneity, clarity, and fluency in the use of language are indications of his sense of security, albeit there are broad normal individual differences in the amount of talking children do. Children who are handicapped in hearing and speaking suffer mentally, emotionally, and socially. Many parents often need help to distinguish between language problems that are temporary and will be outgrown with intelligent guidance and problems that require specialized professional treatment. Many three-and-a-half- and four-year-old children stutter for awhile, often because their ideas and their eagerness to express them outrun their language facility. As a child has more language experience and confidence, the stuttering tends to diminish and disappear. However, stammering created by emotional tensions or other personal developmental problems may require professional diagnosis and extended treatment.

*The sociality of the four-year-old shows improvement.* Unless a child is exceedingly withdrawn or timid, he now makes more social approaches in his play and spends more time in social contacts with members of a play group. In determining a child's readiness for group play, age is not the only factor. Individual differences in rate of development and personal temperament must also be considered. The play pattern of the average four-year-old is co-operative group play with two or three other children. Both boys and girls of this age enjoy dramatic or imaginative play. However, because some four-year-olds are still immature, they are not always able to establish social relations with their peers at the first exposure. They may require help from adults and a well-planned environment that makes social play inviting and easy.

*Preschool education pioneers developed in the nursery school a planned environment in which social interactions are a natural outcome.* The playroom is usually divided by screens into separate areas for homemaking play, block building, music making, arts and crafts activities, quiet play, and a daily rest period. In each section, the playthings and equipment are arranged so the children can play together at times and by themselves at other times. In all instances they can test and practice their relations with their peers. The child-sized wood stove, kitchen cupboard, sink, table and chairs, and kitchen utensils permit a few children at a time to "cook food for a dinner party" and to set the table with appropriate dishes and cutlery. The child-sized doll bed and dresser and assorted dolls also permit several children to play together. Preschool girls and boys eagerly join forces to play at family living. Dress-up and theater arts activities, as well as doll and dollhouse play, thoroughly engage four-year-olds in imaginative role playing. They like also to play simple picture lotto and domino games. Nursery school children rejoice in making music with their age-mates and respond with enthusiasm to rhythmic activities.

The nursery school can help young children handle and express their feelings of aggression by helping them learn how to cope with them in ways that are socially acceptable. Puppets, a punching bag, giant push'em balls, and other such toys make it possible for young children to release their tensions by bringing their pent-up emotions to the outside.

Nursery school playground equipment was also deliberately designed by the preschool education pioneers to further social interplay between little children. Large packing crates require three or four children if they are to be moved about and played with. Eight-foot bouncing or seesaw boards need at least two children for their use. Building with hollow blocks also invites group play. Wagons need a puller and a rider. The ladder box permits group adventuring, as does a jungle gym and a horizontal ladder. The tendency of many of today's nursery schools to eliminate the "packing-crate philosophy" and substitute cheaper, lightweight items curtails important social-physical interplay at the preschool level.

*The five-year-old is comparatively independent.* He is protective toward younger siblings and playmates, and his friendships are becoming firmer. He actively chooses to engage in associative play with two or more age-mates. He wants and needs playmates and enjoys group projects that include the construction of houses, airport and train layouts, and all kinds of community set-ups with blocks and other accessory play materials. He is able to carry his interest over from day to day and has definite intention to finish what he starts, even though it may take a few days. Crayoning has increased appeal, and he likes cutting and pasting. The five-year-old also enjoys dress-up play. He loves to go on excursions that enrich his play. Although he does not yet possess a sophisticated notion of co-operation, he is more alert to social demands. He is learning to play and work in group ways in kindergarten. With advancing chronological age during the preschool years there is an increase in all forms of social interaction. At the same time, the relative proportion of acceptable to unacceptable methods of social behavior tends to increase. Some of this may come about because the older child relies more heavily on verbal than on purely physical contacts.

During the pre-grade school years a child moves from being relatively self-absorbed to becoming increasingly social. There are expansions in the size of play groups, in the duration of co-operative activity, and in a child's ability to follow the rules of a very simple game. Young children are eager to learn, and their play usually shows what they are learning day by day. Play with other children, more than any other activity, helps forward a child's social competence.

Social development can be measured in terms of a child's mobility, communication ability, self-care, self-directed activity, and social attitudes and behavior. The six-year-old, for instance, can attend to his toilet needs, wash his hands and face, dress and feed himself, talk in complete sentences, use and enjoy a bicycle, a scooter, skates, and a sled, get along with his age-mates, wait his turn, and obey simple rules. The closer he comes to this level of maturity, the more he is ready and able to take his place in the world of the sixes. Becoming independent of adult supervision and control is a long, arduous process, which entails years of growing, experimenting, and playing out social situations.

Some of the skills that are acquired as a child learns to relate to others are giving, receiving, and sharing; expressing feelings and ideas; and making choices. Social competency also includes techniques for expressing interest and friendship, for welcoming and including others in play, and for initiating and carrying on group activities. No child enjoys an adequate social life unless he has acquired the ability to play with other children. Every child wants to be part of a group of children his own age.

He achieves stature only as he is accepted and respected by the group members, as he plays or works with them in the attainment of mutual goals, as he makes contributions to group projects, and as he learns that group life calls for initiative as well as conformity.

It is a herculean challenge for children to try to meet the behavioral and learning demands of their parents, the school, and society. "The human is a social creature," writes James L. Hymes, Jr. "His sociality is a quality of the utmost significance. If it were not for this deep-seated social urge, disciplining a child so that he could live in society would be an almost insuperable job. Fortunately children want to live with others and need to live with others . . . The whole direction of their internal maturation is toward the ways of acting that make human society possible."

*Consideration for others is a learned social skill.* How well a child relates to other children and adults depends on his ability to get to know and accept other people. The growing child needs more than beneficial nourishment and good physical care, more than parental love and wholehearted family acceptance, as necessary as the foregoing are to his total well-being. However, if he is to attain his optimal development, a child must also have suitable playthings and playmates and full opportunity for play. Children, if left alone, will seek play and playmates as if their lives depended on it—and perhaps they do!

*A child learns to relate to life and the people and things in it when he is not isolated from the world and its goings-on.* His first attempts at wider socialization come when the family includes others in its activities. People of varying ages, temperaments, occupations, and relationships stimulate a child's feelings, his curiosity, and his thinking. Parents and teachers who are alert to the need for building social acceptance between varying age groups take steps to organize an environment that fosters such social interchange. One school principal we knew insisted on building within the school community close relations between the different grade levels. The twelve-year-olds, for instance, made toys for the three-year-olds, and the eleven-year-olds read to the four-year-olds stories they had themselves written and printed.

Throughout his social development, a child spends less and less time with his family and more in play with children his own age. This gradual transference, which extends over several years, is a major process in a child's social sophistication. Positively, there is more independent behavior and increased participation in peer group activities. On the negative side, it expresses itself in a growing revolt against parental control and often in a critical attitude toward parents and the home. The peer group is a child's very own social milieu, with its special language, mode of interaction, loyalties, values, and acceptable forms of behavior—many of which the grownup cannot understand. The child has equal and at times even superior status with others in this child-sized dominion, not the subordinate role he invariably has with his parents and other adults.

Play groups that form before primary school days begin have some features that set them apart from later play groups. The choice of playmates is relatively restricted in kind and number because the preschool child must accept or reject whoever happens to be available in his immediate area. Once in school, a child may choose playmates from among many children. His increasing self-reliance allows him to play away from his immediate neighborhood. The play group is a child's introduction to a group that appraises him as a child, from a child's point of view, and teaches him rules of conduct from the same viewpoint. Each child enters a new and powerful world when he joins a play group, which is the most informal of peer groupings. It is essentially an alliance of equals to share in a common play experience or the use of a common play space or play equipment. Play groups that tend to be temporary alignments function mostly from the sixth to the twelfth years. Playing in a group of equals provides as well many situations for learning about property rights and taking turns.

Play helps a child try out his social skill. Children have a strong need to get and give love. In their play, young children also find outlets for such wishes as a desire to dominate, destroy, display their prowess, make noise, or make a mess. The child who in real life finds it difficult to construct, to repair damage, to help, or to give of himself to others can find many opportunities to do so in make-believe play, as well as in reality through co-operative play with others. There is really nothing mysterious about the power of play. Play is basic to all normal, healthy children. It provides pleasure and learning and a minimum of risks and penalties for mistakes. Because it enables them to escape the restraints and frustrations of the real world, play provides children with greater opportunity to experiment and dare and more possibilities for the full exercise of the imagination.

The nursery school is in no way a substitute for parents and the home. However, one drawback in the home is limited space for indoor play or lack of a safe outdoor area where small children can safely run, climb, build, or dig. Even in a house or apartment where there is sufficient space and equipment for a child's play, the routines of the household often keep the mother from spending sufficient time with her child. On the other hand, the nursery school teacher is not distracted by house-cleaning chores, doorbells ringing, meals to be cooked, telephone calls, shopping, et cetera. Also, the sturdy, simple furnishings of the nursery school can always be shifted to make big, open spaces as needed. In the nursery school there are fewer restrictions on normal child play, and the nursery school teacher's prime function is to respect what each child is trying to do and to help him do it. Program planning for preschoolers takes into account the wide range of individual differences found within any age group. Therefore, in the nursery school there is a balance of individual and group activities in which each child can find activities and materials suited to his inclinations and abilities. The nursery school provides as well materials that are not readily available in most homes.

The child for whom the nursery school will be most productive is the one whose home life has already enabled him to develop sufficient independence, self-confidence, and ability to get along with his peers. Yet it is the dependent child, the one whose emotional needs interfere with his ability to relate to social situations or whose background of language and information is inadequate to provide him with tools of effective communication, whose need for the nursery school experience is the most urgent.

As previously indicated, a child's social growth is interlaced with his language skill. If parents talk to their child, read to him, listen to what he has to say and ask; if they provide him with interesting activities at home, such as baking cookies, watering plants, helping feed the cat or dog; if they take him to a restaurant now and again, to a firehouse or an airport, and help him develop a vocabulary to fit all his experiences, they will be providing important language support for his social development. Just as parents play a vital role in helping their children build personality, language power, and social maturity, so the nursery school and kindergarten have significant contributions to make. The too-quiet home or schoolroom will not encourage children to attain language command because language must be used to be mastered.

*The four facets of language that every child needs to master are listening, speaking, reading, and writing.* Listening and talking are the most used means of communication, but reading ability is basic to all academic learning. Listening and reading are input processes whereby the child enriches himself by adding to his knowledge and interests. Speaking and writing are output aspects of language by means of which a child expresses himself and communicates his thinking to others. Learning to write does not begin with putting pencil and paper into a young child's hands, with some material for him to copy. Written language usually begins for the young child with the writing down by an adult of the child's spontaneous expression. His first experiences may come through his dictating to his mother messages to be included in letters to a grandparent or favorite aunt or uncle. Or it may be the mother's writing down her child's oral recollections of their visit to a circus, firehouse, or other exciting place. When a young child tells his parent or teacher all about one of his paintings or drawings, he is engaged in beginning "writing."

Some children are slow talkers because they have no need for talking; their every wish is anticipated by doting parents and siblings. The child who has learned to get everything he wants through pointing, whining, screaming, or baby talk may feel little need for speaking. The nursery school teacher who consistently fails to understand such methods of communication and waits for the child's efforts at speech before satisfying his wants will soon have the child wanting to talk. She gives the child the words with which he can relay his desires and get the responses he seeks. If talking brings the satisfaction of his wants, together with appreciation for his efforts, the child will inevitably begin regular talking.

*A young child stretches the boundaries of his world by means of make believe.* In his flights of fancy, he goes beyond the bounds of space and time; he performs feats beyond the limits of his strength. He employs imagination in his social activity because much of his play with other children takes place in fantasy settings. When children play at being the mother, father, or baby, the doctor or nurse, the fireman or policeman, et cetera, they are externalizing their feelings and ideas. Dramatic play gives young children a direct, personal means of communication and co-operation at an age when social growth is beginning to ascend levels of increasing maturity. However, imaginative play has greater reality value for the very young child than for somewhat older ones. The younger the child, the easier it is for him to accept substitute satisfactions when original objects are not available. In their dramatic play, children often reverse the roles they normally assume in real life. An aggressive child might play the part of a gentle mother, a submissive one might relish being a domineering father, and a usually self-reliant child might choose the role of the baby. As they role-play, most children try to break through the restrictions that confine them. Logical thinking and verbalization are difficult for six-year-old and younger children. Nevertheless, they do have ways of expressing their understandings and using their knowledge for purposes meaningful to themselves. Dramatic play is often their language and their logic. Play is still necessary to six-year-olds because they are not yet in possession of complete clarity, and in play there is no penalty for steps back into fantasy. Children consolidate all their learnings in their play.

*An only child can often have a difficult time making social adjustments.* Living with adults and discovering social graces through them are insufficient preparation for the rough-and-tumble give-and-take of social relations with one's peers. Parents have to recognize this by sending their "only" to nursery school. In the home they need to provide an environment of play in which social roles with imaginary peers can be rehearsed. Child-sized brother or sister dolls at a tea table and puppets are some good tools for freely dramatizing interactions with make-believe siblings or friends. By constant rearrangement of his make-believe social setting, the only child can test out his feelings and relationships and prepare himself for ultimate social play with real age-mates. This imaginary playing out of roles and changing of situations can often lead to the development of sensitivities not usually found in children from large families. These sensitivities are often present in highly gifted people. In studies made of American "geniuses," it was found that they were more often an only child who was forced to fantasize relationships with make-believe siblings.

*A few thoughts about sibling rivalry.* The arrival of a second child can throw an older child into a temporary, regressive, emotional tailspin. But whether a child is a first-born who is replaced by a new baby or a newborn who finds older brothers or sisters when he arrives, he will eventually have to come to grips with feelings of jealousy. Writes Margaret Mead, "When a new baby is born, the world of the older child is enlarged but it is no longer his world exclusively . . . he must learn to share his mother's love and care, his father's games, his grandparents' indulgence . . . Whether the older child welcomes the newcomer with excitement and hope . . . or greets the newcomer with resentment . . . he will henceforth see life with different eyes, and in the future his feelings toward all other children will be colored by this response to a younger brother or sister—welcoming or fearful, warm or coldly distant."

Whether siblings are of the same or opposite sexes, the painful sense of loss of undivided love and attention cannot be avoided. This rivalry occurs in all families where there are several children. The most open forms of competition between children at ages three, four, and older are tattling, taking, breaking, or hiding the sibling's toys, as well as teasing and fighting. All brothers and sisters go through normal periods of rivalry with each other, competing for many things but most especially for the attention of the parents. While there appears to be no way of doing away with this, a child's feelings of hostility will decline as the understanding and patience of his mother and father increase. Parents need to demonstrate their ongoing love and interest to their first-born. While the baby sleeps, the mother can read to her older child, play a game with him that he enjoys, and otherwise show him that she still cares. She can have her older child help with the care of the baby whenever this is feasible. She must make every effort not to let her older child feel left out.

Sibling rivalry is faced, too, by parents whose children are spaced several years apart. Profoundly influenced by the much older brother or sister, the younger child will imitate and take on dangerous feats for which his limited understanding and co-ordination may not yet be prepared. Rivalry between children can lead to all sorts of conflicts that can only tax the ingenuity and forbearance of mothers and fathers. Properly directed play can become a helpful outlet and lessen the build-up of hostile emotions and aggressive behavior. Whether sibling rivalry is resolved with or without ill effects is solely dependent upon the attitude of the parents toward all their children.

Research studies show that conflicts between children are more frequent when play space is limited and the equipment and play facilities are not adequate. Co-operation is encouraged by such items as tricycles with a place for a rider on the back, wagons, and so on. Dramatic-physical play with sawhorses, barrels, and pails (some of the tools of community workers) offers limitless opportunities for the interplay of several children. The competent teacher recognizes the needs of young children to use their bodies with ever-increasing dexterity, to learn from each other, and to extend their experiences and knowledge.

The perceptive teacher is able to create leadership experiences for non-leader children through the careful selection and formation of subgroups of non-ascendant children. The child who has self-confidence and reacts appropriately in social situations is the child most accepted in the group. He leads out of an interest in the activity shared with other children rather than out of a need to dominate or have his own way. The teacher also helps each child increase his social awareness and skill through discussions that give some understanding of incidents that take place during each school day. Some children come to nursery school and kindergarten equipped with good techniques for interacting with others. Others come aggressive or withdrawn and find it hard to take their place in the group. However, most children come wanting to count with their peers and teachers, as well as to have fun and to learn.

*The group games that children play.* Usually when children reach about seven years of age, they begin to participate in a form of peer group play that entails child-determined organization, rules, leadership, and boundaries. The forms these group games take are varied, depending upon the ages and interests of the group members, but participation gives each child a glowing sense of self-worth and belonging. With advances in years, there is increasing importance of membership in age-mate clubs and play in team games. Formally organized and competitive athletic games appeal to those children whose feeling for team work and respect for fixed rules are most prevalent and who have some athletic prowess.

For younger children there are hide-and-seek games and the ever-popular game of tag, which include running, chasing, and capturing. Since these activities require no special skills, most boys and girls enjoy them thoroughly. In games of pretend combat and daring encounters, sides are also selected. Either all are pitted against one, as in "Blind Man's Buff," or the group may be separated into two equal opposing teams, as in "Cowboys and Indians."

Intellectual games have appeal for most children, beginning even at the six-year-old level. However, as is true with all games, practice improves a child's ability to play. A few popular board games are checkers and number dominoes and card games like rummy, old maid, and snap, as well as games which can be played with regular playing cards, like "go fish." School-aged children delight in playing games of chance that employ dice, balls, numbers, playing cards, or a spinner. Snakes and ladders, Parchesi, and Monopoly are some of the board games that are still most popular.

Games that require some physical dexterity include marbles, darts, ringtoss, jackstraws, tiddlywinks, and pick-up-sticks. All are good social games because two or more children are needed to play and enjoy them. Temporary defeat is an acceptable part of the games because otherwise the players could not continue to take turns and each game would bog down.

Guessing games are heartily enjoyed after age six. There is an exciting element in pitting one's mental acuity against another's, and it is even more fun when done by two competing teams, as in charades. All children need to learn to win with grace and to lose without too great anguish, both of which attitudes are more easily said than done. Playing for the challenge and sheer pleasure of a game with friends is a basic social learning.

As children approach their teens, they want to engage in highly organized team play. At this time, most are better able to think of the good of the group and not merely their own desires. So it is that children "graduate" from their early unorganized rough-and-tumble physical games to such rigidly organized sports as baseball, hockey, basketball, football, volley ball, soccer, and team swimming.

The very young child plays group games with complete disregard of the rules. In fact, there is a constant rearrangement of the rules of a game to suit the whims or the lack of skill of most young players. With older children, however, disregarding the rules is frowned upon and even regarded as cheating. Of course, children differ broadly in the degree of their interest in group sports, and some who lack experience and practice in motor skills often become onlookers instead of active participants.

*Children are usually most co-operative when engaged in satisfying play together.* They can turn rivalries into make-believe play instead of open conflicts. Social learning takes place in relation to the resolution of conflicts as well as in co-operative play. While adult behavior, criticism, and suggestions serve as part of the basis for the learning of sociality in the young child, the subtleties of sharing, playing, or working together, tolerance of diverse personalities, and agreeable participation in group life come from a long period of early practice in which all kinds of social encounters and obstacles are met and resolved. No period offers more opportunities for practice in social living than the first ten years of life.

CHAPTER FOUR

# Learning Power in Play

When psychologist Dr. Benjamin S. Bloom took a two-year sabbatical from the University of Chicago to begin an across-the-boards look at the child development researches of the previous thirty years, he initiated a chain of events that will have tremendous impact on education in this country for the next hundred years. What he found in his examination of the statistics and curves of child growth, as set forth in his book *Stability and Change in Human Characteristics* was that the period of greatest learning are the years from birth to about age eight (precisely when play is a child's prevalent way of life!). He discovered that 80 per cent of all learning at age seventeen is attained by eight years of age, that 50 per cent is attained by age four. Academic interest, according to Dr. Bloom, comes before the eighth year. (In a sample survey of professionals listed in Who's Who, undertaken by us in 1967, almost 70 per cent of those who responded indicated that their academic interests were evident in the years between five and ten.) *

* "Learning," as we use the term throughout this book, is meant to cover a wide range of self-chosen sensori-motor experiences, emotional behavior, play, perceptual development, and language and other skills that result from the young child's informal interactions with his peers, as well as with stimulating people and things in his environment. Academic learning is a later development that is concerned with the teaching of specific skills—reading, writing, arithmetic, spelling, and so on—generally taught in a classroom in more formal ways when the child first enters elementary school, and thereafter.

Mounting evidence of the tremendous learning power in these early years has resulted in the undertaking of all kinds of research projects to explore how early learning takes place, how concepts are built, how language expands learning, whether infants see and discriminate in the first four weeks of life, and so on. So far none of these surveys vouchsafes our assertion that the methodology that best carries out early learning is the environmental stimulation and active imaginative play that takes place in the home, the preschool, and the kindergarten. We believe, however, that new research studies will substantiate our judgment that there is extraordinary learning power in play and an enriched environment of playthings. After all, children do not play in a mental vacuum; they use and test all their ideas as they play. We daresay that play is the child's most dynamic manner of learning.

Nevertheless, many psychologists who use tests designed to measure verbal facility are reporting that their findings concerning the intervention of play, toys, and playmates do not show "growth in learning" in the nursery years. We seriously question whether IQ alone is a true measure of "learning." There needs to be considerable in-depth research to determine whether language ability is one of the outcomes of play. Fortunately there are psychologists today who recognize that the "old-style" intelligence tests do not measure a broad range of "intelligence"; rather, they gauge one's ability to learn specific academic skills, which is, after all, only one aspect of intelligence.

One must ask what is the real meaning of education? Is it memory and recall or does it also encompass the laying down of such traits as creativity, the courage to try the unknown, wholesome self-image, self-confidence, and inner discipline and drive? If these characteristics are fundamental to fulfilling adult life, then play must be considered a powerhouse of learning. Play needs to be given its due recognition. It must be measured eventually by insightful tests as yet not developed. Until the true learning power in play in early childhood is thoroughly and accurately researched, parents, teachers, and psychologists need to maintain their intuitive belief in the tremendous learning power inherent in child play.

Much learning occurs in the course of play. Childhood educators have always had intuitive thoughts about the learning that takes place during play. They have advocated extensive periods of play in the nursery school and kindergarten in the belief that such experiences help build interpersonal relations, permit children to adjust to their peers, and prepare young children for the inner discipline and resources they will need during the demanding years of academic study and throughout life. However, even today too many educators are not ready to support the idea that play and the use of play materials with age-mates accelerate learning at a rate that few formal institutions of learning have ever attained, even with the most modern teaching technology and equipment.

Lawrence K. Frank, author and lecturer on human growth and development, in an article entitled "Play Is Valid," published in the March 1968 issue of *Childhood Education*, had this to say about play and learning: "With his sensory capacities, the child learns not only to look but to see, not only to hear but to listen, not only to touch but to feel and grasp what he handles. He tastes whatever he can get into his mouth. He begins to smell what he encounters. He can and will—if not handicapped, impaired or blocked, master these many experiences through continual play . . . the most intensive and fruitful learning activity in his whole life cycle." Young children are highly self-motivated to determine the how and why of things in their play. They are almost continuously involved in the process of concept formation and in clarifying and extending their understandings of the world.

The importance of the home and its family members. It may well be that the family and home are a better place for early cognitive development than the limiting classroom. How else can we explain why there have been three-year-olds with a vocabulary of some two thousand words? Why some children come to first grade with the ability to read and write? Why most preschool children can learn a foreign language in a new country in a few months while adults usually take years of hard study to accomplish the same objective? It is now clear that a low IQ may be due, among other things, to the failure of the home and neighborhood to provide the preschool child with incentives for involvement in intellectual activity and abstract thinking. The family and home that give a child opportunities to affect his environment and in which he can feel competent and contributing will be doing more than the very best that any school can offer today's young child.

What makes the home a better place for learning to take place? Obviously there are usually loving parents and stimulating siblings to provide constant example, incentives, and encouragement as well as important language feedback. The home and neighborhood can also provide many more varied opportunities for seeing, hearing, touching, and motor activity than can the circumscribed classroom. For every perception or act of a child in his home, there is a word-labeling procedure by the mother. "Baby has a book," "Baby is eating apple sauce," "This is a dog," and so it goes for several hours a day, accompanied by the infant's seeing, hearing, feeling, tasting, smelling, and other motor-sensory activities. Ideally, in the home there is responsiveness to the child's needs and the individual attention that cannot always be evoked from the teacher who is burdened with some thirty to fifty children. For each stage of physical and mental maturation, there are suitable objects or playthings to manipulate. In the home there usually are no bells to stop what a child is doing and certainly no curriculum pressures. An action or experiment can be tried again and again until mastered to the child's satisfaction, and there are usually appreciative adults—parents or grandparents—ready to give encouragement and support to the child's reaching out.

Many early childhood educators maintain that the earliest a parent should send a child to school is three years of age. Whenever circumstances require an earlier school experience, parents are requested to be close at hand until the child is comfortably acclimated. Through the ongoing years of a child's education, parents' and teachers' roles need to be co-operative. Unfortunately, the involvement of the mother, as well as the father, gets too little attention in the current debate on education. Although certain aspects of a child's development are best handled in the home, others are better accomplished in the school. The sooner parents and teachers define their parts and evaluate what each milieu can do best, the more meaningful will be the child's learning.

To comprehend which environment—the home or the school—can do the best job and where both should share the responsibility, one must understand each stage of child development. Parents and teachers need to know the sequences of the learning process, the particular behavior of children at each successive stage of growth, the most sensitive periods, the best type of learning suitable at each maturation level, and the kind of environment and activity that brings such learning about.

*Some learning theories.* For centuries, debate and controversy have posed the question of whether a child's growth and learning potentials are predetermined by heredity or whether they can be affected positively or negatively by environmental factors. Simply stated, the advocates of the first position hold that (given adequate diet, air, sleep, et cetera) a child's intelligence is set at the moment of conception and cannot be altered by changes in his interaction with the physical and interpersonal elements in his environment. Those advocating the latter point of view argue that interaction with people and objects controls a child's behavior and learning and hence can affect intelligence.

There have been concrete studies with animals that indicate that changes in the environment and stimulation can cause pigeons, for example, to detect and "learn" when food is used as an inducement; that information-processing parts of the brain develop faster in animals that are "handled, stroked, shaken, sung to or stimulated" during the first days of life; that nerve connections in the brain develop more slowly in newborn rats that are left undisturbed in their litters than in rats that are subjected to a variety of environmental stimulations; that newborn mice that are visually deprived by living in the dark develop fewer nerve connections in the vision center of the brain; that the brain of monkeys that play with toys are larger and heavier than those that are deprived of play material and the opportunity to play.

These animal researches have spearheaded recent research on the immediate learning power of infants. We now know that infants see and distinguish at birth; that they can locate and follow sounds; and they perceive depth, distance, and movement. Research on the sensory powers of infants had so excited educators that they took steps to describe and define the stages that an infant goes through to acquire concepts and solve problems. Others assessed the kinds of environmental factors that stimulate babbling, reaching, and visual following. Toymakers developed many modifications of traditional cribs, in addition to manufacturing new manipulative toys for babies.

*Stages of child development.* Dr. Piaget and other child psychologists have attempted to define the stages of child development during which learning takes place. Piaget refers to the period from birth to two years as the sensori-motor stage. From the very first day of birth an infant seeks to affect and master his environment. His early motions are primarily reflexive; he responds in an uncontrolled and undifferentiated way to his surroundings. Everything is lived rather than thought out. At this time an infant's intelligence can be likened to a fixed succession of images, each connected with an action. Through external stimulation in the earliest months—parents and play—an infant attains the following rudimentary knowledge: he establishes a differentiation of himself from objects, localizes himself in space, and establishes awareness of cause and effect as well as of space and time.

During the first months of life an infant shows little but reflexive behavior. His first action is that of seeing, and he looks for the sake of looking. There is sufficient evidence in modern research to indicate that from birth a baby is capable of visually discriminating many features of his environment. In fact, babies follow objects visually eighteen hours after birth. Researchers in infancy have found this out by watching eye motions and the orientation of the infant's head. They find that babies prefer patterns to plain figures, irregular to regular shapes, centered to diffuse patterns, three-dimensional shadowed patterns to flat ones, and moving figures to still ones. Researchers have recently spent much time trying to find out why as early as two months infants seem to show preference for a scrambled rather than a standard face with proper features where they should be. Can it be that from birth infants are challenged by novelty and distinctive detail?

Dr. Jerome Kagan, professor of developmental psychology at Harvard, has done some fascinating work with four-month-olds employing three different kinds of faces: one is the outline of a face, another a flesh-colored sculpture of a regular male face, and the third a distorted version of the same face with the eyes, nose, and mouth rearranged. All the babies paid the most attention to the regular face. When presented to eight-month-olds, however, the greatest response was to the distorted face. The foregoing indicates a baby's progress in classifying his environment. By eight months the pattern of a face is so well established that an ordinary human face holds little challenge.

While most of the research on the seeing of infants is relatively recent and by no means complete, it might be illuminating to summarize some of the findings to date: (1) the human infant can see and discriminate patterns from birth; (2) complex visual patterns are intrinsically more stimulating and elicit more attention than do color and brightness alone; (3) pattern discrimination permits the infant to explore his environment visually and to have increased experience with parts of it, including faces and solid objects, which have potential importance for later behavior; (4) as the result of visual experiences from birth to three months, an infant decreases his attention to familiar patterns and increases his attention to novel ones that give rise to active exploration of his environs; (5) visual perception precedes action; and (6) the infant sees a patterned and organized world which he explores discriminatingly with the limited means then at his command.

*Designing a rich visual environment.* The foregoing researches have set toy designers to exploring how they can vary and enrich the infant's seeing environment during his first four months of life. They have mapped out playrooms and methodically inventoried everything an infant can see. While on his back, there are ceilings, bolsters at the sides of his crib, canopies, front and back crib boards, strings across the crib bars, light bulbs, windows, and air space to see. When the infant is on his stomach, there are the mattress, sheets, a blanket, doors, and windows to see. Piece by piece, the designers have attempted to incorporate in each of these things some colorful detail, some form of perpetual motion, as well as pleasing sound effects. The result of this industrial designing has been the creation of an enriched visual world for babies.

In the sides of protective, clear vinyl crib bolsters and in durable plastic playpen mattresses a variety of colorful details have been embedded. A "sight line," with transparent plastic, snap-on pockets, hung across the crib, offers the infant all kinds of interesting things to see and study. The pockets can be emptied and new family photos, objects, shapes, and textures set into them from time to time. An "inquarium," a tough, transparent vinyl pouch filled with water and live fish, hung on the side of the crib or playpen, provides constant viewing action which never seems to tire even the smallest infant. Battery-powered or wind-driven mobiles with mirrors, sound, and movement also keep a baby in a state of contented alertness. There are new machine projectors that create color patterns to intrigue infants and keep them happy when they are not asleep any time during the night. There are luminescent decals of stars and planets that glow in the night that can be adhered easily to the ceiling of the nursery. Colorful pinwheels that turn as the wind blows can be attached to the outside of the nursery window.

According to today's ophthalmologists, care must be taken to vary an infant's seeing environment. Babies should not always be on their backs looking directly up. They need sights to the right and left of them, and some should be moving from left to right. Many parents are placing cribs close to windows so their infants can watch the out-of-door action.

We believe there are some real questions whether traditional "containment" cribs offer infants the best learning opportunities. Note how aggressively a baby will lift his head up in his attempt to peer over a solid crib bolster. Many parents regard this as a phase of physical development, but actually the infant is trying to explore his surroundings visually. Parents often report that though placed in the middle of the crib for sleeping, their infant usually ends up in a corner of the crib where the bolsters meet. It would seem that the slice of open space invites the baby to try to see things outside his limiting "container." We think such infant movements are deliberate and it would be a good idea for parents to purchase transparent vinyl bolsters instead of the solid ones that block seeing.

Inasmuch as parents do not have ready access to specially designed cribs, it would serve the learning needs of infants if they were taken on sight-seeing trips around the apartment or house. There is some misunderstanding as to why a baby stops crying when he is picked up and rested on his mother's or father's shoulder. What is not realized is that the infant has been offered new sights to enjoy. Watching the world can so engage a baby that he has neither the need nor the time to cry. In fact, the viewing and learning can be so intense and exhausting that the baby will sleep longer hours. This is contrary to present thinking that it is the innate nature of an infant to be passive, that it is natural for him to sleep more than be awake. Actually, a baby is constantly alert when he is well and awake. He actively studies his environment and tries to figure out ways to make elements in it do his bidding.

Crying to be picked up to have a chance to see more freely is one technique that all infants master very early in their lives.

There is growing evidence that the perceptual learning and relationship thinking that develop from intensive seeing and hearing in the beginning months contribute immeasurably to a child's ability to master the difficult abstraction of reading later on. The indication is that programs to increase perceptual horizons might better be applied during the earliest years of life than later on.

It will take alert parents to convert the average infant nursery into a more active sight, sound, touch, and taste environment. Far too many nurseries are models of white cleanliness and barren of movement; they offer too little to finger, hold or savor. Usually they are off-base for the action and noise of siblings. An infant in a crib or playpen is much like a caged small animal. He wants desperately to get out into the mainstream of the life of his home. The sensitive mother methodically changes her baby's setting by putting him on the floor, in a reclining infant seat, or on her shoulders or back. She takes him on trips outside in a securely held car seat or a sling in front of her. She places him in a shopping cart while marketing. In short, she makes every effort to thrust him into the action of life itself.

All seeing experiences should be accompanied by appropriate touching and manipulating opportunities. Touching and tasting are a vital part of the learning process because they totally engage a child. Parents should therefore make it possible for their infants to handle as much as they can with safety.

*The physical attributes of the nursery need to be researched further and remodeled.* Ceilings and walls might be turned into screens for the projection of regular and irregular shapes, forms, and images. TV screens, where available, might get integrated into a crib side since there now is some research evidence that infants enjoy the color and movement of particularly graphic TV programs even more than those of mobiles. It might be possible to provide on educational TV a special program of graphic stimulation for babies. The crib mattress and floor covering might get converted into texturized, multicolored and shaped sound and sight adventure play areas. The baby bath might be redesigned to include water conversion play, with "finger-feeler" areas. A plastic playpen that can be blown up instantly and collapsed could be taken on a trip to countryside or beach. All will help the infant become a part of the world of action instead of being shut out from its excitement.

A recapitulation of the power in a child's visual environment may be useful at this juncture. Most adults have viewed infancy as a period of helplessness when all that was wanted or needed was given. From this they have concluded that the infant does nothing "until he is ready." They have assumed that as far as the outer world is concerned, the infant either does not perceive it, does not respond to it, or, if he interacts, it is purely instinctive or accidental. He sleeps incessantly, and the few hours he is awake it appears that any learning is infinitely small and of short duration. Nothing can be further from the truth! Except when sleeping, he is constantly alert, observing motion, distinguishing detail, and building up his relationship thinking.

*Vital periods in infancy.* Many of the learning psychologists are now saying that how alert an infant is, how much chance he is given to observe, master, and affect his world, and how much he babbles and communicates may have far-reaching consequences for his ongoing intellectual development and general maturation. His will power, his eagerness to learn, his drive and creativity, his body and ego are all affected. Child psychologists indicate that there are times of special sensitivity in the early development of every child, and if the needs of these periods are not met, a child loses interest and stops trying. Thereby his intelligence stagnates. His body control and ability to communicate also suffer.

The normal infant sees, hears, feels, clings, sits up, crawls, locomotes, and talks. If the environment does not provide him with enough to see, hear, and touch, if parents do not provide conditions and toys to make it worth his while to crawl, walk, or take actions in his own behalf, or if they inhibit activity by keeping him in limited play spaces, the resultant inaction and frustration make the infant withdraw into himself. When a child's self-image suffers, deprivation sets in.

There also are critical periods for building interpersonal relations with parents, brothers and sisters, other relatives, and one's peers. At six to nine months, children need a close relationship with one or two family adults—but not too many different adults—who recognize and value their strivings and achievements. At eighteen months, when language and loco-motion enable a child to shape relations with adults other than close relatives, he can approach or avoid individuals; he can influence them; he is able to practice the oral language that is essential for communication.

*The hearing environment.* Hearing is a highly reactive attri-bute of every normal newborn. Abrupt, explosive sounds can convulse a baby; gentle ones soothe him An infant will pick up every sound and relate it to a seeing experience. He will relate his mother's voice to her face. If the tone of her voice is loving, he will welcome it as a signal of reassurance. The baby can detect when his mother's voice is expressing dis-pleasure. A mother's positive action and appropriate verbal response initiate the interpersonal communication between them that helps the infant start building the important feeling of selfhood. His signals of crying or contented gurgling are his first means of social-minded expression.

There is much discussion today among researchers as to how soon the neonate reacts to sound, but all agree that a baby will respond to the sound of a clap after his fourth to tenth day of life. A baby is gentled by soft whispering at his eleventh or twelfth day. The sense of hearing is better devel-oped than most people realize. We still know relatively little about the kinds of sounds which are best suited to the infant under six months of age. However, we do know that most infants will respond to the repetition of continuous single sounds: the ticking of an old grandfather clock, the clicking of a typewriter or metronome, the tinkling of a music box, and the beating of a drum. Infants appear to respond more to high tones than low ones. We know, too, that music is quieting. It can make a baby's breathing slower and decrease his pulse rate.

Parents need to experiment with all types of sounds to discover which ones appeal to their particular baby. Music produced by gifted performers on fine instruments and good music boxes are recommended. High-fidelity records of all kinds of music are excellent. All infants will be stimulated or reassured by pleasing voices, music, and the variegated sounds of the world that are not too harsh, jolting, or discordant.

Before an infant can imitate language, he has to hear his own voice, his own sounds. His babble or cry is often the signal he employs to evoke some desired reaction. When his parents respond with loving sounds, the baby will begin to use his own sounds as expression, signal, or symbol. Amplifying his sounds to let him hear himself may be a good starting point.

*Language learning requires vocal reciprocity.* Having repeated pleasurable encounters with adults' and children's voices, including listening to well-selected phonograph records, may be vital elements in the development in early childhood of oral language fluency. An infant needs internal and external motivation to nurture an appetite for language. Conditions that engender vocal responses from infants include their contentment, attention from the people in their lives, and constant but relaxed encouragement. We know, for example, that an infant vocalizes more when he is smiled at.

At first a baby makes sounds of a random nature. He begins babbling between the age of two to five months. As soon as he perceives that he can produce sounds at will, the baby engages in endless play with his vocal organs. He practices the sounds made by others. He recognizes his name and knows when he is being spoken to or talked about long before he can say his name. He shows his understanding by reactions such as looking attentively at the speaker or the object being mentioned, reaching for or handling the object in question, or complying with simple, familiar directions. Toward the end of the first year, infants understand many words even though not yet able to pronounce them themselves.

There is much research yet to be done in the area of infant hearing and listening and their significance for learning. Note that we make a sharp distinction between *hearing* and *listening*. Listening entails interaction, a baby's interest in persons and things. Therefore, any infant listening program should include opportunities for active play with his parents and musical toys, assorted rattles, and stuffed musical animals. To this end, toy manufacturers are fabricating cause-and-effect toys where handling or pulling by the baby results in a new movement or the sound of a bell. Others are devising automatic ways for infants to turn radios and record players on and off, voice boxes that turn on and off at the slightest touch, music boxes that play a full tune upon easy pressure and release. "Sound rugs" are being designed to allow an infant to test out all kinds of choral tones by squeezing "rubber bumps." To get infants to look and listen intently, many new toys have sound feedback. As the baby handles or pulls at a toy, he is rewarded with the sound of a bell or a click-clack on a tone block, as in an "infant activator." There can be no doubt that with aural feedback, awareness and learning are intensified, that visual and auditory cues are closely linked.

If his auditory mechanism is normal and his environment interesting and responsive, a baby will react to auditory stimuli after the first few days of life. Pitch discrimination can be conditioned within the first year, and the ability to localize sounds at or away from their source also appears to occur during this period. It seems that an infant responds more to the verbalization, tone, and singing of his mother than to anyone or anything else. His interaction with her probably plays a major role in his hearing (and other) development. His auditory memory becomes obvious at about eighteen months. Auricular acuity has a significant relationship to speech learning and social development. Any student of deaf children will tell you that there is a definite relationship between hearing development and the emotional and social growth of a child.

What happens with children who really do not listen is that during their early years they had shut out all the sounds of their environment that they did not want to hear or, because of the confusing cacophony of sounds about them, they were not able to make fine aural distinctions. They had taught themselves to have a "deaf ear" to their mothers' pleadings, their siblings' or friends' teasing, or their teachers' admonitions. To bring such children back to attentive listening in a classroom situation may require them to experience a series of remedial auditory programs that get them to focus on simplified sound discrimination exercises and on picture and sound recognition games.

It is probable that strengthening a child's sensory abilities through concerted practice will build his perception in all modalities. Toy manufacturers have begun to explore toys that combine sight and sound dimensions. The miniaturization of circuits, the use of transistors instead of glass tubes, automatic cartridges, and sight-and-sound recordings now make it possible to give small children this material at popular prices. There is available a new "voice toy" that has a round metal mirror embedded in front. At the lightest touch of an infant's finger or hand, two- to four-second messages or simple questions emanate from the toy in a pleasing, clear voice, e.g., "Look at yourself in the mirror," "Point to your nose, your eyes," et cetera. This is not too far removed from the individual carrel, or language laboratory, now available in many classrooms, in which a child responds to question upon question and soon learns a second language. There are other playthings that offer children pictures and appropriate sounds so that relationships can be concretized into organized perceptual patterns. Such toys satisfy young children because they can use them over and over until they master all the auditory and visual associations they incorporate. Unfortunately, in the attempt to imitate TV or comic book characters, the voices in some of these toys are Disney-type, making it difficult for the young child to understand the voice or learn its emotional tone. Nonetheless, such playthings are a step in the right direction.

Another development is a tape or cassette cartridge system that fits into a portable, battery-operated play-back machine. With such a play tape machine, even a two- to three-year-old can handle his own "phonograph." There is no needle to get stuck by, no record arm to break, no machine to turn on and off. When the child easily inserts the cartridge into the machine, power is automatically turned on, and music or story are promptly available—in the crib or playpen, on a trip, or at the beach. Even more exciting than the tape player are the instruments of the future: a record player that will project slides and motion pictures during some twenty minutes of synchronized sound on a single record and video tape cartridges that will offer thirty minutes of motion pictures with sound that will attach to any existing TV set. These will make it possible for programmed oral language learning to be started in the home during a child's earliest years.

We are convinced that children who have the benefit of such training will be better prepared for the reading and elocution skills taught in the school. Convenient two-way electronic communication between parent or teacher and child at distances apart will also be feasible. A parent will be able to tune in to a classroom, play yard, et cetera, because her child will have pinned to dress or shirt a miniaturized sending and receiving set. What this will open up in the way of oral and auditory training only the imagination can predict.

A *tactile environment builds perceptual schemata*. All children need to acquire general organized knowledge about the nature of their environment. Part of such learning comes from maturing physically, but most of it must be reinforced by action and tactile experiences that a child can organize into his personal sensori-motor schemas. A child cannot begin to realize the nature of objects until he can combine his visual and auditory impressions with the tactile and kinesthetic impressions he obtains from touching, handling, and manipulating.

A striking example of the power of tactile experience is revealed in the recent work of infant researchers with Hopi Indian, Mexican, and disadvantaged slum children. These researchers are proving that at the end of the first year these children are more alert and visually ahead of the middle-class American child who is "locked up" in a safe, clean, white world. The Hopi Indian infant, strapped on the back of his mother sees more and Mexican and slum infants have closer relations with siblings and extended families. The Hopi Indian, Mexican, and slum children lose out in their second year, however, when they have fewer things to touch, feel, and relate to their visual experiences. At this point the middle-class American child moves ahead because of parental interaction and the wide assortment of home objects, toys, books, and other materials that are made more freely available to him.

When infants are ready for grasping (at about thirty-six weeks), a new world of intention and imagery unfolds. At the first stage there are sucking objects, objects to look at and grasp. As previously indicated, touching and handling are accidental and reflexive in the beginning. The infant practices his random movements. Then he begins to discover the world of objects and his ability to act upon them. In the second stage of development the infant establishes relationships between looking, grasping, and sucking as he continues to apply a great variety of actions to the same objects and shows increased purpose in his play. He is building an inner imagery of familiar objects. The infant is starting to organize a sense of physical space, form, and texture. Learning in the real sense has begun. He enjoys feeling a variety of things, exploring their contour, balancing them, and striking them against other things. He turns objects around to view them from every angle. It can be said that he is developing spatial understanding about objects, about nearness and distance, inside and outside, position and placement, and object permanence. Learning is always an active process full of touch, taste, visual, and aural complexities. The infant organizes all of his experiences into usable schemas in the course of his maturing. Carefully selected play materials can encourage and maintain this learning.

Parents cannot afford to sit by passively during this stage. The urge of the infant to explore and manipulate is so strong that to neglect it will deprive him of stimuli that can foster his drive and excitement for learning. Parents must literally "program" a full tactile environment by supplying their baby with multiple playthings to touch, finger, squeeze, and stroke. Variegated textures need to be introduced: smooth, rough, furry, soft, hard, et cetera. Many assorted shapes need to be experienced. Quantity relations need to be fingered. All the attributes of objects need to be compared and contrasted before a child can communicate his feelings about them. The parents help by verbally labeling each object and process for their child. When he is able to associate words with objects and actions, his verbal comprehension has begun to operate. An infant needs to be encouraged in all his attempts at mastery, and when he succeeds, the parent must voice approval—even bells must ring! Acknowledgment of a child's efforts and accomplishments are imperative at all times.

Toy manufacturers, like most parents, are not aware enough of the oral (sucking) and tactile needs of infants. Both are guilty of keeping the crib challenge-free. One of the most sensitive and powerful learning tools of the infant is his mouth. Sucking movements are initiated so the baby can fill the void in his stomach when he is hungry. The mouth admits food and excludes or expels unwanted matter. It serves admirably for the infant's exploration of flavor and taste, texture, firmness, brittleness, and so on. Through his mouth the baby soon makes distinctions between pleasurable and disagreeable tastes and objects. He gets a "first taste" of his power as a choice-maker through the use of his mouth.

Rattles and teethers are overwhelmingly numerous, but many are made more to attract adult attention than to challenge an

infant's learning tasks. Some of the successful first toys are
rubber beads or plastic discs or keys on a rustproof metal chain
into which the baby can rub his gums and, later, his teeth.
Others take the form of easily gripped, smooth wooden objects that just fit the mouth, like Figurettes or the Space
Teether. There are small rubber rings and plastic tube rings
with water enclosed and tiny, colorful floating objects that are
perfect for grasping, sucking, and chewing. Creative Playthings,
Incorporated, makes Jack the Giant Teether, a soft, pliable
plastic teether that has differently shaped protrusions, all fascinating to the baby and easily suckable and chewable. Many
rubber toys with safely embedded squeakers are on the market.
Some of them may frighten an infant if he is not properly
introduced to the sound effects. Sorely needed are sucking and
chewing toys that have cause-and-effect relationships built into
them. Such toys might accompany the sucking or chewing
with sound effects, motion, or a play of lights nearby. Another
good idea might be a rubber Shmoo that would change its
shape every time an infant bit into it or a sucking-biting doll
that would change its facial features with each "attack."

Parents should have "touch toys" handy as soon as the infant can flex his fingers and begin to grasp things. Although
his motions are haphazard at two months, hanging Plakies
or a string of rubber beads within his sight and reach or placing
a rattle near his hand will prompt him to explore and finger.
Small dumbbells of plastic or light stainless steel are ideal
first holding toys because they accommodate the pincer action of the baby's hand.

Snuggling, clinging, and stroking are natural infant movements which are associated with their search for security. Very
early the infant latches onto the softness and comfort of a
blanket or a small furry animal. Most of us know from first-
hand experience that many children refuse to relinquish these
throughout their childhood. This being the case, the mother
should make sure that her infant's first snuggling toy is attractive and that it can be washed or cleaned easily and regularly.
A good investment would be the Snuggler, a washable, at-

tractively designed orange-colored piece of lambswool which has a silk-screened face on its skin side. This is the time to introduce the baby to the softness of a well-made foam-rubber or terry-cloth doll or animal.

As the infant gains control of his fingers, he correlates seeing and handling and begins to show purpose in his reaching for things (usually at three months). While on his back in the crib, he needs touching, pulling, and exercising challenges. All parents enjoy gently exercising their baby by offering him fingers to grasp and then pulling him up carefully into almost sitting position. The Cradle Gym has become a byword in almost every home where there is an infant. He uses this for activity and exploration when mother is not at hand. He relishes fingering the colored beads and rings of this ingenious device, which helps him pull himself up into sitting position when he is ready. Another interesting cause-and-effect infant plaything is the Activator. When the baby reaches for its bright wood knob and succeeds in grasping and then pulling it, a bell rings and a beater strikes a wood tone block. Such playthings help the baby begin to develop a primitive sort of motor intelligence. He learns that when he pulls, something interesting will happen, that he can cause the action, which he follows intently with his eyes and the excitement of his whole body. The end result of this type of interaction between baby and plaything is what psychologists call "kinesthetic feedback to visual input."

When an infant is especially alert or unusually early in responding to his environment, a problem may arise because his precocious efforts to do for himself cannot be supported by his immature physique. Unless his parents are sensitive to this lag, an unbalance may ensue between his attempts and his inability to cope physically. Parents therefore need to provide their infants with play materials that allow them to minimize or overcome their physical immaturity.

For the four- and five-month-old who peers longingly through the bars of his crib or playpen at his siblings playing or at a ball or other play object, placing him on an infant crawler will give him the mobility his "stomach drag" and the weakness of his arm and back muscles preclude. This safe, comfortable crawler will enable the infant to be a more active part of his environment and make exciting sensori-motor experiences available to him.

What happens when an infant's environment is enriched with seeing and hearing experiences? We now know that the more he sees, hears, and does at an early age, the more he will attempt to do throughout his life. What happens to the self-confidence and feeling of mastery of an infant when one pull by him on a string activates a bell or buzzer, a sound system, or a light projector? He will feel that the world is at his finger tips, that it is his to explore and enjoy. Will power is strengthened by repeated efforts, which become satisfying accomplishments. But, say parents, life *is* frustrating; everything in the world is not at one's finger tips. Agreed. However, there is a time later to experience life's frustrations, and early childhood is not the time for this sharp realization. During the earliest years, when physical control of the environment is not easy, parents and other concerned adults must see that the world is brought down to the child's ability to manage it. The environment needs to be so planned that a child feels satisfied that he is affecting it. When he meets success in most of the things he tries and is rewarded by sincere parental approbation, his ego thrives. Unless the environment is sensitive to his maturation level, unless the play, the reaching out and touching tasks are challenging, a child will not invest his energy. Very soon he sees no reason for pitting himself against completely unattainable goals. If he is allowed to develop the conviction that his efforts cannot affect the world, he stops trying.

Our friend Lawrence Frank recognized long ago the power of play. We want to share with you what he wrote with regard to learning through trial and error in the previously mentioned March 1968 issue of *Childhood Education*: "The world confronting the child is, as William James called it, a 'great blooming confusion' which the child has to organize by putting into it some orderliness and meaning . . . The big adult world, the macrocosm, is too large, too complicated and often threatening to the child who cannot cope with it; and so he focuses upon the microcosmic world of play, as Erik Erikson stated some years ago, a world that he can encompass through toys and play materials. To these he imputes his often childish beliefs and expectations and also his feelings, but by repeated explorations he gradually relinquishes some of his more fantastic beliefs. When he tries to make the world conform to his childish beliefs and expectations, he is repeatedly confronted with the actuality of situations and events, and ever-present threats and sometimes painful consequences. But he can do this restructuring of the world only if he is permitted and encouraged to try, to persist until he learns what can and cannot be done; and play provides a minimum of risks and penalties for mistakes. Play . . . is a way of learning by trial and error to cope with the actual world."

*The infant begins to crawl.* When an infant begins to crawl, the number of people, things, and events he must adapt to and assimilate grows enormously. As his seeing world enlarges, his desire to reach and touch everything he sees becomes overpowering. This stage of growth puts most parents in a state of frenzy. The baby's desire to touch and handle everything within sight and reach often results in a tablecloth being pulled down, a small end table being overturned, a filled ashtray being dumped onto a rug, and objects being explored by mouth—all of which offend the sense of order and cleanliness of most parents. Preparing a proper environment for the crawler is the parents' complete responsibility because few toymakers provide playthings for the crawling-exploring set. The crawler loves to hide under tables, under bottom shelves, in closets, or in corners. He pulls at accessible drawers; he often gets stuck between a table and chair legs. There is need for "peek-a-boo houses," contoured surfaces with "nests" in which he can cuddle up, floor and wall "busy boxes" with programmed challenges, et cetera. When it is necessary to keep an infant off the floor, the playpen should be a large one with sides that permit the insertion in its slats of a variety of interesting playthings.

At this stage, the infant moves from being primarily a reflexive organism who responds in undifferentiated ways to his environment to being a relatively coherent organization of sensori-motor powers. He begins to demonstrate intention and goal-seeking. Now his motions are not completely random or accidental. He pulls a knob because he knows this will cause a bell to ring. He drops something on the floor because he wants to hear the noise, or make Mother come running. He builds a sort of sensori-motor intelligence whereby his actions are "lived" rather than thought about. It is the kind of intelligence that comes from a fixed succession of static images, each connected with an action. In time, after much practice and well beyond his second year, he is able to hold an object in his mind with less and less direct contact and handling. There is some question in the minds of educators as to whether children and adults throughout life are ever free of the manipulation of objects in order to build mental imagery. One of the reasons schools provide laboratory experiments is so the children can conceive of abstractions through their own concrete, physical actions.

During the four- to eighth-month period countless actions and manipulations on the environment are the way an infant gets a "picture of things." Parents have to insure each child active engagement with the environment for his optimal development. There are countless thousands of things that must be brought to a child's attention that he can explore with his hands, mouth, feet, arms, and body. From a vast variety of play experiences, he gets a feeling of size, shape, texture, weight, volume, density, distance, speed, and altitude, among other things.

During the first four months, parents usually provide several crib toys. When selecting them, most are more concerned about hygiene and safety than about play and learning. A soft animal or ball usually enters the crib first. Actually, even a ball can be "programmed for learning" by having sewn on it patches of different textures—fur, leather, wool, terry cloth, et cetera. When an infant sits up and peers about, he is apt to see a restricted monochrome world, which he soon finds boring. It takes no more than a bit of resin glue, a canvas or duck contoured crib sheet, and a variety of textures and safe gadgets to convert the sterile nursery into a fascinating world to explore. Metal mirrors, pieces of carpeting or sponge rubber, discs of lamb's wool are a few of the objects that can be permanently glued onto a canvas crib cover. Whether cut out and glued down in daisy patterns or at random, the assorted textures, colors, and shapes will spark a baby's senses of sight and touch. His repeated play will give him a good internal and physical image of rough, soft, and smooth. The cover can go into the washing machine ready for the next day's use.

*Body mastery and communication.* Walking makes an infant literally strain at the leash. He gets into everything, wants to go everywhere, and unwittingly gets into all kinds of "mischief." This is the age that requires especial understanding and patience from parents. The toddler actually thinks and acts through his gross motor ability. He is learning so many new motion skills, and trying to do them all at once, that he often is confused. He needs a planned environment, responsive parents, suitable playthings, and encouragement to help him develop a sense of achievement. Push-and-pull toys help him measure how much he can move, push, or pick up. Building and pounding toys require gross motor actions and contribute to the toddler's refinement of his co-ordination. Fitting toys that entail trial-and-error practice are needed and greatly enjoyed. It is the child's striving and succeeding that build the self, a feeling of autonomy, and the will to master. It is necessary that the infant explore tactilely what he perceives visually. He has deep need to make himself and his choices felt. What effect the early exploration of the physical environment will have on a child's learning ability is yet to be ascertained. But there is little uncertainty that if an infant's requisites for living and learning are adequately met, there is less apt to be a diminishing of his interest and drive.

It is by means of action that infants and children up to six or seven years of age make their intelligence known and felt. Every sensori-motor activity enables an infant to incorporate his learnings into schemas, a sort of assimilation of the environment. The child's schemas are continually modified by fresh data he acquires through each new experience. Adapting well to one's environment entails equilibrium between one's assimilation and accommodation skills. A child faced with a play situation that is novel to him, perhaps getting a watch on a chain out of a covered box with a small elliptical hole on top, may first turn the box over and then try to pull the chain through the opening. He can succeed in pulling up the chain, but the watch may not come out because it remains in a criss-crossed position. The child possesses only two schemas here: turning the box over and pulling up the chain. He may try to enlarge the elliptical hole but fail. If he tries again, turning the box over and pulling the chain out, by accident the chain may turn, and as the watch fits the elliptical opening, out it comes. Actually the two schemas he already had were modified when the turning chain enabled him to pull out the watch, thereby providing him with a third alternative for action.

Repeated assimilative actions and accommodations to the environment build a child's pattern learning. A whole succession of actions teaches a child to look for falling objects, to search for hidden objects. But he must be completely involved in all his actions or he will not perceive and learn. At five months, if an adult drops an object nearby, the infant will not react. But at six months, when he holds an object, lets it fall, and hears it drop, he will search for it with his eyes. After many holding and dropping experiments, the infant will have a schema for searching the floor for every object dropped. The existence of an object to a six-month-old always is directly related to his seeing and holding it. His physical acts give him a sense of permanence in objects and their attributes.

The preschool child's patterns of action come from a host of play activities supplied by materials in the environment. At first they can be the metal or pliant plastic measuring cups, spoons, and nesting bowls found in the average kitchen. However, the home kitchen does not boast enough safe, manipulative objects that will permit a young child to follow the dictates of his curiosity. Preschool children require manifold experiences in putting things in order of size (serialization) and classifying objects by shape, texture, and sound. Likewise, they need to learn to apprehend perspective, scale, weight, quantity relations, air space, cause-and-effect action, and sound discrimination, among other concepts. It is because many of these ideas can be structured into playful experiences that modern designers have been creating toys that incorporate them.

To the young child the world is a collection of events developed from his personal experience as an active agent. His task is to construct cause-and-effect sequences, step by step, as his contact with the real world increases. The responsibility of parents and teachers is to foster this learning by providing materials of investigation and construction and relevant discussion that permit the child to experience and evaluate causal relationships.

New research on the disadvantaged child indicates that his relating and patterning ability is limited because from between eight months and three years—a critical learning stage—he has had too few personal manipulating experiences (fitting, sorting, matching, et cetera) with those play materials that foster relationship thinking. He lacks fitting toys that can give him a sense of accomplishment. Our present-day IQ tests measure a combination of personal actions and word labeling ability. It has been found that a twenty-point IQ increase can come to children before they reach first grade if they receive professional intervention in the home in the form of verbal interaction with a responsive adult and opportunities for play with manipulative toys. The middle-class child has a mother ready with a new play challenge and accompanying words to identify each idea or object. Inherent in the active way of early learning is the kind of seeking which is an essential to all learning. The desire to understand, to do, and to make activates a child and causes him to shape his world in accordance with his own drives. The will to achieve lies in a child's personal actions and interactions with his environment. His success in internalizing his actions into the stuff of thinking, of codifying and systemizing them into schemas and concepts—all of these nurture will power. A rich environment of play generates interest and problem solving. It is this vital will power that is missing in the academically and socially disadvantaged child.

*What toys exist that help build relationship thinking in the early years?* Certainly there are matching toys (with one-to-one correspondence) wherein a cup is matched with a saucer, et cetera. Or a soft ball or cuddly Teddy bear is handled and the mother labels it "soft" or "furry." There are toys for self-identification whereby a child sees himself in a mirror, and the mother labels his nose, eyes, ears, and so on. There are toys for eye-hand co-ordination where four blocks are fitted onto an upright peg. Once mastered, the process is repeated over and over again with satisfaction and delight in achievement. "Eye-hand co-ordination" is more than a textbook phrase; it is a necessary learning process for infants. Learning to roll or stack or fit pieces of toys together are all part of the learning of the creeper and toddler.

At about one year of age, an infant is ready to fit pegs into corresponding holes. Putting peg people into a balancing beam or rocking horse or merry-go-round toy introduces additional learning and dramatic play dimensions. Putting a quantity of pegs into a peg bus adds a feeling for "lots of people" and signals a beginning introduction to quantity relations and elementary number concepts. There are all kinds of toys for simple experiences with motion. The roly-poly will always return to an upright position; a balloon will bounce and fly up into the air; a shoofly rocks back and forth safely; wheels and rolling cylinders respond readily to pushes and pulls.

*Toys for experience with shapes.* Wooden egg and bottle carriers give contact with recognizable shapes that can be handled and even dropped without fear of breakage. A shape-sorting box requires a child to choose, sort, and differentiate fifteen different small blocks because each of the five different holes in the top of the box accepts only blocks of corresponding shapes. There are nesting toys in wood or plastic that challenge the size-discrimination ability of a child because he must fit one inside the other or reverse them and pile them high in proper sequence. The color cone has graduated rings which are fitted in sequence over a central peg. Then come simple jigsaw puzzles in wood or rubber, with size sequence incorporated in animals, people, or fruits. These materials and others provide for active handling and thinking on the part of children and enable a parent or teacher to seize opportune times for labeling the actions with appropriate words or talking with the children about what they are doing. When children begin to build with blocks, a parent or teacher can focus on the mathematical interest in the building, i.e., the number of blocks needed in whole or part, the matching or correspondence of shapes and sizes of blocks, as well as questions of weight and balance. Such discussions lead to counting, ordering, comparing, contrasting and, ultimately, to number, size, quantity, shape, time, and weight, all of which are elements in mathematical learning.

*Play is a self-discovery activity that teaches as it builds ego and creativity.* If play is to be extended to constructive educational purposes, the parent or teacher must be an active participant as interpreter, labeler, and programmer in setting up physical or mental problems to be tackled by the child while the activity is in progress. Young children are dominated by their sensory perceptions and respond most actively to what attracts their immediate attention. Matching pictures, objects, and signs entails encoding and labeling procedures that, in due course, lead to reading readiness. The self-direction inherent in early childhood play is so potent that many educators would like to take advantage of the self-choice and will power of young children to introduce them to symbols (numerals and letters) as well as action. There is extreme danger in prematurely pushing symbols during a child's first three years of life since this can curtail the spontaneity and non-verbal experimentation of early play.

One of the weaknesses of our society is the glib verbality of our children who rely too little on doing and experimenting. The child who uses symbols only too soon usually resorts to rote learning. While he may be able to feed back the words, too often he does not comprehend their meaning. Most young children count to ten but rarely, if ever, before five years of age can they set forth groups that connote sets of three, five, or ten objects. Parents and teachers should think twice before inaugurating a program of verbal and symbol learning without its concommitents of parallel lab learning experiences (handling, sorting, sequencing).

Physical development and learning go forward at twelve to twenty-four months with the maturation of the large and small muscles. An infant begins to creep not only because it is "natural" to do so at six to eight months, but because there is in his environment something challenging to reach for, and perhaps to touch and therefore to crawl to. Unless parents put into the infant's immediate world toys and things to go after or inviting places into which to crawl, he will not be nudged to invest his energy. More children lose will power in their earliest years than most pediatricians lead one to believe.

Somewhere from eighteen to twenty-four months, a child's large muscles develop sufficiently to enable him to walk. His learning to walk represents important maturing of his nervous system. Now that he can locomote, he can explore more freely. Dependence on parents for survival lessens somewhat. Walking makes available a wider array of perceptual and tactile experiences. Now the toddler has to interact with more people than those in his immediate family. To succeed in his interpersonal relations in his widening world, he has to communicate—to talk and make himself felt. No longer can he point to something and expect a hovering parent to understand his non-verbal communication. He has to develop words and then sentences and emotional tone when dealing verbally with strangers, and the normal toddler does so with alacrity.

This is the time to provide toys that encourage a child to practice conversation with his peers and with adults other than members of his family. Fit-together toys enable a parent to label parts that are "bigger than," "smaller than," or "the smallest," "the largest," and so on. Toys which embody placement challenges teach concepts and words such as "over," "under," "in," "out," "more," "the same." Hammer-and-peg toys now feature pegs in varying geometrical shapes which allow parents to name the peg her child is to hammer: "Now hit the round peg," "the square one," "the star shape." This is a prime time for introducing beginner storybooks with touch experiences—"Pat the bunny's fur," "Feel Daddy's scratchy beard"—and cloth self-help books with zippers to slide open and shut, buttons to unbutton, laces to tie, and so forth. Play with finger puppets encourages conversation. Identifying rubber or wood farm and zoo animals and listening and dancing to repetitive folk and rhythmic music are also satisfying activities.

Most toys evoke verbal response, but it takes a sensitive parent to help her offspring expand his vocabulary by subtly intervening with new ways to use playthings and posing fresh problem-solving situations. As the child plays with his toys, he establishes the "inner speech and imagery" he needs for reflective thinking and the mobilization of his memories. Sagacious parental intermediation with appropriate toys and activities for verbal interaction can be an influential contribution to advancing a child's IQ.

In February of 1966, a family casework agency in Long Island, New York, set out to explore whether the IQ of disadvantaged children could be raised by fostering verbal interaction with toys and books. Sixteen families with two-year-old children, living in a low-income housing development, were separated into experimental and control groups. Each child in the experimental group received sixteen toys and seven books, while the control group received no materials of any kind. The result of four months of intensive study, including before and after tests of children and parents, revealed that there was a rise in the IQ of the children in the experimental group of 13.7 IQ points, as compared with a fractional loss of .4 IQ points for the children in the control group. These researchers, and other NIMH (National Institute of Mental Health) researchers in Washington, D.C., Miami, and Philadelphia, are finding that play with selective toys provided during the optimal eighteenth to twenty-eighth-month period has a profound, positive effect on verbal intelligence.

*When children enter the preschool years, their play takes on greater imagination and symbolism.* They throw themselves wholeheartedly into role playing, and it is out of this particular kind of play that their operational and conceptual schemata unfold. This free play, which has organization and structure, involves a child's mind as no formal schooling can. Most preschoolers are avid "doers" and "talkers," but they still have much to experience to extend their verbal skills and cognition. All children require a sufficiency of imaginative play. Young children come to understand themselves and the world through their dramatic play. They play with things and ideas in order to understand more fully and come to active grips with reality. In their dramatic play, children relive the different experiences they have had and, as they do so, they learn more and more words with which to express their enlarging understandings. Dramatic play is a dynamic, completely involving way for young children to plumb their feelings and broaden their ideas and knowledge.

There are two stages during which perceptive play is in operation: the egocentric two- to four-year-old period and the intuitive four- to six-year-old period. Two-to-four-year-olds are completely self-seeking. They use themselves as a standard of judgment and are unable to take the viewpoint of others. They assimilate certain aspects of their environment and build them into a play schema that they want to direct and dominate themselves. They do everything they can to build their self-image and to prove to themselves their power to subvert their needs and desires to reality. These children are not reflective. Their categorizing is based on single characteristics of objects.

Although four-to-six-year-olds are still ego-oriented, they are able now to see more interrelationships in their play. They can use objects and toys and ideas as a basis for their imaginative play.

The period from two to at least six years is then a time of confidence building ("Look at the tall building I made!" "See me ride my tricycle!"), of encouraging curiosity with all kinds of patterns of association (differentiating offered by lotto games, jigsaw puzzles, et cetera), of exploring city and country living (as in building block cities and farms), of thinking through kinship relationships (with dolls and doll play). This is the prime time for giving young imaginations full sway (as in puppetry, store play, and other theater arts activities), for testing manual dexterity (with assorted construction sets), and for helping creativity flourish (by means of painting, clay work, and music exploration).

Our culture allows children to play and experiment with ideas freely at least up to their sixth year of age. However, this permissive period when "a ferment of knowledge is already stirring in the mind" needs to be put into some sort of perspective order. This is a time of incubation, when information has to be utilized, tested, thrown into fresh combinations, and sorted and classified into conceptual frameworks by each child. Out of this playing with ideas come useful insights. Critical self-evaluation and the perfecting of work being done come later.

Most educators and almost all parents support the educational processes that are best carried forward by the active fantasy and dramatic play of children from two to six by allowing them the freedom to be themselves. Adults can help sustain a child's need for searching and finding out. They can support stimulating play experiences by providing suitable toys and materials of play, introducing new materials and experiences as needed, and encouraging discussions that can reveal the strengths and weaknesses of each child's cognitive abilities.

Preschool children learn to represent their world through the use of signs and symbols gradually, i.e., through images and words. Young children constantly reorganize their picture of the world through their imaginative play, talking, listening, questioning, and experimenting. In their make-believe play, their thinking and reasoning operate on a high level. The literal child does not always find it easy to grasp a hypothesis put to him verbally, yet in his play he often can use it well. Children frequently set for themselves difficult intellectual problems in their make-believe play—which is a young child's powerhouse for learning.

After four years of age, the need to use play symbolism lessens because a child finds more opportunities to satisfy his ego wants in his own life. His social circle has expanded, and he becomes the equal of an increasing number of real persons. Make-believe play gives way to games with rules, albeit simple ones in the beginning. Imagination is reintegrated in images, in thought, and in intelligence. Imitation becomes a reflective, not a spontaneous act. Intelligence makes its outward appearance at six or seven years when there is a subordination of means to ends and the child's application of known means to new situations.

*At seven years, children make distinctions between make believe and the world of reality.* In the years after seven, play takes on new learning formats. There are dramatics—puppetry, shadow plays, role playing, et cetera—whereby children are given a set of circumstances or a script to which they must respond. Playing characters from varied environments and facing new problems, they enrich their vocabularies while discovering relationships previously unfamiliar to them. There are group games with set rules for behavior in which more than one child is involved. The "I" has become the "we."

*Preschool play is a powerful medium of internal thinking.* From his early sensori-motor experiences, a child abstracts a spatial schema which becomes part of the internal imagery he manipulates at will in his play life. Play with cars, trucks, fire engines, blocks, and community play people enables a child to formulate a spatial plan for a city or a farm. His cars travel on roads and bridges of his own making; his trains run on or off tracks he has aligned. He lays out roadways and sets up traffic systems and intersperses all kinds of play figures in his community settings. He begins to see the interdependence of country and city—where food is grown, how trucks take food to markets and stores, how stores sell to consumers, how fish is delivered, how food is canned. Most children have limited notions about the system that runs a city. Here is where parent and teacher can carefully intervene in the play to enlarge concepts and help children understand relationships. They take children on trips to the waterfront (where feasible) to see ships from every country loading passengers, freight, fruit, et cetera. They are introduced to fishing schooners, ferries, tugs, railroad barges, barges filled with sand, coal, or bricks. Most children (and adults) know little about the underground empire that exists in every metropolis, the countless miles of gas pipes, water mains, cables, sewers, telephone wires, signal systems, subways, and traffic tunnels. Children enjoy learning how a city functions— how one may clothe the world, how it publishes books, where artists live and work, how the mailman, policeman, fireman, sanitation worker, and longshoreman function. The complicated, fascinating interrelationships in a city are thus made more meaningful and alive to the average child who rarely leaves his own nieghborhood. Parents and teachers read dramatic stories to the children, which helps them digest the new material and add it to their dramatic play in some form of activity. The adult enters the play only when it lags or to channel it into new learning directions. For example, the adult can set a new scene by dramatically announcing a fire, boldly noting the delivery of a truck loaded with food for the school lunchroom, or the arrival of an ocean liner. At all times it is important that the parent or teacher know whether it is fresh information that would enhance the play or whether repetition of an activity is called for.

To re-create a physical environment effectively, the child has to be familiar with all its details. He will relate a passing truck with its warehouse or store destination, a department store or supermarket with the consumers they serve, or water in the home with its original source. In order to play out a situation fully, the child is much like a playwright. He researches every element in a physical setting, every nuance in a social situation. "Shopkeepers" need information on farms, orchards, canneries, fisheries, and so on. "Cloth merchants" need to see the relationship between bales of cotton and cartons of wool on docks to finished goods.

When children play together to reproduce the physical environment they know, they also are re-creating their social milieu. They bring to their play (in various forms) their family members, themselves, their friends (and enemies), their school life, and other play experiences. They reveal what they know of their overt social relations and their inner fantasy life. Children change roles frequently in their dramatic play: "I'll be the father," "I'll be the doctor," "I want to be the baby," and so on. As the play ensues, most children air their feelings and problems. The child literally turns himself inside out to express and understand himself and the people in his world. The learning inherent in this form of dramatic play is limitless.

Children crave using their hands in their building and construction play. To build a whole out of parts is a challenge to all children. Common to building activity is the imagination to envision a finished structure and the ability to hold the image in mind as the child gropes for methods and materials for its execution. Good construction toys are those that small hands can manage well, that permit the imagination to soar sky high. Numerous toys are available that enable a child to construct a whole out of parts. This activity usually starts at about three years of age with simple pattern play with colored parquetry blocks, five- to six-piece jigsaw puzzles, embossed colored cubes, magnetic basic form boards, et cetera.

The child is able to make a design with a minimum of help from an adult. Four-year-olds will attempt to master other construction sets: Tinker Toys, nuts and bolts, Snap Blocks, Blockraft, Block City, Bolt-It, Lincoln Logs, and so on. For six- and seven-year-olds there is intricate creative designing with Lego, Geo-D-Stix, Flexagons, and so forth. Children enjoy using hammers and nails, first for the sake of handling the material and then for manipulating, experimenting, and constructing with pieces of wood, nails, saw, and hammer. Sevens, eights and nines engage in constructive play such as sewing, weaving, making puppets, fashioning clothes for dolls, playing musical instruments, and making simple toys.

Painting and clay modeling afford children pleasure by giving them a sense of control over raw materials. When pursued beyond the stage of manipulation and experimentation, these lead eventually to art expression and communication. Clay makes its initial appeal through the pure delight children experience in its handling. After a time, most children learn to make objects of beauty and use. Painting is analogous to clay modeling, but it is more flexible. Painting, like clay modeling, can be a form of play, and every child should be allowed to go through the stages of growth and satisfaction with these materials. The spontaneity all mature artists search for comes so naturally to children that superimposing adult standards and requiring "finished products" can make a child so self-critical and self-conscious that his interest in creative expression wanes and dies. Parents and teachers can see that art materials are readily available to children and sincerely appreciate what is produced.

*Internal thinking in the play of preschoolers.* Active dramatic and creative play, no matter what form it takes, is the way young children express their inner lives in a socially acceptable manner. During the early years, the thinking out of an idea is all action through play. Then the child supplements his imagery with words. He talks to himself as he block builds or to another child nearby. He pretends to be a driver who has had an accident or he plays a policeman to be a "boss." The expression of vague feelings through such dramatizations fulfills the same function for the child as thought does for the adult. As a child dramatizes, he talks, probes, and tries to clarify his confused feelings.

*Early language is an important and creative play tool.* The child, talking to himself as he plays, produces sounds and a form of poetry to fit his play: "Toot, toot, I am a tooting train," "Choo, choo, chug-chug, clear the track." He uses language as he uses clay or builds with blocks. He makes every sound or word express all shades of feeling or action. He plays with word patterns as he does with his designs in painting or parquetry blocks: "Splishes, sploshes go Suzy's galoshes." Patterns in words offer great satisfaction to a child; he will repeat them endlessly to his own delight. If encouraged to listen to their own play with words or to the poetry of playful adults, children will have the confidence to continue playing and experimenting with language forms. Unfortunately this free expression flowers for only a short time. Before long, a child's language has to become grammatical and have prescribed structure, particularly as it becomes the medium for delivering factual information in the elementary school years. We appreciate the need for good grammar, but imaginative ways of expressing oneself need also to be nurtured.

*Singing is closely connected to language as creative expression.* It can become a pleasurable part of the enriched play of young children if parents and teachers minimize singing techniques, voice control, or perfect pitch and emphasize action songs with repetitive patterns. These are found generally in folk songs which can be repeated by children until they master their words, spirit, and rhythm. Cowboy songs, sea chanteys, ballads, and songs of workers have tremendous appeal for children, who like these songs because of the quality of dramatic action in the words themselves. Such singing forwards their language learning.

*The collections and hobbies of older children.* For the six-year-old, collecting is a play form he associates with being an adult. It is extremely miscellaneous and undifferentiated, focusing mainly on trading cards, Christmas, birthday, and other greeting cards, bottle caps, comic books, Matchbox toys, fancy paper, or other odds and ends; but later on, collecting becomes more discriminating and serious. Some older children collect or make artifacts that reflect a specific historical time period. Of course, some collections are more educational than others. Rocks, minerals and shells, coins, stamps, maps, and dolls often bring a child into a historical period, and help boys and girls see valid evidences of man's adaptations to technology and change. The learning is intensive, sometimes influencing vocational choices made in adulthood.

*Group games children enjoy playing.* Anagrams, dominoes, Chinese checkers, and simple card games require simple matching and single concepts and can be handled well by six- and seven-year-olds. Games such as Monopoly, checkers, and chess for eight-to-fourteen-year-olds (and older) require coping with varied concepts at a time and demand decision-making with alternate consequences.

Older children enjoy complicated group games and competitive sports, which usually are played between two parties or whole teams. These children relish the prizes for winning and most are able to take the tension and uncertainty of such competition. From early childhood through all of adulthood, the strongest incentives to perfection are praise and honor for excellence. Doing something well means doing it better than someone else. We would prefer to see young and even older children engage in sports for the satisfaction that can come from mastering skills for their own sake and the pleasure to be derived from attaining physical skills. With the transition from pure personal amusement to systems of the Little Leagues and organized clubs and matches, the rules become increasingly elaborate and strict. Something of the intrinsic play quality is inevitably lost.

*Competition does not have to take the form of physical strength or skill.* There can be contests in words, wit, and the mind. Older children like this form of competition also. It starts with six-year-olds asking questions about the mysteries of being—"What is dead?" "What makes water run?" "Where does the wind come from?" "What makes the world turn around?" It goes forward at seven and eight to the memorization of riddles and posing puzzlers to peers and adults. Riddle solving can be a hearty form of social recreation. Often it encompasses some of the questions and answers inherent in religious and philosophical thought. All children love riddles. They use them with great animation to test the wits of adults. Games of questions and answers in verse also enable children to store up much amusing and even useful information. Jokes and "magic" seem to follow naturally as children grow older.

*Play in academic learning.* Commonly accepted practice in many American schools even today is that upon the entrance of a child in the first grade most kindergarten play stops and curriculum work begins. Along with this, emphasis and reliance on words and symbols develop and interaction with things, especially playthings, becomes taboo. Replacing the self-choice interest corners of the nursery school and kindergarten are the traditional desks and work tables of the elementary school. Reading, writing, and arithmetic are pushed in a full-scale teaching program.

Learning and self-direction inevitably falter in such a rigidly structured environment. From his sixth through ninth years, the period when a child can make the greatest advance in academic skills, he can lose his interest in learning to learn because he is no longer allowed to explore challenging subject matter at his own direction and pace. No longer is he free to play with academic ideas for now he is a part of an institutional system that he cannot easily affect. The result is often rejection of academics by many children.

In a research project on the growth and development of Head Start children as they leave the kindergarten and enter the primary grades, it was found that they lose their advantage in the early grades because they cannot adjust to the demanding curriculum imposed upon them. Unless a play element is introduced to academics, unless a child gets more actively involved in his studies, unless there is greater manipulation, experimentation, and discovery, academic interest withers away.

Traditional education, with the teacher up front lecturing, conceives of the young child's mind as a tape recorder or camera that records what it hears or sees. If the child can feed back on a test what he has been told or read, he is said to have "learned" the subject matter. However, there are many educators who believe that this is not the way children really learn, that verbal recall is not the way to retain learning. Many contemporary psychologists believe that the mind of a child does not make a photographic copy of reality, but uses active experiences and associative verbal labeling to come to grips with the raw data of the world. Each child builds his own concept and model of the world not merely by assimilating words but by means of innumerable direct experiences with the people and objects in his environment. The mental models obtained from these self-motivated discoveries constantly undergo revisions until the child attains mastery. Although memory is helpful, learning based on rote memorization will ever remain shallow and empty.

*Children learn well only when they work concretely.* This natural learning process must prevail in the early elementary grades. A first-grader works on academic problems best when he is allowed to manipulate at his own desk physical models that will help to organize and describe his experiences. Learning is conducted on a subverbal level of experience by observing, measuring, weighing evidence, recording findings accurately, until a child arrives at his own academic decisions. At each stage the child is asked to communicate his understandings. Thus he gains mastery and is in control of his learning. Being in control means being able to convince oneself of the validity of one's academic ideas by translating them into concrete operations with physical objects and models.

Children generally distrust abstractions that are not arrived at through their own manipulation. Hence every mathematics, science, geography, history, and art problem must be subjected to dissection and reconstruction if necessary. There cannot be

only one way of seeing a problem; there must be many
concrete and manipulative ways developed so that fine nuances
are firmly grasped by every child in some meaningful way. We
believe the use of tangible materials permits each child to grow
at his own pace, motivated by his own curiosity.

*"I hear and I forget. I see and I remember. I do and I
understand."* There is strong evidence in the research in learning going on today that children need to experiment with
models in order to abstract an idea. They need to manipulate
a device to get a "diagram" to guide their actions. There is
ample indication that even pictures require practice before
they can be used as substitutes for the real thing. According
to Jean Piaget, cognition at all developmental levels consists of
actions performed by the person. At the early levels of development, actions or operations are overt and physical. As the
child matures, the actions are internalized until covert actions
—verbal, symbolic operations—dominate his process of cognition.

We are clamoring for bringing the self-discovery, educative
powers of play into early academic learning. We ask that
academic subjects become less teaching procedures and more
playful, self-learning, manipulative endeavors. We would like
to see the learning of major ideas arise from a foundation of
experiences and interactions with the real world. When this is
not feasible, we need to structure into the early primary grades
simulated play and laboratory experiences that present problems in raw forms to be explored and researched by each child.
Needed data can be presented by means of academic games,
manipulatives in mathematics, dramatic role playing in history,
rearranging panoramas in geography, and so on.

Standard classroom teaching is a way of insuring passivity in
the learner, of presenting ready-made problems with set solutions. Children too often lose interest in beginning mathematics and science because they have nothing to say about the
content and have no sense of involvement in the learning they
are expected to do.

*Laboratory techniques in mathematics.* As presented by

those seeking to make beginning mathematics a meaningful and not a rote subject, mathematics is not concerned with stock problems and answers as outlined in a textbook, but rather with "playful" situations in which the children can themselves find solutions to interesting problems. In kindergarten, for example, they are encouraged to look for answers with jumbo tools: computing rolling wheels that click off feet and yards, giant outside calipers with non-numerical units for measuring head and body dimensions and inside calipers to measure the internal widths of containers, giant shadow sticks to discover the lengths of shadows at different times of the day, giant balance scales to compare the weight of a cup of beans with a cup of sand.

Preschool children are given giant color rods to put in sequence, varied geometrical units for shape-fitting operations, number lines to arrange in numerical order, and so forth. Their optimal interest and ability are engaged as they seek quantitative answers through their play and experimentation. They play in a "math corner" or "math laboratory," where they fill varying containers with beads or water, learn to make change while playing store, and weighing pounds or half pounds of toy fruit and other miniature items. The communication of results, in mathematical symbols and the correct vocabulary, parallel such experiences.

As children enter the primary grades, the number and variety of active mathematics play experiences increase. To guarantee that a child arrives at a qualitative concept or model for organizing his thinking, many diverse experiences have to be provided. He cannot see all the relationships in mathematics with only a number line; he must be given a host of "desk-top laboratories" and models—colored rods, scored rods, counting frames, tens boards, Chinese and Japanese abaci, pattern boards, et cetera. He is enabled to grasp mathematical ideas physically with varied devices that heretofore have been presented verbally. In a playful manner, he matches a colored eight-stick and discovers how many different color combinations of sticks make an eight. He uses a bead frame to count by ones to fifty. Then he is encouraged to speed up the counting process by counting by twos, threes, and later by fives. Then come addition and subtraction. The teacher does not demonstrate, lecture, or verbalize anything that the children have not handled and verified with their own hands. The children convince themselves as they manipulate their own learning. They have little chance of being bored or indifferent.

Children are asked open-ended questions that sometimes require several days of "research" before a conclusion can be reached. Which is a better unit for measuring the area of a piece of paper or a room—a circle, a triangle, a trapezoid, or a square? Which is a better unit for measuring the length of a desk—a small rod, a medium rod, or a long rod? Children are encouraged to try out each unit and support their conclusions with laboratory work. They record their observations in much the same manner as the scientist keeps a daily log.

Children provided with such active ways of learning mathematics are completely involved in research and discovery and are asked to exercise their judgment more than in rote-learning situations. The "self" in learning is more prevalent. There is more seeking, more investigation, and more conversation about ideas. There are more "hunches," "trying out phases," and "good guesses," which lead to the kind of successes that fortify and satisfy a child. The teacher does little demonstrating and no lecturing. However, she goes about the room labeling all ideas and processes with their appropriate vocabulary. She asks questions that will extend the learning: "What were you really doing?" "What is a ten combination?" This method of guiding the learning process is contrasted with teaching per se, whereby instruction is given in advance of the child's own questioning or thinking and without opportunities for testing tentative ideas. If learning has come in response to a child's own desire to know, if he has grasped a process "physically," he will hold the concept in his mind. Later on in his academic life, he will be able to reconstruct the method best suited to attack and solve new problems as he confronts them.

*Experimentation versus verbal learning in science.* The

highest form of research is essentially play. Einstein is quoted as having said, "The desire to arrive finally at logically connected concepts is the emotional basis of a vague play with basic ideas. This combinatory or associative play seems to be the essential feature in productive thought."

The play and laboratory approach to learning is most appropriate to science. The weakness in much of today's science teaching is that it consists of the teacher performing experiments to prove what she has been saying, often something already known. Rote learning inevitably ensues, and the failure of a child's memory can result in his total loss of appetite for learning. Rote learning is sterile because it adds nothing to the mind or to life.

For the primary grade child, only his own active search for a solution to a scientific problem will hold his interest. Asked to make a judgment as to how to go about estimating how many beans there are in a jar, for example, or to record the walking patterns of a mealy worm in a matchbox, a child is permitted to shape his own procedure of investigation. In such a case, a child will accept the "drudgery" of studying science. He will eagerly try to find out what actions bring about what results, what obstacles will have to be overcome, and how to deal with interfering factors.

*It has been said that one laboratory experiment is worth a thousand words of teaching.* Especially for the early grades, science study must permit children to experiment, sort, classify, and then codify their observations. They can be given small animals to care for and asked to note their behavior. Cages for small animals, an anthill, insect cage, aquarium, egg incubator, greenhouse, and terrarium are useful apparatus for such study. A View Master with a good supply of nature films would also support and spur interest. Children can weigh air, solids, and liquids with drinking straw balances and record their findings. They can collect things in their neighborhood and record what they have found. They can experiment with a compass, magnets, siphon and water, and low-voltage electricity from safe storage batteries and play with pulleys, levers, magnifying glasses, prisms, color paddles, telegraph systems, et cetera.

The foundation of a child's learning rests on his own actions, which he internalizes to form "the stuff" of his thinking. As the child matures, he has need for laboratory work that involves interdisciplinary experiments out of which major ideas and models of matter and energy are refined and concretized. There is a fundamental connection between play and discovery, between action and learning. Play and activity are basic elements in all early learning. A child comes to school with the urge to play and discover. The grade school should not suddenly shut off this strong desire nor fence out direct manipulative experiences. All schools need to set up learning environments that will inspire the open, playful mind of the young child, enable each child to actively relate things as they are with things as they might be, and stir the imagination.

*The physical world is not limited to what can be seen with the naked eye.* It is also a microscopic world with minute plants, animals, and cells. At the same time, it is a telescopic world of outer space with planets yet to be explored. The invisible structure and activity of the world of matter determine its visible characteristics and behavior. Extending a child's perspective requires dynamic experiences with basic tools in science—the magnifying glass, microscope, telescope, flexible mirrors, et cetera. Young children need to be introduced early to magnification in its simplest forms. Light holds great fascination for all children; it can be bent, reflected, broken up into the spectrum, or made to move in visible waves. Light can create shadows, reverse itself with mirrors, distort, and do countless playful tricks. The child, like the scientist, can experiment with light, observe its behavior, and draw conclusions.

Of course, science study is more than nature study or the observation and care of animals. It is more than collecting or naming things. More nearly, science study requires operating on one's environment, devising and conducting experiments, testing validity, making predictions, and recording data. In our period of rapid technological change, when finite laws lose their absolute character, children need to be encouraged to experiment and arrive at their own conclusions. Science exploration is an area that lends itself especially well to childhood fantasy play and a sense of adventure.

*Play involving ideas in geography and history.* Social studies, as taught in elementary schools today, includes broad listings of geographical and historical data concerning places, people, events, dates, and so on, which the disengaged pupil may or may not commit to memory. The teacher assigns a textbook to be studied, which is a recording of the conclusions of others. Discussions take place to help the child retrace the steps that led to the conclusions. Work books and tests are used to ascertain whether the material has been memorized. History and geography thus become a fragmented, telephone directory-type of experience for most children.

However, a great revolution in methods of teaching geography and social studies is taking place. The elements of play and the self-discovery of major ideas are replacing the indiscriminate demand for the sheer memorizing of facts. Elementary school children in the third and fourth grades are encouraged to be data collectors, first observing objects, events, and pertinent phenomena and then isolating and analyzing them. They record changes in the weather daily. Temperatures are noted. Clouds are classified. Traffic is counted and graphed. All findings are compared with statistics in other regions, and before long the children classify the information they accumulate themselves into an ordering or regional system. They are encouraged to study man's adaptation to differing environments. The children are given panorama boards and three-dimensional artifacts representing topography, people, animals, and vegetation and are asked to re-create environments that fit data cards listing climate, growing seasons, the soil, bedrock, rainfall, the terrain, and so on. Even problems on the location of mythical islands may be posed so the children can themselves be "discoverers." On a huge globe they are asked to trace the sea travels documented in the early diaries of real explorers. Longitude and latitude problems demand the use of mathematics. Diaries describing island discoveries are avidly read. The children eagerly play out situations that require their making judgments about the kinds of people, animals, and vegetation that could exist there. Social studies and geography study are thus made living, involving, exciting subjects.

*History can be an absorbing field of study for young children.* The historian does not memorize unrelated, irrelevant facts; rather, he "re-creates periods of time." He collects data and assesses credibility about events, institutions, land usage, family composition and life, political systems, and technology. He gets his information from actual documents, diaries, artifacts, old maps, letters, et cetera, and with these he reconstructs a meaningful picture of a period. If the schools are to make the study of history more vital and useful, they will have to make it more playful and thought-provoking adventuring for children. They will have to let children use the techniques of the historian, researching original diaries, census tables, reading old gazettes, looking at antiques, and evaluating all for "patterns of relatedness" as typical of a given time period. For example, a class could research certain industries, grist mills, asheries, or distilleries that indicate a specialized farm crop. This, in turn, might lead to a study of transportation, the degree of technological development, et cetera— in short, a pattern of life in a particular historical period of time.

*Researching original data is but one technique of discovery.* Children must literally play with and manipulate an environment in order to comprehend the complex ideas in history and geography. To understand the changes that occur in a specific physical setting as a result of new technology, they must re-create (play out) with miniatures how the introduction of new tools and inventions changed an environment from hunting in a wilderness to a clearing in the woods in a pastoral society, to a semi-agricultural social order with the introduction of the plow, the rise of economic exchange with the introduction of the steam engine, and the beginning of cities as a result of the Industrial Revolution. Playing with properly scaled toys and building materials, the children are able to trace road building, the utilization of land, and developing technology.

To conquer the concept of a period of time, children carry through "archaeological digging" games in which they actually dig up layers of Plasticine "earth," and from the miniature artifacts and skeletons they find, they present a picture of how they think life went on during that period. After listening to taped cassettes of master storytellers, they are able to picture the events on "time lines." More advanced learning through play programs introduces the children to various cultures to verify patterns of relatedness between technology, family life, land utilization, or political systems. Such patterns are not presented orally; rather, they come from class experiences with game play in which land, wives, and goats are exchanged on a kind of Monopoly board (Githaka) to illustrate an exchange system among the Kikuyus, an agricultural tribe in Kenya. Or each member of the class is designated a Nigerian Benin tribal member by hanging a "role-playing card" around his neck and simulating actual situations he must act out in the "tribal council." These play and learning techniques show children the elements that make for historical change and how they work. Their active engagement in manipulating the activity gives the children a sense of chronological progression so essential to the understanding of history. They discover that each age has its own peculiar character, its own special style and significance.

In a play and discovery setting there are no right and wrong answers to a finite number of questions. When children are in control of their own learning, they are not so much concerned with "right" answers as they are with asking the right questions about the setting they are studying. The teacher joins in this quest, regarding herself not as an oracle but as a fellow seeker.

We urge minimizing the memorization of questionable facts in the teaching of social studies in the primary grades and giving greater emphasis to the mastery of major ideas when children tackle any academic subject. Such mastery must come before a student reaches high school because secondary schools are departmentalized by tradition, and interdisciplinary ideas do not have a chance to flourish in such fragmentation of learning. In the primary grades, with one teacher directing the learning, patterns of relatedness in social science can be abstracted from multiple play and discovery experiences. Structural models that help a child organize and describe experiences can be used for practicing skills or for problem solving. But play and laboratory experimentation must always precede practice.

*Academic games.* In recent years game play has become a supplementary technique for motivating learning, spurring intellectual initiative, and organizing students' concepts and intuitions. (Businessmen use games to present industrial case histories; psychologists employ game play to build interpersonal relations; academicians use simulation games to get over the structure of a subject.) A simulation game is a way of partitioning off from the complex stream of real-life activities a portion of the action that requires special investigation and study. There are set rules in academic games, a particular segment of time, a framework in which the action takes place, and a group of players with a predetermined set of role-playing activities. Above all, there is a goal for which the game's content is relevant. After the student learns the rules of play, he has to make judgments and act. The player has to assimilate the information in order to compete efficiently and enjoy the game. Moreover, the game provides a series of interrelated actions that build up into a structure that not only facilitates achieving the game's goal, but also becomes the framework for retaining and using information. An educational game can structure human actions in the social sciences, the humanities, and mathematics. Underlying most academic games is a model of the real process they are intended to simulate. The games are especially well suited to the development of the problem-solving skills of students, while calling into play their analytical and intuitive abilities.

Academic games encourage group discussions of rules, information, and actions. Failure to win an educational game does not upset the participating students as does a low or failing subject grade. The use of simulation games in academics reinforces our hypothesis that play introduces a fundamental positive change in the learning tasks of the school. Among some of the more successful games are Wff'n Proof and Equations in mathematics and Market Place and Githaka in social science. We believe the academic game field will grow considerably in the years ahead because it is one of the best ways to get across to children the structure of a subject while minimizing irrelevant information.

*Play in art education.* Inasmuch as art expression has in its scope so much play with ideas and new materials, and because it has positive values for furthering the creative processes, it has become increasingly suited to the dynamics of our changing world. It deserves attention in early academics equal to that given mathematics, the language arts, science, geography, and history. In the preschool years art is a spontaneous process of creation and discovery. Any art training during these years should minimize the value of an end product. The home and school should merely provide those raw art materials that enable children to accomplish their creative art expressions freely and easily.

Too many parents and teachers still believe that after the first five or six years of life, a child's spontaneity and imaginative powers diminish. This point of view needs to be reversed. What is wrong is that the environment may not provide sufficient "adult" art challenges for children. The form and construction of things, both natural and man-made, are of consuming interest to children in the primary grades. If parents and schools would feed this interest, art expression and art appreciation would grow and grow! The continuous sharpening of sensitivity and the development of techniques come as the result of play with all kinds of materials and ideas and exposure to beautiful things. The very moment when childhood spontaneity gives way to adult-imposed art standards is the time to bring playfulness back into the art education picture.

We need to find and provide manipulative art experiences that make children keenly aware of line, color, shape, texture, space, and design. Children like rubber-stamping textured areas, patterning with crayons and paint, creating curved, horizontal, and vertical lines, exploring motion with roller-printing devices, investigating proportion with transparent overlays, experimenting with shadows using projection techniques.

It is when volition begins to lessen that children need to be encouraged to study the physical elements in art, to isolate them and consider them separately and in relation to one another. Children need to experiment with the rhythms of lines and points, with the massing of forms and space, light and shade, color and texture, and with their dynamic interaction with balance, proportion, motion, pattern, scale, value, mood, composition, and unity of design. Children need to be exposed to contemporary art as well as works created by earlier artists.

*Music education.* Music as a creative subject too often lags behind all other creative play endeavors in the home and the primary grades. Children respond to music almost from birth. They move and dance to its rhythms and are especially fond of folk and band music, eager to have it repeated interminably in order to learn melodies and beats. They will play avidly with simple rhythm instruments to accompany the melodies. Spontaneously they will act out the slowness or the fastness of the rhythms and, if called upon, can act out the exact mood of the music.

More needs to be done to get children to experiment with sounds in the "raw" state, to get the feel of pitch (high and low), rhythm (long, short, and staccato), velocity, and all other aspects of musical awareness. There are two important aspects of musical exploration: the making of original patterns in sound (improvisation and composition) and the re-creation of musical patterns created by a composer (performance and interpretation).

Toy manufacturers and musical instrument makers need to do more to encourage the exploration of sound. Only recently have one or two of them showed concern for this area of music education by making xylophones with interchangeable notes or pipes so a child can play with the sequences of sound. Electronic technology has so improved that true sounds and notes can now emanate from a push of buttons or sensitive "pens" pointing to musical bars. The kalimba, an African thumb piano, and a Haitian drum permit children to engage in exciting musical improvisation. The electronic amplification of music has also given the young child a feeling of great power while attempting to make music. More experimentation with transisterized devices would permit greater musical play and creativity in composition.

There should be some time each day for listening to classical and folk music, whether played by the parent or teacher or by means of phonograph records. Inasmuch as the listening span of young children is fairly limited, the choice of music and the time for listening are important considerations.

*Play is a vital learning process.* It provides the subject matter for activity, thinking, and learning. The play element gives energy and motivation to learning. It is the freedom to experiment that spurs the learning. Whether the play is with concrete objects or purely mental, there is always some plan in a play activity, and the end result is almost always likely to be the acquisition of satisfaction and some insight. The moment when things go together, when ideas begin to click, that moment is an exhilarating one for the learner. In every academic lesson and most especially during the early elementary grades, there must be some time for playing, for allowing a child's imagination to forge ahead, for letting children "try the impossible," and for their toying with the infinite. Play, like nothing else, has the power to infuse learning with dynamic purpose.

*Structuring the play environment for academic learning.*

Most laymen and even many educators and scholars have long considered play to be non-constructive behavior and not sound from a learning point of view. The average teacher, trained for structured learning, is aghast when he visits the average nursery school. "The activity is kaleidoscopic," Dr. Millie Almy of Teachers College, Columbia University, points out, "as children flow from one small group into another." Domestic play themes merge with transportation themes as "play husbands" from the housekeeping corner become "truck drivers" in the block-building area. To the nursery school educator, this kind of free play has the most learning power, but the average educator sees in it no beginning, no end, certainly no structure, and, what is most evident to him, no teacher leadership. Most educators believe that equipment should teach specific concepts, with appropriate accompanying language to describe every activity. While it is true that pre-school play lacks rigid structure, the nursery school teacher values it highly because of what a child can accomplish with his own imagination and motivation.

For over fifty years, many nursery school educators have been trying to explain to grade school teachers what vast learning power there is in spontaneous, unstructured play. Drs. Anna Freud and Susan Isaacs, among other Freudian child analysts and therapists, tried early to define this kind of play as being "bound neither to logic nor reality." Others described it as "childhood wishful thinking" and therefore put it on the opposite side of intellectual reasoning. Still others maintained that a child freed from the restraints of reality, time, and space during his early years could through his free play try out his growing intellectual power.

Nursery educators have often found strong emotional and interpersonal validation for spontaneous play, but have had great difficulty defining the exact cognitive aspects of this play. An indication of this is the fact that the material and equipment in the preschools are the same for the three-, four-, and five-year-olds. What is lacking, according to the proponents of structured equipment, is that there is no clear sense of developmental direction. Those who prefer a more structured program for the early years are suggesting that one might bring into the child's environment more prescribed learning activities initiated and directed by the nature of the equipment and a more planned environment and program.

We are indebted to many psychologists and education leaders for their clarification of the roles of "activity" and "things" in the learning process. Maria Montessori introduced a system of interaction with didactic materials that brought preschool children to a stage of readiness for mastering quantitative and mathematical relations, geometric comprehension, and tone sequence in music. Jean Piaget suggests that the seven- to eleven-year-old group is at the stage of handling concrete operations, which means that the child is able to operate on the concepts he has formed, but he is more likely to be able to do so if assisted by repeated and varied interactions with physical things. In the early academic years a child cannot reason hypothetically. He must have concrete situations or at least firm images of such situations. Suitable structuring of the physical environment and encouraging the child to interact can sometimes hasten the arrival of the verbal and non-verbal hypothetical reasoning stage.

We are also obliged to those education pioneers who espoused the principle that a child learns best when he is active. This does not mean that he be violently active; rather, that he be an active participant in all his learnings. Too often traditional learning has required that a child adopt a passive role, that he sit quietly and listen to the teacher and, at most, be able to answer a series of questions "to see if he has understood what he has been told." Piaget has suggested that the development of a mental structure parallels physical activity of a very personal kind.

Dr. Jerome S. Bruner, director of the Harvard Center for Cognitive Studies from 1960 to the present, has also been exploring the relationship between physical handling and concept formation. Physical handling, and especially two-handedness, may be a prelude to language transformations, according to Bruner. Somewhere around the age of one year an infant will master a "two-handed obstacle box." Seated on the mother's lap, the child will suddenly use one hand to push and hold a transparent cover while the other reaches inside the box for a toy. To Bruner this is extraordinary because it shows that an infant can now distinguish between two kinds of grips: a holding and an operating grip. After that, many routines can be devised by the child for holding an object with one hand while working it with the other, which is the precursor to the distinctively human use of tools. Bruner speculates that this distinguishing and differentiating between two physical operations carries over into language transformations. Thus, developing "clever hands" may be a prelude to putting other things together, like language and speech.

We appreciate, too, Bruner's explanation of how an infant learns to control his environment en route to his mastery of motor and learning skills. An infant can look at a toy long before he can reach out his hand to take it. His motor system has "more slack, more degrees of freedom for movement than he can control." The baby begins to learn how to reduce his neuromuscular freedom—"the complexity of response"— in order to gain control. If an object crosses his visual path, the infant moves his head and feet; his body becomes tense. He attempts to lift his trunk, "pumps his arms, shoulders and head, and closes his fist" while staring at the object, working his mouth at the same time. The infant tries many side-swiping movements toward an object. Intention and attention thus call forth ten to twelve responses. At two months a baby's physical abilities do not permit him to cut down the number of responses. It is only at six and seven months, or later at twelve months, that he is able to limit his responses to six jerky motions of his hand in order to grasp a cup and bring it to his lips. By twenty-seven months his actions are reduced to one smooth movement from hands grasping to drinking. This behavior indicates that the infant must now have enough control of his attention to keep a goal in mind while he decides how to carry through his plan. All these strategies prepare a child for other more demanding learning tasks, like language, numbers, et cetera.

We are beholden to Anna Freud for her analysis of the capacity of the child to derive pleasure from completing a task and solving problems posed by play materials themselves independent of adult praise and approval. Most psychologists tend to ignore this phase of play as developing intellectual competence. Many child psychologists are so preoccupied with the emotional aspects of play that too often they deny its intellectual connotations. Most nursery school teachers also seem to be unaware of this.

The playing child advances each year to new stages of development, one associated with the nature of the play materials and the other to a relationship with his peers. In a sense, as Erik H. Erikson puts it, "The child moves out of himself to confront reality more effectively." Most nursery school educators do not appear to see the cognitive aspects of spontaneous play or to see that play and reasoning have several common elements. We are convinced that spontaneous play can add to the building of intellectual skills. A unit building block construction will not stand unless it is properly balanced. A toy truck will not pass through an opening that is too narrow. Out of such reality-based play encounters come not only mastery of construction principles but also understanding of the larger physical world and one's place in it.

We owe even greater appreciation to Piaget for his studies of cognition in the play of children. In his book *Play, Dreams and Imitation in Childhood*, published in 1962, Piaget illustrates from close observation of his own children how encounters with the environment help children build a pattern of action (schema) and relatively stable concepts with which to view the world. According to Piaget, attaining mature logical thought processes depends not only upon a child's interaction with things in his environment, but also with his interrelations with his peers in the give and take of free play. He describes the first approach as an "accommodation process" in which a child's thinking conforms to the outer reality. The child discovers the environment by means of what he can do with it. Then he integrates (or assimilates) this into the systems of meaning that already exist for him. The two procedures are reciprocal, though at any given point they may not be in equilibrium. When accommodation is more heightened than assimilation, Piaget identifies it as "imitation." Where assimilation takes priority, the child is "playing with an idea." Play, therefore, constitutes the "extreme pole of the assimilation of reality of the ego" and permits imagination to go to work, which, to Piaget, is "the motor of all future thought and reason." Through the manipulation of objects in reality, he would also have older school-aged children discover the properties of objects and how they can be classified.

Piaget believes that structured play may not be sufficient for the young child, that the youngest one has first to "assimilate reality" in his own way, in his own time, before he can adapt to adult ways of thinking and seeing things. We think a preschooler's spontaneous play is his initial preparation for this kind of assimilation. Structured sorting and arranging are probably best suited for children who have had some background of fantasy and "accommodation" play.

*Teaching aids versus learning aids.* Teachers have used things to demonstrate what they have been talking about to their pupils, but in the main these physical objects have been used as "teaching aids" rather than "learning aids." The teacher manipulates the object and the child remains remote from both the teacher and the aid, adopting the usual passive role. If we are to accept the theories of Piaget, we need to replace demonstration props with real learning aids. This means, of course, that there must be sufficient objects for each child to be able to use so he can be personally involved according to his own needs and interests.

Structured aids are usually created by education experts who are aware of the specific concept they are designed to embody in a concrete way. Ideally they are presented in a number of different embodiments and in as many varied ways as possible.

It is necessary to understand that children learn not only at different speeds, but in different ways as well. Hence the need for all kinds of learning aids and sufficient time to allow the slower child to catch up to the quicker child in abstracting useful concepts. When higher stages of insight are reached, we need to rely on experts to design challenging materials that are structured so that the child using them will be led forward to the abstraction of even more complex notions. The average classroom teacher usually is not able to design such aids. Fortunately, top-notch mathematicians, scientists, and historians have been employed to develop purposeful learning aids. For use in elementary mathematics learning, such materials as the Stern apparatus, Cuisinaire rods, and Dienes multibase equipment have been made available to schools. Lab work in mathematics and science has been developed by scholar-administered curriculum development centers in Syracuse, New York, Berkeley, California, and Newton, Massachusetts. Simulation games have been developed at Harvard University in anthropology and other social sciences. Regrettably, no such research has as yet been undertaken to develop play and learning materials of an unstructured type—or to structure early learning ideas into the playthings used in the preschool and kindergarten. Because kindergarten children are playful and spontaneous with any materials presented to them, educators despair of combining learning with playthings. They make such a sharp distinction between learning and play that young children find it difficult to make an adjustment to academic tasks in the early elementary grades.

*Free play.* Every young child who is introduced to some new learning material needs to be allowed as long a period as he requires for free play. The length of the period and the way in which it is employed will if course vary from child to child. No child should be hurried through this stage because a great deal of implicit learning takes place here, even though the results will not be readily available to the teacher. For example, a child first using a set of graded colored rods quickly becomes aware of the rapid increase in the size of the rod and uses this information when building with them in the free-play stage. Playing with parquetry design blocks, the child becomes keenly aware of shapes and colors, sees which of the shapes go together and which combinations of colors most please or displease him.

At a later stage these very same materials begin to be used in a special sort of way. A teacher can structure a lesson in numbers with these materials, and from such experiences the child can abstract a particular math concept. To be able to do this, however, the child must have a considerable number of experiences with many different kinds of aids, and he must be free to discard the irrelevant until he has decided upon the one concept to be abstracted. It is at this time that the expertly designed structured materials prove more effective than haphazard interaction with environmental materials because the former are designed so that there is minimal distraction from the desired end result. Thus, children are led to the precise concept that is desired—toward a general overview. After this plateau of understanding is reached, the child is led through more experiences with the same or related materials. Each variable gives the child an added perception of what has already been learned, thus reinforcing the learning.

What we have tried to illustrate is that in all true learning there are several stages. (1) First, there is a playing-around period, a somewhat groping stage during which situations are handled more or less randomly in the course of the child's explorations. Enriched materials channel the free play into purposeful "games" which lead to heightened awareness and interest. (2) Then follows an intermediate, more structured stage of play and learning. (3) This, in turn, leads to the child's promulgation of insights, accompanied by his desire to use his ideas in many different situations. The use of insight through analysis and practice will firmly anchor the child's learning. (4) A wealth of concepts (or models) is established, which a child can call upon at will. (5) The concepts are then defined by words and/or symbols, and are communicated by the child by letters, numbers, et cetera.

In all learning, unstructured play experiences need to be followed by structured activities—still play! A well-planned and balanced program of both kinds of play experiences, followed by the use of symbols, is far more effective than attempts to give symbols their meanings by verbal explanations alone. This is one of the prime reasons for the new emphasis on more game play, more laboratory work, and more active, personal involvement in beginning academic learning.

# CHAPTER FIVE

# *Creativity Through Play*

Have you ever noticed how often "non-intellectuals" turn out to be creative leaders of industry, opinion-molders in government, science, and daily living, as well as creative producers in art and music? Take a survey of the top men in government, commerce, and research, and you will find that in college many achieved only average grades. Many were probably the second child in the family. Left to their own devices, they learned early to use their inner resources. Or they were an only child who played alone in a fantasy world of their own creation. Often they had greater closeness to one parent. If you could get them to answer a personal questionnaire, you would find that they had parents who cared as much about their early play life as their later formal learning. In fact, in most instances their parents entered into their early play life. They made costumes for their children's playlets, played fantasy games with them, told them bedtime stories, sang to them, and in general sought out the kinds of play materials that encouraged creativity and fantasy in their offspring.

In March of 1967 we circulated a "play questionnaire" we composed to two hundred and sixty-five people we selected at random from the 1964–65 edition of Who's Who. Forty-one graciously replied:

37 men from all fields of endeavor
and
4 professional women

They answered detailed questions about their early play lives and subsequent academic years. While this is certainly not a definitive piece of research, we think the tabulation below is of pertinence to our play thesis.

Most of the forty-one indicated that one of the reasons for their success could be attributed to sensitive parents or relatives who were close to them during their preschool years.

31 of the 41 spent their early years mostly in the city
3 spent their early years in the country
6 spent their early years in the suburbs
1 did not answer

6 of the 41 attended preschools
26 attended kindergarten
15 had no preschool or kindergarten experience (4 were ill during the earliest years of schooling and spent time at home)

15 of the 41 felt their parents were perceptive about good playthings
18 felt their parents were indifferent
8 did not answer

18 of 37 men
1 of 4 women claimed that among their favorite toys were the large building blocks

15 of 37 men
4 of 4 women considered painting a favorite early creative activity
(8 became painters
2      "      sculptors
1      "      an art historian
1      "      an architect)

17 of the 41 claimed their parents read to them considerably or more than average

36 of the 41 claimed they read intensively in their early years

29 of the 41 claimed their career interests were evident in their early years (9 before 5 years; 13 in years between 5 to 10 years; 7 in years between 10 and 15; 12 after 15 years)

23 of the 41 had mothers who gave full time to the family

What is most interesting is that more than half of the group was exposed to unit building blocks and considered painting a favorite early childhood activity, and twenty-two of the forty-one claimed that their career interests were formulated by them before they reached ten years of age.

What is it that often puts the B student ahead of the A student in adult life, especially in business and creative professions? Certainly it is more than verbal skill. To create, one must have a sense of adventure and playfulness. One needs toughness to experiment and hazard the risk of failure. One has to be strong enough to start all over again if need be and alert enough to learn from whatever happens. One needs a strong ego to be propelled forward in one's drive toward an untried goal. Above all, one has to possess the ability to play!

One also has to be able to see relationships easily and clearly, to pick out the relevant, and to put ideas together; in short, to play with ideas until insight, or "the moment of truth," comes forth. Insight and creativity do not come as a flash of genius; rather, they come from a long period of playing, of looking at a problem from unusual perspectives, of holding a situation open for review until several approaches have been found, or from rearranging things in new ways that please one better.

Playing with ideas is hard and often frustrating work. Being creative involves trying to find something without necessarily being able to say clearly what it is that you are seeking. You have to be willing and able to let some things stay unresolved for a while. You have to break with stereotypes and try new approaches. You have to be willing to challenge what is considered to be true. You need to have tolerance for individual differences and to understand that each being must develop his own style of behavior. You have to be able to share tentative ideas with others. Most importantly, you have to be able to dream!

Have you ever surmised what would happen to American ingenuity if creative people were robbed of the precious sliver of time just before arising in the morning? This seems to be a special time for prolific playing with configurations, for daydreaming, for letting the imagination soar, for unfettered mental gymnastics, and for daring to take risks that are rarely approached in a reality framework.

The ability to fantasize, take risks, lay things down and pick them up again is a fundamental potential of all children. It gets its greatest impetus from play encounters and explorations of one's environment, both animate and inanimate. While motivation to explore may come from interpersonal relations, it comes equally and perhaps more readily from the examination of the things in one's surroundings. A child's creative development requires extensive interpersonal and nonpersonal involvements.

Some children learn early how to exploit adults and their peers to get what they want. They develop tricks and put much time and energy into seeing if adults and children react to what they are doing. They often expend so much time on this type of game play that they have little left to get involved in anything else. As a result, they are often left out in the cold. If they could forgo this "game" and get involved in active playing, they would then have an experience that is liberating. If they do not free themselves from manipulating persons and maneuver objects instead, their way of life could even border on the neurotic. For some children, encounters and involvements with inanimate things are needed to activate their creative ability. They are able to develop socially only by first coming to grips with the inanimate objects of the world of play. The world of things is not restrictive. In fact, it encourages fanciful and non-threatening thinking—the free play of the mind. In this wonderful world, neither parent nor teacher places restraints on childlike wonder and play. There are no facial reactions, no threats that communicate "no" and "yes" lights on what can be done.

*Every young child has the capacity for make believe.* While the degree varies from child to child, it can be repressed or constricted. Children need encouragement to speak freely, to make believe. Even more important are opportunities for a wide range of artistic and aesthetic experiences and challenges with the raw materials of imaginative play. Have you ever thought what would happen if children did not have long periods of fantasy play?

Dr. Lawrence J. Friedman, a senior faculty member of the Los Angeles Psychoanalytic Institute, points out that regular television viewing has rendered children passive, thus denying them normal outlets for their fantasy and aggression. In a recent book he wrote: "All television, except in small doses, feeds children ready-made fantasy at a time when fantasy making is crucial for their development . . . We are just beginning to see the results of long exposure to television in adolescents today. This is the first TV generation and much of its violence can be traced directly to its early TV habits . . . a generation that grew up just pushing a button to be entertained is finding it extremely difficult to establish an object relationship with others. A child who watches enough television will become violent because he has nowhere to go with his normal aggressive energy that he should be working off in creative activity."

What is there about fantasy play that gives a child such full release to the development of self and imagination? Fantasy play is a freeing of oneself, a reinless activity which allows a child to test out the absurd; to "change the rules" frequently; to be illogical or infantile. Fantasy permits the creation and shaping of elaborate, imaginary worlds. It is a kind of un-hampered flight which "lets wit grow into a sense of the world as it is and as it should be." In freely dramatizing the world as he sees it, the child is reliving it on his own terms, and he is finding it full of delight. He projects his own pattern of the world into his play. He is building the feeling that the world is his to understand, to puzzle out and make over.

*Laughter, love, and learning are most closely related to fantasy.* Because there is a physical giving, recognizing, and releasing of the self in laughter, much humor abounds in the realm of fantasy. The child has full control over his imagined world. Often parents are not able to be responsive to or to enter into the fantasy play life of their children. It seems too pointless, irrational, or even maddening to most parents to submit to the infantile whims of such play. Yet most knowl-edgeable teachers and child psychiatrists know that intervening in this play can be one of the most powerful educational tools they possess. It is the flexible change of the rules of play, as well as the complete manipulation of the child's personal and physical environment, that gives fantasy play its great power.

Because there are differences in each child's environment and decided variances in early experiences with playthings, some children become creative adults who are bold and free to explore and take chances. In fact, we believe that because of the nature of play materials, or the lack of them, in the early years, some cultures have creativity and drive while others lack the creative force to handle their problems. An intensive study should be undertaken by the United Nations to ascertain whether there is a direct relationship between the nature of a nation's play materials and the drive of that nation. Some surprising research facts would no doubt be revealed that would cause every nation to take a second look at its materials of play for its young and set as high standards and controls for their content and quality as for food and drugs.

In what type of man-made environment does a child's playfulness and creativeness seem to blossom? An environment that can be moved about and changed to a child's satisfaction encourages creativity. Such an environment may even be the most impossible aesthetically. We saw children revel in creative play in bombed out areas of Frankfurt am Main in West Germany back in 1953. The movable bricks and stones, crater holes, and rough terrain were conducive to manipulation and free physical and dramatic play.

A construction site is a dangerous place, but it is a type of man-made environment that would encourage the creative free play of children. That is one of the reasons nursery schools and kindergartens have sawhorses, wood blocks, nail barrels, sand piles, wheelbarrows, and so forth, all of which suggest limitless construction and house-building play ideas to the imaginative child. A barn permits fanciful physical play: climbing, rope swinging, jumping in the hay, experiencing the smell and texture of new-mown hay, and sliding down a hayloft. A junk yard is also a gold mine of play opportunities for any child, especially when he can collect and combine bits and pieces to his heart's content. What is common to all these environments is that they reflect the adult world. They have variations in terrain. They have movable materials that can be handled and arranged and rearranged in ways that delight a child. The elements are unpredictable and full of challenge. The spatial boundaries of all fantasy play settings enclose a "secret" or "mystery" world in which the child has complete autonomous power.

Unfortunately, most children live in technologically stamped-out environments that offer very little in the way of creative challenges or "happenings." The mobility of a child in today's cities and suburbs is severely circumscribed. Indoors there are generally less than one hundred square feet of bedroom space, with its immovable bed and furniture. Out of doors there is a clean backyard or an asphalt playground with "no touch" signs well-ingrained in a child's consciousness. Grassy areas of the neighbors are taboo; heavy concentration of trees for hiding or climbing are off limits; brooks are considered too dangerous. The child is confronted repeatedly with "the actuality of situations and events, with ever-present threats, and sometimes even painful consequences." He learns soon what he can and dare not do. He must cope with a restrictive world.

*A child needs a long period of make-believe play to strengthen his spontaneity and self-expression.* He needs at least four years to build an "as if" world of his own and to pretend freely and revel in his fantasy and dreams. He needs freedom to play with carefully selected playthings and equipment, with ample "living space."

Are some environments and play materials better for creativeness than others? What play materials encourage more exploration? What materials lead to creativity in the arts, drama, the dance, and role playing? What situations evoke the creation of one's own ideas rather than of models of adult-imposed patterns? What stirs play with words, with sounds? What playthings free a child's imagination and build will power? What play materials are structured for teaching? Just as there is a difference between academic and play environments, so there is a difference between the "unstructured" playthings that encourage creativity and those that are "structured for learning."

*Structured playthings.* Dr. Jerome S. Bruner, professor of psychology at Harvard from 1952 to the present, in an oft-quoted statement, claims that one can teach a young child almost anything. Yes, one could structure almost any learning concept into a playful experience. However, greater care and ingenuity are demanded when one uses play materials to get ideas across. Words are easier, but then the learning results are questionable. Since play experiences are self-chosen and self-directed, they are more believable, more involving, and less threatening to a child than word learning superimposed by a teacher. Learning via play experiences usually invokes inductive processes. Ideas have to be analyzed for their varied subideas, and these then have to be translated into a variety of different play experiences from which meaningful associations can be gained and subidea platforms built. This kind of intensive planning seems more readily associated with word learning than with play experience. For this reason, play is neglected by educators as a structured technique in learning. We label toys as "educational," but in truth toymakers and educators, with few exceptions, have not devoted much time to the planning of educative playthings.

It is encouraging that play is being given more prominence by today's educators who are beginning to look to play as a way of deeply involving children in their own learning. Many are researching such techniques as simulation games, role playing, matching, sequencing, counting, et cetera. Structured playthings are those materials that come to the child with prearranged, adult-set outcomes. They may have academic implications. The outcome may be learning shapes in the alphabet, ascertaining sequences of time in clock movements, seeing simple associations in parts of the body in a jigsaw puzzle, matching groupings of domino dots to teach sets in mathematics, or putting together circular picture-story puzzles to prepare a child for sequenced picture reading. The outcome is programmed; that is, there is generally one set way the child can complete the task. There are few opportunities to make alternate judgments. A child cannot "play around" with such "playthings."

Of course, if the child is provided with enough of such structured playthings, if they are varied versions of the same idea, a concept is bound to be learned. This concept of variability of experiences is an important one for parents and teachers to learn. A child does not learn from one or two play experiences. The more experiences, the easier it is for him to deduce an idea. Counting and adding are complex mathematical ideas. Before a child can use symbols or words for numerals, he has to master a host of preliminary, non-verbal mathematical ideas.

Reading is another complex skill. It takes preliminary training to see simple picture associations. It requires word sounding and phonetic ability. It takes shape and size recognition skill before one can sound out letters and then read words in sentences. Passive TV viewing and listening to the radio or others are not enough. Children need to match wholes and parts, put things in proper sequence, know colors, et cetera. There is a definite sequence of steps, each a specific skill dependent upon those that came before. Seeing differences between *in* and *on* depends upon recognizing the differences between *i* and *o*. In turn, this awareness stems from recognizing the separate characteristics of straight and curved lines.

Designers have to research the learning tasks to be performed, analyze their structure, and break concepts up into varied, short, successful play experiences. It would be necessary to incorporate all elements into non-verbal playing games or tasks. With sufficient ingenuity, all learning tasks in mathematics, social science, the sciences, et cetera, can be structured into challenging play materials. Most structured playthings have their reward in the finished problem-solving task or completed product. A finished number puzzle gives a child a pleasurable sense of accomplishment. A circular sequence puzzle that pictures the evolution of the building of a house when properly positioned has its reward in a self-correcting color match on the reverse side. A word lotto game perfectly picture-matched marks the child a winner. This is the nature of structured material. There needs to be some reason to finish the activity, an academic skill to master, or a reward that impels a child to undertake a learning project. For the demanding tasks of reading or mathematics, structured playthings may be the preferred way out. But for stimulating a child's creativity, unstructured play materials should be chosen.

*Unstructured play materials.* In an unstructured plaything or play material, the reward is in the excitement of discovery and in the playing itself. There are no preconceived goals engineered into unstructured playthings, no adult-imposed objectives. Such toys are generally raw materials of play which include unit building blocks, clay, sand, finger paints, water, poster paints, brushes, paper of all kinds, pegs and pegboards, design cubes, collage material, scissors, paste, and so on, for which there are no blueprints to follow. All of the foregoing encourage, even demand, creativity, and the end result (whether houses and community scenes layed out with the blocks, a figure sculpted out of clay, a picture painted, or an assembled construction) is in the eyes of the experimenter.

Initially the child "fools around" with the material. He sets the blocks in long roads or stands them up on end and topples them. He tries filling a piece of paper with broad brush strokes of paint. While no one can foretell exactly what the end result of such free play will be, we know that a child gains pleasure and a sense of confidence in himself every time he masters the elements in his play world.

Unstructured play materials are not necessarily pliant or molding materials per se. They can take finished form. An electrical invention box for nine-year-olds, for instance, provides buzzers, bells, sockets, wire, switches, and a dry-cell battery. It comes without limiting instructions while providing the raw material needed for safe electrical experimentation. The child discovers and tests out his own circuits and circuit breakers. Before too long, he will have hooked up a burglar alarm system or a Morse code transmitter. End results are limited only by the child's own imagination and dedication. Provide a set of instructions with such play material and you have a "structured plaything," one which requires precise following of electrical plans formulated in the instruction sheets.

*What makes unstructured playthings so popular with children, and why do they involve them over long periods of time?* Anyone watching a child playing with such material will observe that they lend themselves to trial-and-error activity. There can be no failure and no disapproval if a project isn't finished according to adult standards. Because there are no set goals or restraints, a child will try out new ideas again and again until he establishes his own schema. These materials say to the child: "Here are things that lend themselves to the creation of any of your fantasies. You are in full command. You can manipulate them freely. With blocks or paint or clay, you can make anything you wish. You can roll the clay into balls, the balls into snakes, the snakes into pots, and the pots into people, if you wish. You can make your blocks form roads, your roads form fences, and your fences form a town."

*Unit building blocks.* These are probably the most widely accepted unstructured play material in nursery schools and homes for the use of children from two to about nine or ten years of age. Block building satisfies the universal urge to give form to ideas and feelings. It also furnishes the setting for dramatic play through which children clarify, extend, and test their understanding of the world they live in. Blocks add immeasurably to the muscular co-ordination of children and to their skill in manipulation and imaginative play. Blocks enable a child to construct a small toy world over which he has full control.

Blocks are free of the embellishments that inhibit constructive imagination. They are heavy, unbreakable, and made of natural hardwoods. Only properly cut, architecturally modular unit blocks work well—those cut in 2¾-, 5½-, 11-, and 22-inch lengths. Children consider poorly cut or designed blocks or miniature blocks to be so much junk to be tossed carelessly about, not played with. Many parents are disappointed when their child tosses about his new bag of blocks. The best testing technique is for adults to try building with the blocks they buy. If they can build big and high and the blocks go together easily without toppling, the blocks will afford their child limitless hours of pleasurable play. If not, the blocks should go back to the toy store or the manufacturer!

By merely removing building blocks from the shelf, a child already begins to make an impression on his environment. The unique combination of creative expression and mastery that block play initiates seems to be practically irresistible to all children. Sometimes very young children use blocks for aggressive and not constructive purposes, and they delight in flinging them about. The need to "let off steam" comes on occasion from the pressures that are exerted on children to conform to adult standards that have little real meaning for them. Even happy children enjoy knocking over their block structures. Often they build only to destroy. A good deal of "destructive" play actually reflects a child's quest for novel effects. Blocks offer children a chance, without the usual consequences, to do exactly what is forbidden in other areas of play. In the process of growing up, children are constantly warned to be careful not to throw things, not to break things. They are often punished even when destruction is accidental. In the benign world of the block corner, the child can build, destroy, and repair to his heart's content—until he has had his fill.

Building blocks can be used by all kinds of children to satisfy all kinds of needs. Blocks are so totally indestructible that a child feels safe in playing out both his fears of disaster from without and his destructive impulses from within. Projecting his feelings on something so real and concrete, a child is able to rob them of their power and possible threat. Whether constructive or destructive, the dramatic play which building blocks help to implement serves to round out the personality of a child.

When children build airports, bridges, skyscrapers, et cetera, they are not merely reproducing objects. They are (in fantasy, at least) gaining control over things that ordinarily dwarf them. Along with the satisfactions of block play, children learn invaluable concepts: balance, form, height, distance, and matching shapes and sizes—all of which will stand them in good stead in their later work in reading and mathematics. The late Frank Lloyd Wright, world-famous American architect, used his childhood unit building blocks throughout his productive professional life.

Most unstructured play materials bring forth results quickly and assure a child the emotional satisfaction and success associated with achievement. These raw materials of play are abstract, without signs or symbols that dictate a rigid purpose. A truck, with or without wheels, in natural wood can be an exciting tool of play and manipulation for the city-oriented child. He is able to use it for any set of circumstances, today as a train, tomorrow as a barge or any kind of vehicle. Detail and reality can be a hindrance to free, creative play for the very young child, because he can use the toy only for what it was originally intended.

Sometimes to get a child to play creatively, it may be necessary to provide in some of his toys evidence of the reality he finds in the world about him. Often this "reality" is only a stimulation to play. After awhile it gets in the way of a child. An early pioneer in unstructured play, Caroline Pratt, provided silk-screen painted figures to represent family members and assorted community workers. These were made of wedge-shaped wood to stand easily. Preschoolers delighted in using their building blocks to house them. They built firehouses, garages, railroad stations, et cetera, for the community wedge figures. After a few years of this community play, Miss Pratt insisted that the wedge people be removed and that the six-to-eight-year-olds be left to their own resources with only the shapes and sizes of the building blocks themselves. The result of this removal of detail was the children's amazing flow of fantasy and creative constructions with the blocks themselves. The abstract block forms became people figures and were used most effectively and freely in the wholly inventive play of the children.

Trips to local community centers of interest expand the use of unstructured play material. Especially rewarding are the community supermarket, bakery, shoe repair shop, pet store, florist, and service station. Later on, the post office, firehouse, police station, and building and road construction sites offer food for thought and fun. Trips outside the neighborhood might include a museum, farm, zoo, railroad station, airport, and harbor with its docks, boats, and trucks. Children return from such trips so full of information and enthusiasm that they relive these adventures over and over again in their play.

We associate a quality of "pliancy" with unstructured play-things, that is, they can be more easily manipulated or a child can make them do his bidding more freely and readily. Blocks, clay, and paint, for example, permit great freedom of use. The same pliancy can be given to more structured toys, like dolls, community figures, construction sets, and so on. If a doll or community figure has a wire armature so that it can bend easily and its feet are weighted to stand firmly, this would enhance the toy's play possibilities. A child could make such a figure do exactly what he wants it to: stand, sit, bend, kneel, climb, or even hold a baby doll. Now if facial features were removed on some kind of bendable abstraction of a doll, it would have even greater play value because this would increase the number of roles the child could make it play. Although abstract toys may be good design for children's play, the chances of such playthings getting on the market are minimal since most toys for children are bought by parents, grandparents, and other adults. Most adults are attracted to toys with perfect detail; usually they shun abstract playthings. If doll house furniture is an exact replica in miniature, one can be fairly sure that adults will buy it. If children were allowed to pick their own toys without parental or TV commercial dictation, we believe they would select the simplest cars and trucks, bendable figures free of facial detailing, plain doll house furniture, and other uncluttered play materials. When most adults give toys to children, their choices reflect not so much play value as adult enchantment with minute detailing.

Creative toys do not dictate any one kind of action; they permit many different operational ways of playing. On the other hand, a toy electric train on a track operated from a remote-control switch is not a satisfying experience for the three-year-old who must be the engineer himself and push the train. The track itself is restrictive. Inasmuch as the child is not supposed to take the train off the track, he cannot make the train go where he wants it to. Also, the exact detailing of an electric train leaves little to a young child's imagination. Experimentation is also restricted by complete detailing on a wooden truck. A basic shape with wheels that move easily offers multiple, flexible transportation play possibilities to eager, imaginative, young "engineers." For the very young child (from eighteen months to three years of age), simple floor trains and cars without wheels can be maneuvered most easily. In fact, wheels can get in the way of the very young child and limit the action.

Creative toys give a child sufficient basic shapes which can be combined so he can create his own interpretations of city or country living: wooden house shapes, tree forms, vehicle and boat shapes, building blocks, et cetera. The more kinds of fanciful construction and the greater possible combinations such shapes suggest and permit, the more inventive will be the response of the child. We say the play material is unstructured when it comes to the child without "telling" him what he can do with it. Building blocks with apartment house window detailing printed on them, for example, might make the play less meaningful to a country child.

Bendable people, assorted animals, cars, and trucks expand the play possibilities of unit building blocks. The parent or teacher who watches a city or country scene unfold before her can forward the learning and encourage imagination by introducing signs to identify streets and buildings, and ferries and barges for food and other waterway transport. She can intervene with suitable stories and trips to local places of interest to keep curiosity alive and perking. Intervention is a positive role that all parents and teachers need to play with great care, however. Children relish interchange of playfulness with adults, but only if not heavy-handed. There is a profound effect on creativeness in later life if a child has enjoyed adult support for his playful fantasies and efforts. The right suggestions can deepen and enrich each experience. At the same time, the child's wondering and resolving spur his imagination.

*Unstructured playthings are difficult to design.* They represent suggestive, abstract forms with which a child can create for himself all kinds of playthings or play settings. The child can use them to define space in imaginative ways, creating varied environments in which he can playfully act out all sorts of situations at will. Whatever the experimental objective may be—to play with color, geometrics, design, texture, et cetera—the end result will depend largely on the unstructured forms that are available to him. If we desire children to play with color, we have to design play elements that go together to permit the most extensive color experimentation. If we want children to play with art design, we need to develop three-dimensional elements relating to texture, size, shape, motion, et cetera, all of which can go together to make possible the creation by the child of infinite design possibilities. If we wish children to explore all kinds of constructions, we have to provide those parts and connectors that offer full freedom and satisfying building accomplishments. If we would have children test geometric patternings, we have to evolve lines, triangles, cubes, and squares in three-dimensional form. Unstructured toy ideas tax the skill of all toy designers, very few of whom are successful in this challenging field.

*Unstructured materials for art expression.* Children need many and varied raw art materials that are suitable to the developmental level they have reached. For example, if the child can handle a brush and paint adequately, he is ready for painting. Most three-year-olds are ready and eager for this activity. Even some younger children can manage these materials and derive great pleasure from doing so.

Many three-year-olds can cut with scissors and handle paste quite well at their own level. In brief, each child should have his first art experience when he shows that he is ready for it. Art materials offer a child great freedom and choice of creative activity. With these, he can communicate his individuality and come to appreciate himself as a person distinct from other people. He finds that he has manipulative power and control over the material because he can make many different things with it. He can make the material do his bidding!

*From scribbling to drawing.* While pencils and crayons are less costly and less messy, they do not stimulate a young child toward exploration and experimentation as poster paints do. Also, a child is prone to grip a crayon more tightly. Often he becomes tense as his interest in what he is making increases, rather than to relax as in painting. Most children start to scribble at about age two. As a child's muscular co-ordination improves, his marks on the paper become more than random movements. He enjoys making the lines go where he wants them to go. Large pencils with blunt, soft leads are easy for the young child to hold, as well as large wax crayons. However, neither pencils nor crayons can substitute for the sweep of feelings and ideas that a paint brush allows.

In recent years, non-toxic, odorless water color pens have been replacing crayons. These markers feed ink evenly into broad felt tips so that a child can make free, broad lines with an assortment of bright colors.

Children should be free to play with ideas without spatial restrictions at a very early age, which is one reason we do not like coloring books. Their ready-made shapes and the need to color inside the outlines can block the development of a child's creative powers. Some coloring books have a colored picture on one page and the same picture in outline on the facing page for the child to fill in. Other coloring books contain outlines of animals or people or just designs. Our objection is that all these cramp creativity. Young children are naturally spontaneous and free. Any activity that inhibits this tendency dampens their ardor for creative expression. In addition, giving a child someone else's drawing, whether it be of fine or poor quality, implies that he cannot draw well enough for himself and this can undermine his confidence in himself.

*Painting is a liberating adventure.* The years between two and four are especially appropriate for the introduction of painting as a medium of expression because these are the years when children's painting is least representational and the most direct response of each child to the material itself. When the young child begins to paint, he paints his feelings, not things or people. Instead of delineating his ideas, he tries to show what and how he feels. He does not regard the painting materials as a means to something else, not even the expression of his feelings, but rather as a challenge to investigation and a source of immediate experience. Thus he will bring the paint into contact with his eyes, nose, skin, and even mouth for greater personal discovery and involvement. The next step in a child's approach to painting is still exploratory in nature, but he now begins to focus on objects outside of himself. At first he may see no reason for putting the paint on a piece of paper; rather, he wants to see how he can spread it over everything. He cannot understand why he should not put it on table, chairs, walls, or himself. He has to learn that he is expected to paint on the paper provided him. He is not yet interested in producing a "picture."

A child can paint with great blobs of color and feel that he has created something wonderful. He finds he can invent colors, and mixing them is a great adventure to him. He can draw or paint a shape and appreciate it as something he knows. If he wishes, he can even give it a name. As he continues to form other objects, his mental images grow stronger. This is the beginning of the creative process at work. Painting is one of a child's best means of expressing his feelings about himself and his world and of communicating his ideas to others.

There is something special about raw art materials that free a child to create spontaneously. The forms the child makes may have meaning only to himself. In fact, very young children never regard their "finished" art work as adults do. Yet a deep impression is made on the child as he works with the material. Each child paints in his own way. Some splash large strokes across the paper; others use staccato strokes; some paint in patches; still others make linear pictures. Gradually their paintings take on form. As help is needed—and only then—the parent or teacher can show a child how to dip his brush into and against the paint jar so that there is not too much paint on it. If parents and teachers keep in mind that painting is another form of play, they will let children go through their own stages of growth in painting. A parent does not walk and run for her child; she should not paint for him!

Poster paint is the best kind for children because it flows easily from brush onto the paper. Since it is water based, it is washable off faces, hands, and clothing. Red, yellow, blue, black, and white are adequate because almost any color can be made by mixing two or more of these together. Paints must always be kept tightly covered to keep them from drying out. Three brushes, ¾, ½, and ¼ inch wide, are all that the young child needs. Long-handled, short, flat bristle brushes are best. Brushes need to be thoroughly washed after each painting session and stored bristle end up or lying flat, in order to keep the bristles in good shape. There are different kinds of paper suitable for painting; white drawing paper is the most expensive and the best, but 18×24-inch sheets of unprinted newsprint paper are usable. Powder paint is less costly than poster paint and is almost as good when it is mixed with water to the consistency of heavy cream. Because mixed powder paints spoil quickly, they should be mixed in small quantities for each use. Water colors that come in hard little cakes lack the freeing quality of poster paint and are not recommended for young children.

In painting and drawing, a child's first recognizable symbol is usually a human being. Two circular shapes used may be eyes; two lines may represent arms; two other lines suggest legs. A body as such comes after. With slight variations, their symbols become animals. Adults need always to keep in mind that the young child paints and draws what he feels and what is meaningful to him. To a very young child, for example, the head is more important and therefore he gives it greater relative size in his drawing or painting than the body. He also uses colors imaginatively; for instance, a cat can be green; a house, purple; a person's hair, blue.

Children can paint independently when the room arrangement and organization of materials make this possible. The easel should be sturdy and placed in an area that cannot be harmed by paint, with the floor protected by linoleum. The tray of an easel will hold small jars of poster paint. An empty jar will hold the long-handled brushes. Pads of 18×24-inch newsprint paper can be held in place on the easel board by spring clips. In the home, of course, a low table large enough to hold the large sheets of paper and a tray for the poster paints is adequate. One advantage of a painting easel is that the child's paper is up where he can readily reach his painting as he works. Newspapers can be spread on table and floor to make cleaning up easier. A smock of plastic or cloth will protect the child's clothes. Low shelves nearby can hold all the materials the child needs. If art materials are well kept and easily available, a child will be free to paint whenever so inclined.

A child can be shown how to wash his brush before dipping it from one color to another and how to press it on a sponge in order to get rid of excess dirty water. In time he will learn to keep his colors clean. Techniques have no value in themselves. If imposed before they are needed, they only confuse a child for they have no meaning to him. A child learns to paint, model with clay, and make constructions as he learns to talk—slowly, developing in his own very personal way. It is much more important for a young child to *enjoy* painting than to learn the best techniques or to observe rules of order and cleanliness, all of which will be learned in due time.

Provision needs to be made so that fresh paintings can dry. This can be accomplished with a clothes line and spring clothespins. When paintings are dry, there should be a large bulletin board available for displaying them. Since children and parents often wish to save paintings and drawings, portfolios are available that can hold a child's growing collection of his works.

*All young children have potential for creative development in the arts.* According to R. Buckminster Fuller, bold thinker and innovative architect-designer, "A great many children are perfectly willing and capable of artistic development, but their environment inhibits them." We believe that parents and teachers are responsible for providing children with a stimulating environment and making readily available to them the materials of creative art expression. They can help immeasurably by learning to understand each child and his strivings and by showing him the mechanics of creating in the various media when he expresses the need therefor.

A child's first painting is his initial step in learning a new language of expression. His first efforts at drawing or painting might actually be likened to his beginning efforts at speech. Both call for praise and encouragement!

*Play with clay.* Among the three-dimensional art materials, an inexpensive, non-firing moist clay is the best plastic medium for children of all ages. It hardens when it dries and can be painted. It is unlike Plasticine, which is clay mixed with oil and does not harden. Moist clay is a powdered clay mixed with water. Because it is easy to mold and responds readily even to tiny fingers, moist clay can be used by the youngest children, who enjoy squeezing it, pounding it, and even smelling and tasting it as they explore its properties. They will roll it into simple coils or pat it into pancakes or balls. Often the shape of the clay itself may suggest an animal or figure to some children, and they will play with it as a toy. Eventually they learn to fashion recognizable animals and people, as well as small candle holders and very simple bowls.

Play with clay permits children to interpret their ideas, experiences, and reactions to life—and to make something. The emotional implications of the use of clay depend upon the needs brought to it. It seems to offer the best outlet for aggressive impulses among the creative materials available for very young children. Clay adapts itself well to a variety of fantasy expressions and is used for this purpose by troubled children, as well as those whose development seems to be proceeding smoothly. Clay encourages construction with satisfaction or destruction without feelings of guilt. Most children derive deep pleasure from the creative process itself as well as from the things they produce.

Proper working conditions and tools are also needed for clay work: a good working surface, a clay board, tongue depressors, simple modeling tools, and sponges for cleaning up. The clay can be stored in a large covered can to keep it moist and pliant. As a child's experience with clay increases and as he matures, he becomes aware of its many uses in society, and its working accessories of plaster of Paris, rubber molding, the potter's wheel, glazes, a kiln, et cetera.

When clay is used by young children, the enjoyment in manipulation is more important than the finished product. Offering models for a child to copy or showing him what to do with the clay before he is ready for the discipline of technique can discourage his creative efforts. At around nine or ten, however, children who wish to create artistic products may require technical help, and they should then get it.

*Finger painting.* With its lack of arbitrary standards, finger painting is another medium that encourages freedom of artistic expression. Like clay, finger paints can be manipulated easily. Finger painting is a satisfying means of expressing feelings as well as design ideas. Its use engages a child's visual, tactile, and kinesthetic senses. The tendency to smear finger paints on themselves at first is common among young children. In fact, in the beginning it is often more intriguing than the painting process itself. Finger painting quickly frees inhibited children for greater spontaneity. Its main gratification lies in the sensory experiences it allows, including the chance to smear and be messy.

The response to finger paints normally follows a general sequence that starts with pleasure in feeling the material and with indiscriminate color mixing and smearing, then going on to experimentation with abstract forms and patterns, and finally evolving into an appreciative exploration of all its possibilities. Children value the aesthetic aspects of finger painting and show considerable response to the color mixtures they can produce. Many older children create finger-paint pictures of real artistic appeal.

*Collage and construction.* Most children enjoy choosing all kinds of materials of different textures, patterns, and colors and combining them in pasted pictures, or collages. Collage and construction projects are popular three-dimensional art activities. Young children get a great sense of control when they change a sheet of paper by cutting or tearing it. Paper and scissors respond perfectly to a child's desire to invent because he can produce new shapes with them. Scissors should be blunt-nosed for young children and of good quality so they will cut well. Paper for cutting must be firm for inexperienced fingers. Colored construction paper and heavy wrapping paper are perfect for this purpose.

Collage and construction materials increase a child's possibilities of choice as they offer him all kinds of alternative ways of seeing and expressing his ideas of his world. Such materials include scraps of plain and patterned cloth and paper, newspaper, wallpaper samples, burlap, felt, feathers, leather, fur, tissue paper and cellophane in varied colors, paper clips, pipe cleaners in many colors, multicolored and varishaped beads, swab sticks, tongue depressors, glitter, et cetera. Some "creative" materials that usually can be found in the home include salt, bottle caps, net bags used to hold onions or oranges, all kinds of buttons, dry cereals, colored string and yarn, beans, rice, crushed eggshells (dried and dyed various colors), broken pieces of jewelry, and so on. Other useful materials found out of doors are leaves, bark, small twigs, sand, nuts, acorns, pebbles, weeds, seeds, flowers, pine cones, et cetera. It would help to organize the various materials and store them in separate labeled boxes or other containers, for ready availability and safekeeping.

Children like also to experiment with play dots, corks, pegboards, play tiles, glossy colored gummed paper strips, circles and squares, paper doilies, bits of colored ribbon, and colored rubber bands for making their collages, space designs, mobiles, masks, and so forth. Clay can also be used as a base for constructions using such things as Popsicle sticks, twigs, acorns, swab sticks, and tongue depressors. Cardboard, Masonite or thin plywood boards, wire of different gauges, glue or paste, and a stapling machine with staples are also of imaginative usefulness. Plasticine, papier-mâché, soap, synthetic carving materials and plastics, and sheet metal can be used by older children to make figures, animals, and abstract art forms. Children enjoy as well sewing and carpentering to make things that satisfy them. Big needles, heavy thread, cloth, and big

1. A giant magnifier enlarges the small world and gives a sense of power.

2. Hollow blocks enable toddlers to build big and fast.

4. Non-complicated cars and trucks provide a manageable fantasy world.

ide-em toys put the child e driver's seat.

5. Water play with a harbor set is a favorite activity of infants.

6. Oral satisfaction comes from having ples to suck on.

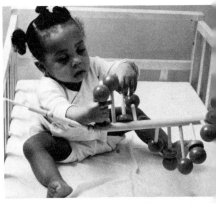

7. Three unbreakable mirror surfaces make baby responsive to his own image.

8. Turning knobs and clickety-clack so come from baby's own actions.

9. Crawling at 3 months with the aid of a body-fitting "dolphin" on casters opens up a sensory world of touch.

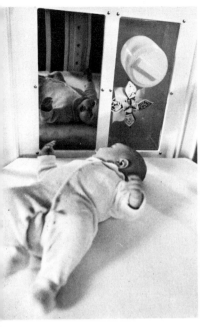

Who is that? Baby begins to discover f" when he recognizes his own bodily ons.

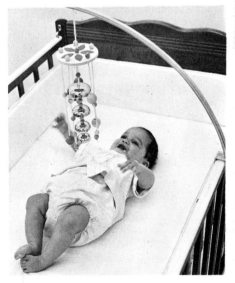

11. An infant never tires of watching nature, especially live fish in a crib aquarium.

Turn one gear and thirteen others rot at baby's command.

13. "Reaching" takes place with eyes as well as hands and causes pleasing sounds.

14. Manipulating a fantasy setting is almost like running the real world.

15. Re-creating family play is a way of experimenting with and understanding social relations.

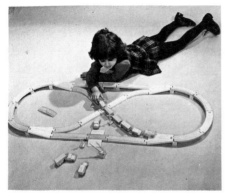

16. Actively pushing a wooden train on a wooden track is better than passively watching an electric train go around.

17. With a ride-em tractor and trailer child can control the action and play.

18. Large Caroline Pratt unit blocks build dramatic city and country play and promote interpersonal co-operation. They are the finest playthings for 2-to-8-year-olds.

19. Body management gets tested with movable metal sawhorse, cleated walking planks, and seesaws.

A concrete façade and a sliding pole ill children need to start firehouse and intergroup co-operation.

21. "Rub-a-dub-dub, two girls in a tub" requires help and co-operation from others.

22. Testing balance on a walking beam builds self-confidence.

24. Art and design can also mean ~~ancing~~ and experimenting with sp~~~ arrangements.

23. Matching and naming objects in a lotto game is fun as well as preparation for reading.

25. Sturdy rhythm instruments encourage musical play and expression in children.

26. Every home needs an adjustable ready for action along with poster p and wide-tipped brushes.

. A child-size log cabin stimulates group
d sibling play and encourages practice
housekeeping arts.

28. Running a store—making change,
weighing vegetables — is preparation for
arithmetic and writing practice.

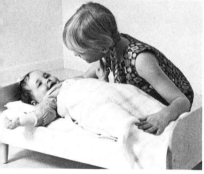

A doll bed must be sturdy enough to
netimes hold a real baby who refuses to
npete with a make-believe doll.

Giant hollow blocks allow division of
ce for playing school or house.

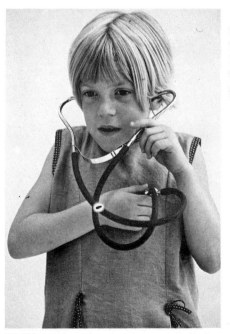

31. Listening to her own heart and playing
doctor with a real stethoscope eliminate a
child's imaginary fears.

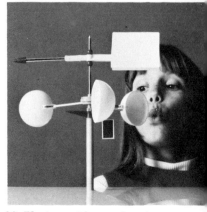

32. Setting up and testing wind and water-mills provide a basis for learning about dams.

33. Playing with weather instruments one way of understanding the element

34. Weighing and balancing are steps to explaining the force of gravity.

35. Learning is made more meaningful when the voyage of Columbus can be re-created on a giant globe.

36. Game play while blindfolded he children comprehend the problems early navigators.

box nails and large pieces of softwood are some of the materials these activities require.

All children gain in independence and confidence when encouraged to work in their own way. As they work with increasing assurance and absorption, their ideas flow more freely. They become more sensitive to the wealth of shapes, forms, and colors in their environment and gain in the ability to express themselves artistically. An important part of the pleasure is each child's adventure in looking for and finding usable things himself.

Adults generally think of art in terms of painting pictures or making sculptures. Children are more nearly interested in the process itself. Whenever a child makes new combinations with the raw art materials he has at hand, he is furthering his creative powers. When children get a bit older, some adult or a peer thinks that it is time to criticize the reality of a child's painting or other art effort. This can make creativity suffer, often forcing a child to perform for acceptance rather than to express what he feels or imagines. More children are lost to the fields of art and music because insensitive adults make impossible reality demands on them. What we must do is offer exciting new art play projects and provide children the freedom to work at them. Papier-mâché, for example, offers an exciting opportunity to make large-sized modeled forms that can be easily preserved. Size helps give importance to a child's work. Sculptural experiences can range from modeling forms in clay to creating stationary or moving metal abstractions.

We need to give older children challenging design problems. We can give them interesting rubber design stamps with circle, triangle, square, and free-form shapes and varicolored ink stamping pads. Can you imagine what fun it would be for children to tell the story of William Tell, using only four basic shapes in repetitive patterns and two or three colors of ink? Or the response that creating wallpaper patterns of their own could evoke in children? Making their own holiday greeting folders would be another free and satisfying form of art expression for children. Even six-year-olds can make simple puppets out of discarded socks, yarn, and buttons or small shells for the facial features.

Children like to use real tools, learn to measure, discover the special characteristics of wood, learn to master the necessary skills and the adult way of doing things when they are ready. Artistic ability is the result of a combination of such qualities as manual skill, ability to devote considerable energy into completing a piece of work, perceptual facility, creative imagination, and aesthetic sensitivity. Parents need to recognize their child's effort each time and not expect finished products. Disparagement can swiftly destroy a child's desire to make things. Greater skill usually comes with time and experience, as do increased strength, co-ordination, and concentration. As children learn, they develop useful standards of work and a deep sense of achievement.

*Enjoying and making music.* That children have a natural love of music is evidenced by their irrepressible singing and dancing and their pleasure in listening to and making music. All normal children relish physical activity, and there is a strong rhythmic quality in their chanting games, rope skipping, and ball bouncing. Music is a universal medium of self-expression and enjoyment, and every child can have deeply satisfying adventures with music. However, a child's capacity for enjoying music must never be stifled by the imposition of technical facility too soon. The songs his mother sings to him are a little child's introduction to music.

A varied assortment of well-chosen phonograph records will provide opportunities for listening, singing, tune making, dancing, rhythms, and dramatic play. Creative dancing frees a child to express his moods and thoughts through body movements to music. A fine way to sharpen a child's aural perceptions is through the use of real, child-sized percussion instruments. Most children enjoy using a musical triangle, rhythm sticks, a tambourine, jingle bells, a drum, cymbals, castanets, and a tone block. Even little children delight in experimenting with a true-toned xylophone or a marimba. Older children relish strumming the strings of an autoharp or guitar.

*Fantasy and creativity are also extended through role playing.* Play with ideas comes from role playing. Most nursery school children have to physically act out roles in order to comprehend them. They have to play the baby—get into the doll bed or doll carriage, drink from a bottle, and be rocked to sleep in a doll cradle. Nursery schools have learned the foregoing from experience, and all doll carriages, beds, and cradles are ruggedly constructed to bear the weight of the child who wishes to "play the baby" himself. As they grow older, from four to about eight years, children accept the doll as the symbol for all baby roles and put their dolls through imaginative play activities. They become mothers or grandmothers, fathers or grandfathers, and are able to shift characters and moods. If children lack the ability for fanciful play, the parent or teacher usually stimulates this by providing all kinds of dress-up costumes and accessories. Especially favored by children are the adult worker headgear of the fireman, policeman, nurse, coal miner, et cetera. When children grow older, there is the disguise kit with its stick-on beards and mustaches, eyeglasses, wigs, and so on to quickly transform a child into new roles to act out. A big trunk or box of costumes, accessories, and props puts the child in charge and allows him to play any character of his choice. He can also work off fear and anger in his role playing. This is one reason child psychiatrists and play therapists often employ costumes and puppets to help children get into roles rapidly to play out what disturbs them.

Recently we observed the play of young American Indian children in New Mexico. The Indian reservation and the parents provide the young child with little active participation in their adult society. The young do not seem to help their mothers bake the bread or weave or help their fathers make jewelry or paint kachina dolls. The adults appear to do all the gardening. We saw little children sit in front of their mud houses sifting sand endlessly through their fingers, an activity that does nothing to build confidence in a child that he can affect his world. However, participation in a colorful, dramatic event—festival dancing—does give even the littlest child a role which helps rescue some of his self-image. The child is proud of the magnificent dancing costume that his mother and father make for him. With this beautiful costume of perfectly worked skins, feathers, and ankle bells, tomahawk or rattle, the child enters the adult society on an equal footing. He dances well, with great abandon and grace and with complete adult approbation and acceptance. His costume and dancing skill have made him count to himself, which is even more important than winning the approval of the adults of his world.

Children who do not have several years of active, fantasy play experiences are not able in later years to imagine or create. We believe the Mexican, Asiatic, and Indian child for whom there is no lively play during early childhood loses the ability to create imaginary situations. An examination of the play materials of these cultures shows them to be made of clay, papier-mâché, and flimsy wood, none of which lend themselves to active use. These playthings are generally put on shelves to be collected and adored but never handled! Introduce the rubber or vinyl doll, building blocks, and other unbreakable toys, and we maintain that the innate playfulness of these children would quickly be given active support. At a meeting in Brighton, England, in October 1960 of the International Council for Children's Play, a Mr. Doublé of the Bureau of Educational Research in Paris reported on a little experiment on play undertaken in Dakar, Senegal. One hundred three- and four-year-old children were given carefully selected European educational toys. He said they found that the toys that were best suited to the play needs of these African children were the same as those that would be chosen for European preschool children. It seems that little children the world over, regardless of their race, like playing with the same type of sturdy toys.

A child's ego gets a big push at two to three years of age when he starts out to master the big world. Creativity gets its greatest spurt forward at four to six years of age, when our American culture allows each child to play actively. Play is tied up primarily with interactions with inanimate, unstructured things and secondarily with people. The kinds of materials and the kinds of play and the duration of the play period can determine the personality and learning development that takes place.

Surround a child with tiny toys only, and we are convinced he may develop a warped personality—too much ego and too much aggressive feeling and behavior. A child with overlong exposure to minuscule playthings that he maneuvers into a "whole world," the life pattern of which he easily dictates, may well develop the desire to want to dominate everything and everyone. We have often wondered whether the German obsession with miniature toys may not have contributed to their drives for world supremacy? In Germany, kindergarten toys (people, animals, cars, boats, planes, trees, et cetera) are so tiny that they are sold by the kilo, and in no time flat it is possible for a child to feel like the "master of the universe." This total involvement with miniature toys often continues throughout adulthood. Miniature electric train systems and model soldiers and forts in perfect detail are an excessive preoccupation of many German adults.

In the United States, Sweden, and Denmark, where educational toys are large, a child can create and manage only an environment of a few buildings, not a complete world. Often nursery school and kindergarten play materials are so large that they require the co-operation of several children to manage them. Big packing crates, for example, need four children to carry them. Interpersonal relations begin to build up, and democracy flourishes. Parents and teachers need to supply a well-balanced assortment of large, miniature and tiny toys.

We think that the kinds of toys you give a child may even determine his fantasy, personality development, ego power, and creativity. Some toys encourage ego and drive, others build playfulness with ideas and patterns of thinking. Some help build social relationships. Others help develop logic. Still others actually teach quantitative number relations. Almost anything can be structured into a child's play materials. Provide a child with toys that make sense, and he will "get the message" in no time.

*Fantasy versus reality.* As a child grows older and becomes part of a social group and shares his play with others, he gradually "internalizes" his fantasies. If parents accept his early flights of fancy, a child's imagination and creativity flower. However, as children grow older, they must be able to distinguish between reality and fantasy. Very young children are not always able to make this separation.

Children in the middle of large families are less inclined to fantasize because they are caught up in direct imitation of the other children. The only child is more apt to have the need and time for fantasy play. Not having brothers and sisters, he imagines the siblings of his friends and may talk constantly to his Teddy bear or doll as if it were part of his family or peer group. The only child often develops sharp awareness of others and greater sensitivity. Usually he is more introspective. Often, in adulthood, such children become our poets, writers, artists, filmmakers, and actors.

*The right mix of playthings.* The challenge is to find and provide a properly balanced assortment of playthings to meet each child's many needs. The shy child may require toys that encourage interpersonal relations—for example, a housekeeping play corner with child-sized pots and pans, a toy stove, child-sized table and chairs, et cetera, or puppets and marionettes that require more than one child if a show is planned. An insecure child lacking in ego may benefit from the ease of mastery inherent in miniature toy play. A dominant or aggressive child may require long periods with those tools of play that would make him a part of the big world which he cannot yet really affect. The child without an apparent spark of creativity may get stimulation from the feedom to play with unstructured materials of all kinds and the encouragement of the adults in his life. Finding the most suitable combination of playthings for each child requires infinite patience, understanding, and sensitivity on the part of parents and teachers. In addition, the adults need to know when they should intervene in the play. It is possible to overwhelm or distract a child with too many play ideas and so take initiative away from the child.

*Humor and laughter.* Humor in the form of jokes may also be considered as belonging to the realm of unstructured materials of play. Riddles and nonsense rhymes expose a child to new word relationships, as well as to adventuring with the absurd. According to Herman Helmer, in an article in *Psychology Today,* "Words form one of the basic order carriers of a child's world. Every joke or departure from the norm means an attempt to shake up this order himself or to hear it pushed around by others. But in the final analysis the order remains unscathed. The child's relief that order has remained unshakable breaks through as laughter." While play starts with playthings, it soon becomes concerned with ideas and assumptions and words and riddles with which a child carries on verbal play, poetry writing, and "thought experiments." Many fruitful ideas in science and the arts have been developed by those adults who were unfettered enough to countenance unexplored ideas and translate them into formal programs of action or products. Such adults have retained from childhood a capacity for imagining and creative thinking. They no doubt found their inspiration in "idle fancifying" and "non-logical thinking"—the free play of the mind. Often free play with models occurs when thought or imagination temporarily gives out. Models are the toys of the adult scientist and mathematician who send fantastic machines into outer space and to the moon, areas far removed from the reality of experience.

*Play and creativity are synonymous.* Play in childhood supports the experimentation and drive necessary for creative leadership and living in adulthood. Play releases the self and nurtures the imagination. If we would have inventive adults, then parents, teachers, and society must provide play settings and the best mix of unstructured and structured play materials that will foster the fullest development of every child.

*Play is healthful for children and all living beings.* Fantasy is not limited to early childhood. Imagination, fantasy, and playfulness must be encouraged throughout life. When students come home from college on vacation there need be no embarrassment if they take out their childhood blocks and design an architectural structure. Building a puppet stage, making puppets, and putting on a show is an activity that adolescents and adults alike cherish. All forms of play are interlaced in adult life—sports, games of chance, dancing, singing, drama, humor, festivities, and rituals. Among the many forms of life, man is the supreme player. He appears to play from birth onward. If he has difficulty playing, he may resort to induced states of psychological transcendence, such as that resulting from the use of alcohol or drugs.

Play is tied up with human survival. When play is suppressed, man and society suffer. The impulse to play seems virtually irrepressible. Monkeys and apes are most playful. Man plays even more. The more advanced a species is, the more varied and intense the play life.

Play provides the change of pace so desperately needed in a technological society. Whenever there is a change in work, a completion of a project, a change in social status, there is a reason for celebration, festival, or other social observances. Such events usually include rich play activities.

Adult play in many societies in the non-Western world is completely acceptable behavior. It is encouraged on special occasions, although kept regulated to some extent. At festivities, where people dress up and a reversal of traditional personal conduct is permitted, customary rules of moral behavior are often suspended—but for a set time only. Everybody knows when the festivities begin, when make believe and fantasy, and even sexual license are permitted, and when the rites are at an end. These rites—whether a Mardi Gras or other religious festival or tribal dance of initiation—provide a valuable safety valve for the individual and society. Aesthetic expression is often a by-product of these play activities. At the end there always is a strengthening of the propriety of the ordinary rules of conduct.

In America, since the beginning of the industrial era, we have tended to suppress and discourage play. The grip of the puritan ideal of "six days of work and one day of rest" has begun to relax. There is evidence that the young people of today are abandoning the old prejudice against play. They are openly stating that play and fantasy are natural to human behavior, serving an essential role in maintaining life. They have adopted fantasy in their clothing, in their dancing, and in their "little theater" movements. They are giving play a place of importance in daily living. The authors applaud this course of action and believe the time is at hand to honor play with a Museum of Fantasy and Play. To this end, they are collecting the play artifacts of the world.

# CHAPTER SIX

# *Programming Play and the Environment for Childhood Maturation Levels*

It is perhaps on the confusing side to categorize play by age levels and stages of development because inherent in this is the suggestion that all children of a certain age conform to a set pattern. This we know to be untrue. Nonetheless, a study of ages and stages in the development of a child can provide some useful perspectives on the role of play in a child's maturation and on the various and pertinent requirements and play opportunities that need to be made available. At each level of growth, certain bodily and sensory powers of a child unfold and can be strengthened through play with suitable materials. Understanding these maturation levels and intervening with the right mix of stimuli and environment planning are paramount tasks for both parents and teachers.

"*Ages and Stages*." The reader may question our repetitive use of "ages and stages" throughout this book, but each presentation is designed to show another important facet of a child's growing up. In this chapter we seek to show how each advance in physical maturity calls for new stimuli and environmental changes. Sequences in behavior have been identified by psychologists, pediatricians, and psychiatrists and illustrate significant developmental transitions.

Psychologists like Piaget, Flavell, Bruner, and others spend their lives analyzing and documenting the "critical" ages and stages in a child's growth. Piaget believes that each age has its own intellectual limits beyond which stimulation and education cannot go. From birth to eighteen months is a period of neural and physical maturation during which the child operates on his external world with his sensori-motor system, acquiring notions of space, time, and cause and effect. With the conversion of his sensori-motor schemata into language, a new stage begins for the child. This stage, from two to nine years, is a period for acquiring symbolic thought, when the child can understand the relationship between reality and the symbol or word for it. The final stage comes at ten to twelve years, when adultlike reflective intelligence and concept building are attained. Piaget has pointed out that if one tries too early in a child's life to teach him words that require complex reflective thinking, one is apt to waste valuable learning time.

Pediatricians like Arnold Gesell, Benjamin Spock, T. Berry Brazelton, and others spell out in excellently documented works the ages and stages in the physical development of a child. They define and describe the stage of reflexive actions; visual and auditory following; fingering, reaching, and manipulating; oral gratifications of sucking and tasting; sitting, standing, crawling, walking, and talking.

Psychoanalysts and psychiatrists like Anna Freud, Bruno Bettelheim, and others refer to the ages and stages when ego and self-image mature. They describe in great detail the nature of the interpersonal relations between mother and child, in peer groups, and in school and how one's personality develops or fails to mature. They describe those periods that call for the most sensitive attention or intervention.

Whatever ages and stages one can agree upon, one thing is

clear: each level presents a new set of competencies and environmental conditions, and each one is sufficiently different from the other to require its own special "curriculum" and "environment" of play and learning. How "critical" each stage is or how closely we define chronological age boundaries does not seem so important as recognizing that each stage necessitates a difference in activity and learning opportunity. Knowing how to arrange or rearrange the conditions for permitting maximum potential growth is an indisputable asset to parent and professional alike.

*Prerequisites for an environment of play.* Play, which is a pursuit self-chosen by the child (and adult), requires an environment that makes playing possible. At the same time, play challenges need to be integrated into the setting, with many alternative choices so that the child can find activities in which he can succeed more often than he will fail. The play area needs to be arranged to give the child the feeling of being apart from the ordinary world. What others do outside this milieu is of no concern to the child. Inside there are no adult-set rules of conduct. The rules of play are child-ordered. Within the bounds of safety, everything is permissible.

Buckminster Fuller wrote in an article published in the November 12, 1966, issue of *Saturday Review:* "It is possible to design environments within which the child will be neither frustrated nor hurt, yet free to develop spontaneously and fully without trespassing on others. I have learned to undertake reform of the environment and not to try to reform Man. If we design the environment properly, it will permit child and man to develop safely and to behave logically."

Play materials do not have to be toys and objects; they can be an environment that allows the child to create his own imaginary situations. Such an environment can define space in a very personal way, which the child can occupy and use at will. The space and its appearance suggest to the child how he can form his own play world. It can be a tent, a tree house, or a gym frame, or it can be a playroom or a balcony. However, the environment needs to be one the child can subvert to his own ends and control. He needs to be able to turn it on or off by himself if it is an "electronic" world. Playthings need to be in proper scale to the child's size so they will not overwhelm or thwart him. They need to be easy to get at and easy to put back. Like the shop of a competent technician, the containers of play material need to be arranged and stored so that they communicate to the child their availability and their proper replacement locations.

A play space can take on many forms. It can be a permanent area, as in a playground or nursery school, or it can be created out of a figment of a child's imagination. It can be public space, like a cave or social club in which special activities and child-imposed rules of play prevail, or it can be built by the child, as in a play corral formed with large blocks or loose bricks enclosed by a wood screen. For the infant it can be a crib, playpen, or large play dome. The shape, size, and contour of a play area can often suggest the nature of the play. An inclined plane can be for running up and down. Enclosures can make great hiding places. Marked lines on a flat surface can be for hopping or skipping games. Raised platforms can provide for theater improvisations. It is possible to sculpture into an outdoor play area aesthetic forms that elicit spontaneous physical or dramatic play.

Environmental psychologists and early childhood educators talk about playful interactions with the environment as a strong element in the learning process. An environment is more than physical space or enclosures. It can also be made up of people: mother, father, relatives, and peers, with whom the child interacts and from whom he picks up cues about behavior and one's culture. The environment can be the objects that every child encounters early in life, whose operations, textures, purposes, and names must be mastered ultimately and integrated into his intellectual store of experience and knowledge. The physical world of each age level needs to be as intensively researched as developmental stages. At some periods, encounters with people seem most important. At others, exposure to objects takes precedence. We need to examine all encounters carefully in order to prescribe the best arrangement for growth at each age level and stage of maturation.

*The ages and stages of infancy.* The birth of a baby begins a fabulous year of adventure and discovery for every parent and child. In the first twelve months a baby changes faster than at any other period in life. In about half that time the "helpless" little baby will probably sit alone, recognize a familiar face, reach for and grasp a toy, smile, laugh, and hold up his end of a conversation by babbling and cooing. He will be halfway on the road to standing up, walking, handling a spoon, and being a thoroughly sociable person. How is all this accomplished? To some extent it is the natural process of unfolding, with a sequence of stages that occur in all babies. But there are variations in the timetable of these stages. Not all babies sit, smile, and babble at exactly the same age. Therefore one cannot expect an infant to conform to any set schedule of development. Every infant develops at his own very personal rate.

Infancy researchers find that significant differences do exist among babies within moments after birth, in all ways that can be measured. For one thing, newborns are not really the same age. Age is counted from birth, but actually not every infant has already been developing for exactly nine months. Premature babies may lose months of prenatal growth, and some "full-term" babies may be born a week or two before "due" date. Also, each baby starts off with different inherited characteristics. In short, each baby is a unique individual. Differences soon become apparent and determine the reactive behavior of baby and parents. All at once, a fascinating, demanding, challenging entity becomes a vital part of the parents' lives. Not only does the neonate affect his environment and the people around him, but the environment also influences him. What this environment is and what it should offer the child will be set forth in the following pages. It is our belief that the environment, physical and interpersonal, affects desires and needs. If it provides love as well as sensitive custodial care, it encourages enthusiasm and drive and stimulates growing and learning. If the environment is sterile, if parents are not responsive, then there is nothing for a baby to interact with. He becomes frustrated, gives up, does not try, and his maturing and learning are impaired. Research with institutionalized babies has shown that when a baby is *not* encouraged to crawl, to stand, to walk, to babble, or if there is *no* inducement to move to new places and things, he may not necessarily be able to follow the optimal sequential development pattern. He may not even want to walk or to talk. Lack of stimulation is a devastating experience for every human.

From the moment of birth the neonate begins to explore his environment. He finds ways to manipulate it to his desires and needs and to control it. He is "turned on." With his eyes, ears, mouth, hands, and fingers, he scouts his world and searches out what is novel. He strives to put everything that affects him into usable form, to make sense of it all.

To understand how he reacts to his environment, we need to know more about the physical make-up of a baby. What is he like? From head to heels he may be about twenty inches long. His head is about a quarter of his height and about the same width as his chest. His system is in a delicate state of equilibrium. He reacts with his whole body to sudden changes in temperature, pressure, touch, light, and sound. He cries and is less active when he is dressed or wrapped. He is powerless at this stage to control his sensitive reactions to the many little changes in the atmosphere around him. It would appear that clothing seems to provide him with some insulation from the outside world. As he matures he gradually comes to control his behavior. In the beginning most of his movements are inborn, involuntary responses. If you place a finger or a rattle within his immediate reach, he will open his clenched fist in an awkward attempt to grasp it. If he is suddenly jarred he startles with his whole body, throwing back his head and arms and clutching at the air. When placed in water, he makes swimming motions with his arms and legs. At a touch near his mouth or his cheek, he purses his lips, moves his tongue, and turns his head toward the side he was touched on. He is ever ready to find the nipple and suck.

Just as physical growth depends on proper foods at regular intervals, emotional and learning growth needs environmental stimulation and interpersonal nurturing. Without them, an infant will pass through periods of development without appreciable progress. Institutionalized children clearly demonstrate the effects of lack of stimulation. These babies may start out normally and make natural demands, via crying and smiling, but if there are no parental responses, no toys, no stimulation, they begin to respond less and less often and their cries become weak. The institutionalized child turns inward. He stares emptily at barren walls. He becomes apathetic.

A Swiss psychiatrist took five hundred pictures of infants in institutions at three and four months of age and was able to select by their facial reactions those who were likely to be depressives in their later adult lives. He was convinced that emotional depression tendencies are imprinted in the crucial first three months of an infant's life whenever there is little or no environmental or interpersonal stimulation.

What are the inner forces that propel an infant from one stage to another? Dr. Brazelton lists them as (1) a drive to survive independently in a complex world, (2) a drive to mastery, and (3) a drive to identify with and become part of his environment. From his environment a baby picks up cues that indicate to him what he desires to become a part of and how he can go about doing it. As long as the environment and people give him choices, he will develop the desire and power to select.

Interaction with the environment starts earlier than most people used to think. Recent studies suggest that the newborn can see patterns better than light and dark or color, that he can hear sound and distinguish differences in pitch. A day-old baby can follow a moving object with his eyes and turn his head toward the source of sound. He is born able to hear. (Recent research reports that even a seven-month fetus reacts to outside noises.) The infant will stop moving at the sound of a bell as though "staring" in the direction of the sound. He feels changes in temperature, especially around his mouth. He distinguishes tastes and is already beginning to show preference for sweets. (Dr. Lewis P. Lipsitt, director of the Child Study Center at Brown University, has made much progress in his research on the taste preferences of infants.) We cannot be sure how well the infant can distinguish smells, but we do know he is very sensitive to touch and pressure.

How a baby responds to sights, sounds, and touches depends on how long they last, and especially *how important they are to him*. A sudden, short noise may startle him; a continuing soft sound may quiet and calm him. In the same way, sudden jarring may unsettle him while rhythmic rocking will have a soothing effect. The infant appears to be less aware of sensations from the outside world when hungry or sleepy. The newborn can react to and tune in or out appropriate or inappropriate stimuli. He will shut his eyes if a bright white light is shone in his face. He will respond to a bright red or yellow object dangled directly in front of him. The neonate is perpetually bombarded with stimuli, and each stimulus adds to his experience and learning. Much repetition goes into this learning process. In the face of this, the infant must have the ability to select those stimuli he wants to react to. Soon he develops preferences and dislikes. Even while he receives these stimuli, he has mechanisms that can suppress disturbing ones. Sleep is a successful way of shutting out unwanted stimuli and withstanding disconcertion from the environment. Although too much stimulation can evoke excessive crying or even colic, as he matures, the infant can handle and assimilate these stimuli. For most babies too little stimulation is far worse.

An infant is capable of hearing at birth. He is sensitive to the location of sounds and also to their frequency. Low frequency (200 to 600 cycles per second) causes increase in motor behavior; high frequency (4,000 cycles per second and up) leads to fixed behavior. Sounds of less than one second's duration have minimal effect. Sounds of five to fifteen seconds' duration have maximal effect on the level of activity. If a sound lasts too long, the infant becomes less responsive. Low-frequency rhythmic sounds tend to stop a baby's crying. Sounds are part of the infant's environment and are listened to with great attentiveness. He devotes his full attention to distinguishing one sound from another and to figuring out where it came from. Each day there are some regular time intervals in the sequence of sounds he hears: Mother's voice saluting her baby with a happy "Good morning," a bell ringing, the sound of the mailman, the sanitation man's pick-up truck, brother or sister leaving for school, Dad leaving for work. The baby has to make associations to put the sounds into some sort of order. He has to relate faces to voices. He will recognize mother's voice with a smile, others with puzzlement in the beginning.

Parents need to take an inventory of the sights, sounds, and tangibles available in their baby's nursery because these are the first stimuli he interacts with, and they have to be organized as carefully as when a teacher plans her lessons. The amount of eating and sleeping time and the periods of alertness need to be taken into account. The position of the crib, the color of the walls, rug, crib sheets—all are part of the baby's "seeing" environment. The sounds inside and outside, the nearness of the record player, the kitchen noises—all must be considered. Parents are obliged to ask themselves how much their baby can see when he is on his back, turning his head from one side to the other. Should his crib be in the middle of the room or against a blank wall? What can parents do about blank walls, the solid wood head- and footboards of the standard crib, the opaque bolsters set inside the crib to protect the baby's head, the sterile ceiling? Plenty! Parents can demand that bolsters be transparent, that crib boards be made of clear plastic that can hold live fish in an attached tank or a small terrarium that enables the baby to watch animal or people activity. Parents can counteract the empty ceiling by "bringing it down" within focus of the infant's range of vision, about eight inches above him, and suspending from it a colorful mobile or changeable grid of translucent colors. It is a good idea to hang brightly colored infant toys on one side of the crib and to alternate them frequently from one crib side to the other. An encounter with an interesting or novel sight will activate a baby to rapt attention. The young baby is more responsive to patterns (the arrangement of details) than to color. He will stare intently at the outline of a face or a bull's-eye pattern. When awake, the newborn has long periods of seeming to stare into space. If you move a toy into his field of vision (eight inches away), he will move his head and follow it with his eyes. Reaching for it comes later on. Toward the end of his first month, his staring is replaced by a new kind of visual response. He will become excited when he sees a familiar person or toy and demonstrate this by moving his arms and legs, vocalizing, and even making faces that look very much like smiles. What you are witnessing is a kind of response readiness. Parents can meet this phase by playing with their baby and talking to him and fueling his world with sights, sounds, smells, and touchable tangibles. The more stimulation the baby has a chance to get used to, the less easily will he be "turned off" by new experiences.

As the baby explores his environment, the number of activities that grab his interest increases. Here is a perfect opportunity for parents to provide fascinating encounters. Crib sheets need not be white; they can be colored and have varied facial (and other) patterns; they can have textures for the baby's searching fingers to feel. There can be bells for wandering hands to sideswipe accidentally. Booties can be eye-catching, maybe with bulls'-eye patterning or colorful pompoms and safe bells firmly attached at the tips. While the new baby is not able voluntarily to take hold of an object, parents can take advantage of his reflexive grasping. An infant will open his fisted hands and learn to close his fingers around anything small enough that is placed in his palm. Parents can try differently shaped rattles, smoothly sanded small wooden figures, fingering toys with "in-and-out" areas, and small washable soft animals and dolls.

The neonate does not only see with his eyes and hands; his most powerful tool for perceiving and learning to comprehend is his mouth. Sucking gives an infant a sense of control from birth. It takes him no time at all to accomplish this function of self-preservation and pleasure (if he is a normal baby). It is by means of sucking, licking, and biting, co-ordinated with touching, handling, and eventually moving things about, that a baby secures his working knowledge of the realities of his small world. The infant uses his oral sense by means of sucking, feeling with his tongue, licking and biting to explore the softness, hardness, taste, and shape of things. Therefore, the baby should be given all kinds of safe, attractive teethers in different shapes and different materials and textures, for instance, smoothly sanded hardwood, rubber, neoprene, et cetera. New vinyl rubber casting and production processes are producing playthings of all types of textures, shapes, and degrees of softness and hardness.

Psychologists believe so much in the power of sucking that they have used it as a means of ascertaining how infants react to other stimuli and how they use it for other ends. E. R. Siqueland at Brown University and others at Harvard University have encouraged babies to suck on electronic pacifiers which activate mechanisms to bring about visual clarity, to increase the illumination of a picture in a darkened room, or to bring a picture into focus. Watching them suck has taught these psychologists how infants learn to co-ordinate two ordinarily different acts—sucking and looking. According to a report by Jerome S. Bruner, "a six-month-old child will suck the picture into focus, but then he starts looking and stops sucking, so that the picture drifts back into focus again." The infant works at the problem and organizes a strategy of responses that keeps the picture in focus.

*Games babies play.* We are indebted to Dr. Justin D. Call for his analysis of the games infants play with sucking and babbling, which appeared in the January 1970 issue of *Psychology Today*. He points out that neonates emerging from the womb are not capable of playing anything that one would call a game. One of the necessary conditions for playing games is a certain familiarity with the routines of an environment. Another condition is an optimum level of attentiveness; an infant overwhelmed with tension, food deprivation, or insecurity cannot give his full attention to a game. A third condition is having control over the parts of the body used in the game. Since the baby's mouth and sucking are one of his most developed motor systems, it is natural that games of parent-and-child interaction start at nursing time, when the baby's immediate desire is satisfied and his mouth is being stimulated. Near the end of the nursing period, the mother can gently withdraw the nipple to see if the infant will go after it again. This interplay is the beginning of infant game play. The ten minutes after feeding are when an infant's "attentiveness to the external world" is exceptionally sharp. This is the perfect time to introduce the baby to play, socialization, and games. Interplay with him can take the form of putting gentle pressure on his cheek, fingers, and toes and to sing songs like "This little piggy went to market," et cetera. Such reciprocal experiences develop strong attachments between mother and child. The nursing period is also the time when babies develop strong attachments to external objects: a "security blanket," Teddy bear, or favored rattle. Happy is the infant who has safe, loving anchorage to his mother. Most babies appear to develop especially intense attachments; they cannot part with their first possessions. In fact, infantile attachments can remain throughout adult life.

If the mother does not want to live with a tattered security blanket or beat-up rag doll interminably, she must think about the object associations that go on at feeding time, especially during the earliest months. She needs to make sure that her infant's toys are completely washable, that they will remain attractive until no longer desired by her child. There are available on the market today the Snuggler made of lamb's wool, charming Teddy bears with formed foam-rubber insides, terry cloth-covered dolls and animals, all of which wash and wear well.

According to Dr. Call, one of the rudimentary forms of interaction between mother and baby is called the "cough game" —"It begins when the baby coughs and mother out of empathy or experimentation imitates him." At first the child merely smiles, but later he coughs in return. This starts an interchange, with deep satisfaction on both sides. It can be initiated by either parent or child. This cough game is the first form of positive communication. Later on it may lose its significance for the infant, but he will have learned how to communicate oral sounds, an essential to language learning.

By the fifth month the baby is babbling constantly. He laughs with glee over some action or interaction with his parents. He is beginning to master inflection and can imitate adult voices. He can also distinguish different sounds. Toys that make a noise or play music help build his "vocabulary" of familiar sounds. There are bells, chimes, music boxes, rattles, records, and sound tapes. There are cassettes of music and sounds that appeal especially to infants. Appropriate audiovisual experiences keep infants' attention for long periods of time.

Grasping, like sucking, is one of the early tools of a baby. By the time he is four weeks old he can automatically grasp and hold a small object. Some researchers say this is a voluntary action; others claim that it is a response to the environment. Dr. Bruner believes that both of these explanations ignore the crucial aspect of voluntary control, *intention*. He indicates that grasping begins with diffuse activity (wormlike activity of fingers, toes, hands, and feet) before voluntary action is initiated. The infant has much more freedom of movement than he can control. He soon develops a strategy for increasing his control by imposing restrictions on his freedom. As an object is placed within the visual field of the one-month-old, he will move his head in pursuit, become quiet, and increase his attention. At six weeks he will attempt to lift his shoulders and arms. At ten weeks the approach of an object will make him pump his arms and legs, and he launches sideswiping actions with his closed fist. At four months he has enough control to execute a slow reach, and he extends his arm to an object with his hands wide open. His mouth and tongue are working, and his intention is clearly to put the object in his mouth. As with all early development, all processes that become internal first manifest external motor representations. This "doing" behavior be-

comes internalized into inner codes that ultimately get translated, in the second year of life, into speech and language,
with their attendant communicating behavior. In short, there is
active, non-linguistic behavior that shows the infant how to
use "tools" as the means of accomplishing ends.

Dr. Bruner points out that the differentiation between *holding* and *operating* on what is held follows the same rules as the
differentiation between focal and diffuse attention and that
both "presage the use of topic and comment in language."
What he is indicating is that these early six months of sensori-
motor mastery are essential for attaining the verbal expressions
inherent in language and, later on, in reading ability.

*Critical stages for sensori-motor learning.* The early months
of sensory learning are a crucial stage for the exercise of the
infant's intention and attention, relationship thinking, visual
and aural acuity, and manipulative skills. The mother will benefit her baby's full development by planning and encouraging
sensory play. When we say that a child is not sensitive to the
sights, sounds, and touch of his world, we are indicating that he
has missed periods of early play and physical control when they
counted the most and came most easily. The healthful, happy
baby possesses fantastic drive toward the accomplishment of
tasks all his waking hours. When he is older, recovery of underdeveloped sensory powers is difficult because drive, intention,
and attention are then not so powerfully self-motivated. Such a
child is more easily distracted from these elementary tasks. It
takes much longer to achieve progress in remedial work than
to provide welcome practice periods throughout the earliest
months of life.

Hence we need to program the sensory play of the first six
months with great care. As each motor skill matures, we must
seek new ways to encourage further exploration and mastery.
Toys, mobiles, objects, decorations, and visuals have to be
changed so a child can use his sensory powers to his fullest potential. Dr. Lipsitt, who has done much research on visual
stimulation with infants, believes that you can capitalize on the
visual curiosity of a two-month-old. In an experiment with in-

fants, he allowed two-month-olds to fix their eyes on a mobile of colorful objects. Each time they kicked, a string attached to their feet jiggled the mobile into movement. But when the string was detached and kicking no longer produced fascinating movements, the kicking subsided. Reattaching the string brought on the resumption of active kicking. These experiments demonstrate that when given the opportunity, an infant will seek out visually stimulating things. By the same token, when an infant has learned that his own behavior makes a difference, it will lead him to what is visually stimulating. Dr. Lipsitt's experiments with infants are supported in part by the animal experiments of Dr. F. Valverde of the Instituto Cajal in Madrid. He found that newborn mice that were visually deprived by living in the dark developed fewer nerve connections in the vision center of their brains. If applicable to man, these findings imply that children deprived of visual stimuli early in life may well have a diminished ability to read.

How do we program visual stimuli in the earliest months? Obviously by providing the infant opportunities to see and to follow with his eyes. Parents should take an inventory of their baby's visual environment. Can he see uninterruptedly through the sides of his crib? Is his crib so placed in a corner that he can only see out on one side? What about visual stimulation above the crib? What can he see outside a window? Can the crib be pushed near a window so he can watch nature in action? It soon becomes apparent that cribs, as they are designed and manufactured today, were never meant for visual stimulation. Possibly dangerous bars require solid bolsters that shut out visual experiences. If we are going to make any headway, we will have to redesign the crib so that sides are transparent and latticework on an overhead canopy can permit hanging objects in proper focus for an infant's eyes. We must encourage the rear-view projection of colorful pictures that are integrated with infant voice, foot, hand, or foot-activated switches. We may have to place the crib in the center of the room instead of in an obscure corner. We must not shut out voices and sounds in the infant's room. The more voices and sounds he hears, the more there is for him to distinguish. Strapping an infant in a suitable baby chair attached to a table in the middle of a family gathering proves far more stimulating than the "quiet, keep away" atmosphere of most nurseries. We must experiment with all kinds of sounds and develop many kinds of musical games that will invoke an infant to listen as well as to follow with his eyes.

Why are we so intent on programming the sight, sound, and kinesthetic experiences of infants? First, we are eager to promote self-motivation. Motivation is triggered by an emotional state that generates the type of feelings that provide the go/no-go switch for all behavior. Emotional feelings commence the very moment a baby is born. Motivation is nurtured, too, by the love a baby gets and feels from the important people in his world. To grow in every way, he must immediately know that he counts. Scientists working with animals have discovered the secret of the proper mixture of elements that build drive. Psychologists dealing with humans are working overtime now to try to find this combination in human learning. They have found that if an infant or child is constantly faced with tasks beyond his competence, he will become so frustrated that he will simply give up and stop trying. If there is no challenge or pleasure in it, he will ignore a task. If there is too much challenge that is unfamiliar and therefore frightening, the child will do everything he can to avoid it. However, if novelty is combined with a promise of possible achievement, if his life is a series of successful approaches to solvable problems, the child will eagerly seek out and approach new problems as they come along. To guarantee against early failure, it is best to properly structure the sight, sound, and kinesthetic experiences of early infancy. Of course, you cannot program a child's life so that he never experiences frustration at one time or another, but by adopting the pleasure and novelty principle, parents will be helping their children become self-reliant and courageous.

There is yet another reason for structuring an infant's sensory experiences. Since so much of a very young child's life is spent in learning about himself and his environment, it is essential that he be able to concentrate on a particular thing or activity and at the same time to shut out elements that distract him and interfere with his learning. Dr. Boyd R. McCandless, professor of psychology at Emory University in Atlanta, and his associates, put it this way in a recent report: ". . . the importance of such selective attention for later learning, such as school, is obvious. The child who lacks the ability to exert self-control is largely at the mercy of his internal needs and environmental pressures. He cannot voluntarily control his own behavior." Because learning to pay attention and control impulses is among the most important factors in academic studies, we must take every opportunity to help the infant focus single-mindedly on a particular problem. By carefully structuring the sensory activities of the infant with appropriate playthings for hearing, touching, and seeing, we are singling out a specific activity for his full attention, and his reward will be success as he achieves mastery. If we make the environment favorable for concentration, if we control the noise level, remove irrelevant and distracting material, and provide consistent rewards for achievement, we encourage the important disciplines of attention and impulse control, two vital tools for developing learning power.

How can we help the infant to attend to specific objects in his environment? We can pass selected objects across his visual field so that he can track them with his eyes. We can expose him to the projection of large pictures in his crib, that is, if one side is open and has a screen. We can take him out of his crib and on a tour of the apartment or house where he can see and even manipulate some new objects. We can make it possible for him to manipulate toys and objects that are suspended over his crib. We can allow him to explore and handle objects and toys that have varied textures, make differing sounds, or even change shape. The development of attention begins the moment a child identifies and concentrates on a particular object while simultaneously ignoring other potentially interesting stimuli.

A great deal of psychological research has centered on

"stimulus deprivation." People working with disadvantaged children often believe incorrectly that children from deprived homes do not receive enough sensory stimulation. This is not always the case. An infant in an overcrowded home may be suffering from stimulus bombardment (too much and too intense stimuli). Many children from these homes rapidly learn "to tune out" the majority of sensations that deluge them. For example, if a baby has become accustomed to a high noise level in his home, he may have difficulty singling out particular sound differences. This deficiency in auditory perception may seriously handicap his language development. If an infant has not learned to pay close attention, his speech formation may be slow and inaccurate. Parents and teachers need not only to protect children from being deprived of stimuli, but also to keep them from drowning in too much self-defeating excitement. The level of stimulation, its type, and its difficulty are also important and should always correspond to each child's maturation level. Contemporary research with neonates indicates that the three-day-old can turn his head to the left to obtain "rewards" when a bell rings and to the right when a buzzer sounds. But for three-to-four-month-olds, such static responses no longer suffice; something else has to be added as a source of motivation. That "something else" may be very simple problem-solving challenges. The normal infant has a built-in thrust for growing, and as he grows, he feels, perceives, thinks, learns, and exerts himself. Researchers are showing that ongoing actions of the infant depend upon changing the components in his environment, for instance, the need to learn a sequence of movements in order to turn lights or music on and off. The infant seems to be testing almost from birth his ability to affect his environment. Repeated successes afford him pleasure and energize him to continue doing and learning. Hence, a baby will benefit from suitable challenges in a responsive environment.

*Programming visual perception.* How can we program an infant's environment with experiences in simple and complex visual perception? Visual awareness involves two integrated

actions: the eyes receive the stimulus and then send the image
to the brain for interpretation. Inasmuch as the first three years
of life include 90 per cent of the physical growth level of visual
perception, it is necessary to provide learning situations that
will help the child develop skills in two basic areas: (1) figure-
ground relationships, and (2) stimulus discrimination and integration. "Figure-ground perception" refers to the ability to
separate or single out forms from their background. If an
adult looks at a white sheet of paper with a black dot in the
center, he immediately focuses on the dot. He has discriminated
the dot from the white background almost immediately. Not so
with an infant. He may be able to make rough discriminations
at the beginning of his life, but fine discriminations need to be
learned. To distinguish one object from another in the same
background and identify differences between objects require
the visual ability to see the object and the interpretation ability
to make a judgment. "Stimulus integration" is the process of
perceiving a variety of individual elements (or subparts) as
an integrated scene (whole). For example, a picture of a farm
scene may include a variety of objects. The adult automatically
integrates all the elements into a meaningful whole. Not so
the infant. This skill needs to be developed through as many
experiences as we can provide. It starts with three-dimensional
objects. Ultimately the child learns that pictures stand for
things.

It takes a lot of parental intervention to assure that a child
will become equal to the visual-perception skills of reading.
During infancy he will have to be provided with such activities
as (1) fixating on an object that is centered on a visual field,
(2) tracking or following horizontally and vertically moving
objects, (3) tracking an object moving in a circle, (4) discriminating objects as distinct from their backgrounds, (5) perceiving objects in an integrated and meaningful fashion. Some
of these can be encouraged by presenting moving objects in a
transparent tray over the top of the crib, as well as by figure,
line, and dot film strip projections presented to the child
sitting in his infant seat. It can be done by the baby's pulling

cords that impel objects to move vertically or horizontally in his field of vision. It can be done, too, with beams of light on the ceiling directed by the infant's hand. The motion of mobiles might also be just the right stimulation.

Hearing is equally important to the mental growth of a child. Spoken language is one of the major sources of communication and learning until reading ability is established. Inadequate hearing skills and listening habits can be devastating. If an infant does not have appropriate sounds, voices, and music to listen to, if he cannot discriminate between groups of sounds and unscramble them, he will suffer from his inability to fully understand and enjoy language. To assist the infant to develop auditory acuity, parents need to be concerned with the tonal quality and clarity of their own speech and help their child learn to interpret the meaning of all sounds in his world.

*Tactile experiences.* Skill in touching, fingering, handling, grasping, reaching, pulling, and holding is attained only when the environment provides a wide variety of tactile experiences. Development in this area of physical maturity is most rapid during the first two to five months. Infants discover touch by uncontrolled sideswiping movements at the edge of their cribs. If toys are provided that react to these uncontrolled actions, if pleasant sounds result from grasping, if reaching and pulling are rewarded by movement, sounds, or music, then a baby will be impelled to keep on trying. Touching teaches an infant to register the qualities of texture and the intensities of pressure. From such experiences he develops kinesthetic information about the position of his body, posture, movement, distances, timing, and reaction to moving objects. Appropriate kinesthetic experiences should be introduced progressively. Bringing objects close to the baby, moving them away, encouraging the baby to reach for them, then to reach further as they are moved, and then advanced so he can touch them—all are valuable tactile adventures.

Most parents do little to provide their baby with suitable "touch toys." Once a chain of teething beads or a teether-rattle is given the baby, it rarely is changed for another experience until the teething has stopped. The same mobile will remain attached to the side of a crib for six months or more. A Cradle Gym is slung across the crib, and that is that! Once the child has mastered a toy and it no longer satisfies him, the toy should be removed and a new challenge presented. Parents spend too little time selecting grasping toys for their baby. Too often things are either too big or too tiny for the baby's limited co-ordination. Too few toys have any feedback in the form of noise-making, sounds, or actions that encourage reaching, pulling, touching, and handling. What fun for a baby if he pulled on a cord and colored balls began to move down a maze! Infants need many more cause-and-effect playthings than are presently on the market. The horizons of every child can be reached in some measure by means of matching challenging and changing environments to his emerging skills. At each stage of growth, as physical and manipulative abilities become more certain and refined, parents have to keep up with their child's potential by expanding his play and learning opportunities.

*More about maturation levels and learning power.* An infant who is discovering brand-new sensory powers can only practice one sensory power at a time. When he is sucking at his mother's breast, his eyes usually are closed. In the earliest months when he is looking, he is not sucking. In short, he concentrates his full attention on one sensory modality at a time. He looks at objects placed in his field of vision as if his eyes might pop out of their sockets. He gives his full attention to listening and trying to unscramble noises. He learns to recognize the footsteps of his mother, and his feet start responding by his kicking with joy almost as soon as she leaves the kitchen for the nursery. This intense concentration, as if there were no tomorrow, insures a kind of learning concentration that exists at no other age level. As the infant begins to put together what he sees and hears, he is practicing the act of relationship thinking.

The environmental stimulation we have been discussing calls as well for the infant's interaction with sensitive parents. Realistically, very few mothers can devote sufficient time to the developmental and play needs of their babies. Leaving an infant in his crib or in a playpen to gain time for homemaking tasks and other chores, therefore, requires carefully planned environments that complement and enlarge a mother's responsiveness.

*What constitutes a play environment for the infant?* In the first year of life it can be the crib, the infant seat, the bath, and the playroom. It can be the sides of the crib, the ceiling and walls of his room, the nearby window, and the rug on the floor. It also can be the more interpersonal milieu of expressive parental faces and voices. The play environment can include a fish tank, a mirror set into a side of the crib, or modules containing colorful, moving, sound-producing infant toys placed in crib and playpen sides. The crib environment needs some changes at each new maturation level: newborn, three-month-old, six-month-old, nine-month-old, and twelve-month-old. Elements in the environment must keep pace with the infant's growing by offering fresh playthings and play sequences that reinforce his increasing physical and other abilities.

From the protective, soft confines of his mother's womb, the neonate abruptly enters a temporarily stunning world of air space, clothing, hospital bassinet, and his mother's arms. With his ability to see and hear—and then to distinguish what he sees and hears—the few-weeks-old baby requires a planned visual and auditory setting. Three- to six-month-old infants have the ability to mouth, grasp, finger, follow with their eyes, pay some attention, and even vaguely comprehend simple cause-and-effect actions in a most rudimentary way. They need opportunities to experience beginning notions of spatial relations. The six-to-nine-month-old can crawl and stand up. The nine-to-twelve-month-old usually starts his motile career by walking in an uncertain, wobbly fashion.

*Is the standard crib the best first container for the infant's changing needs?* There is some question about a new-fledged baby's immediate adjustment to the vacuumlike spaciousness of a crib. Many mothers intuitively seek out a bassinet, mother's antique cradle, or even the top drawer of a commodious dresser to make their brand-new infant's sleeping quarters a snug space. By tradition, American Indian, Russian, and other peasant mothers tightly swaddle their infants. This firmness, they believe, smoothes the baby's transition from the womb to life in vast, open space. Many hospitals now provide a transparent, plexiglas bassinet for each new baby. These are a great improvement over the opaque containers because they allow the infant visual interaction with the light and shadows in his immediate world. Some hospitals are even beginning to play with the use of "stick-on" graphics on each bassinet to bring color and pattern into the infant's visual arena. Such perceptual interests seem even more urgent for premature babies who often have to spend sequestered months in transparent incubators with overhead windows.

If you could place yourself on your back in a crib, you would realize how sterile the visual environment is for the average baby. You would discover that an infant sees only the bottom of a mobile (usually the tail ends of flying birds or the tips of the feet of figures). The bottoms of things can be dull and lead a baby to give up trying to use his eyes. Among the first things that an infant sees are his parents' or siblings' faces. An infant associates food, pleasant voices, relief of discomfort and distress, and affection and approval with faces. All babies are intrigued with faces and can't seem to have their fill of them. They seem to like to "read" the emotional tones of faces—a happy one, a sad one, et cetera. Decorating the sides of the crib with pictures of all kinds of faces or exposing an infant to a mobile or stabile with faces that he can see is a good way to vary the ocular elements in his surroundings. However, such a mobile or stabile needs to be placed within the baby's field of vision and varied in position as time goes by to take into account his increasing focal range and control. All normal infants are attracted to things in motion. In addition to the fishes mentioned previously, turtles, birds, and even hamsters in suitable containers would delight a baby. Movement related to light or reflections could be integrated into mobiles with mirrors, transparent colored gels, or even exchangeable petals on a flower mobile. If parents can afford the cost of safe, electronic devices, changing the reflections of colored light can be projected on a lowered ceiling panel or on a special crib canopy. An adjustable crib canopy seems to be a good environmental accessory for babies. From it a parent can hang a colorful mobile, insert special "windows" with all kinds of designs and colors, or provide a screen for reflections. However, such a canopy needs to be positioned so it will not interfere with the care routines carried out by the mother. The canopy could be an integral part of the crib or set up on a criss-cross pipe arrangement. It could be a transparent plastic tray slung across the side of the crib. The parent could change the things her infant can see by cutting varied shapes and facial patterns out of multicolored, transparent gels and interchanging them intermittently.

The slatted cribs now on the market interfere with an infant's "see-through" experiences and make the housing of visual or other manipulative materials very difficult. One pioneering company, Edcom Systems, Incorporated, of Princeton, New Jersey, now makes provision for inserting twenty-two-inch square picture windows in the sides of the conventional crib, as well as nine-by-eighteen-inch play inserts that enable the parent to change play modules every three months or so, or whenever a baby's new physical or sensory powers require practice.

Some manufacturers make straps with springs to tie onto the top of crib sides. However, these often interfere with the mother's control of the sides of the crib. What is called for is an adjustable device that can hang from a properly placed canopy or easily removable, sturdy bars that conveniently fit over the crib sides. An overhead, bar-type device, adjustable in height, can hold an activator, an infant exerciser, a Cradle Gym, or other infant cause-and-effect playthings.

*Flat on his back, the newborn needs a periodic change of scene.* At the outset, color changes will do. As he grows and begins to perceive and "study" detail, however, he needs many different kinds of visual graphics to distinguish—bold lines, bull's-eyes, et cetera, in bright colors and all against a contrasting color background. These graphics can be posters that are taped to the ceiling, cutouts that adhere to a transparent overhead tray or lowered Plexiglas ceiling or integrated into protective transparent crib bolsters. A canopy can also be programmed for motion. Strings can be pulled which set clappers into motion and sound, turn mirrors in merry-go-round movement, make bells ring, and activate colorful wood or plastic pecking chickens. A pegboard inserted into a canopy can hold exercise rings, clacking balls, a clock pendulum, bouncing birds, and other intriguing objects.

The carriage is also a vehicle for broadening an infant's seeing horizon. If sights are shut out by opaque sides and canopy, visual experiences are precluded for the baby. Some European manufacturers are now setting into the sides and canopies of their cribs and carriages "areas of transparency" with see-through, safe "windows." Many of today's young mothers are using back and front cloth carriers to give their babies full charge of their seeing possibilities. Car seats for infants have also become popular, another means of expanding their visual (and auditory) environment.

*The sitting-up infant also requires a planned environment.* Most parents are delighted with today's portable reclining infant seats which permit the baby to become an active member of the family. The fact that he is happily enthroned in an "observation post" does not necessarily mean that the infant is using his time most effectively. Some form of physical play challenge needs to be made a part of the infant seat, especially if the baby spends more than fifteen minutes at a time strapped into it. Toymakers should find a way to clamp appropriate, challenging toys onto these seats. The reclining seat might also be placed in the center of a baby play table whereby he could finger sensory and other suitable play materials. A play table has to also offer a variety of sensory-manipulative experiences. Deep trays filled with varied textures, shapes, sound-making devices, and teether-rattles can keep a three-to-six-month-old busy for quite a long time. As the baby grows older, the play table can be equipped with a pegboard and large pegs, a form board, and other engrossing playthings. Of course, a good play table should grow with the child's enlarging size, interests, and skills.

The sitting infant requires a dramatic change of pace from his crib and infant seat. Playpens and play corrals are containment devices, and to make them stimulating play and learning centers, parents should integrate into their sides available play modules and infant toys. Some playpens have special places for inserting such modules. In others, these may have to be attached specially. Criss-cross bars can also be built into playpens and play corrals to hold overhead exercisers. Pockets or baskets slung on the sides to hold playthings will free floor space for crawling. At such time as the space gets too limiting, there are expansion fences on today's market that will enlarge the infant's area for floor activity. Some play corrals can be expanded infinitely by fitting in additional side panels.

*Catering to the needs of mobile infants.* Crawling, standing, and walking bring new problems and challenges to infants eight to twelve months old. An infant usually begins to crawl about on all fours when he reaches his eighth month. First he conquers the space in his crib. If his mother is adventuresome, he is allowed greater latitude on the floor or in his playpen. The desire to crawl needs stimulation also. If we are to nurture the intention to crawl, we need to provide objects that make getting to them worthwhile—a rubber or cloth clutch ball in bright colors, a clear plastic ball that contains colorful turning butterflies on gyrowheels, for example. These invite grasping and pushing. The slightest touch brings on a blaze of action and color. Interesting textured rugs or a sunken glass-covered floor terrarium will entrance a curious infant. Alcoves or emptied bottom book shelves that are secure are exciting, inviting hideaways to crawl into. Heavy cloth playhouses that slip over bridge tables create great hideaways. One of the most satisfying places for the crawler is Mother's kitchen, with Mother about, of course, and low cabinets that open easily to reveal their treasures of pots and pans that clang delightfully when banged together. It might be a good idea for parents to get down to the eye level of their crawling infants to figure out how to make their floor-bound experiences more wonderful. We think, too, that they would be dismayed by the hazards of furniture bottoms, the possibility of tumbling end tables and lamps, and so forth.

To vary and to enrich the world of the crawler require careful planning and designing by industrial designers. There is little on the market now that satisfies the needs of this particular age and stage. The crawler needs a substitute "Mother's lap" on occasion, as well as undulating surfaces to roll balls down and for chasing after them. He might enjoy handlebars that "go places" yet are stable enough to give him holding-on assurance. Floor surfaces that respond with sounds to foot tapping or squeezing might be great fun. The crawler would be stimulated by a washable, furry rug with metal mirrors and soundmakers securely inserted for him to happen upon.

The crawler needs encouragement to search for hidden toys, as well as playthings that roll easily when pushed along the floor. He is ready for toys with rollers or ball-bearing dome casters that will respond readily to each one of his physical commands. Although the crawling period is of short duration—and some infants skip it—it is an important learning time. Physical co-ordinating, learning to follow, and searching and finding are experiences that are basic to later reading skill. Some child study specialists (Dr. Carl Delacato, for one) actually attribute reading and other academic learning difficulties to an infant's missing these experiences at this stage. Therefore, it behooves parents to choose toys and set up challenges in the environment that give incentives to the crawler in and out of doors. With the new foams and blow-up plastics now available, it is possible to create a "creeper's playscape" that will provide a safe physical environment that precludes the danger of falling but offers enchanting surfaces for walking, sliding, et cetera. The usual playground today offers nothing to the crawler but a sandbox, with the sand a serious temptation for tasting, swallowing, and throwing.

Many infants are kept too long in their carriages—immobile

—and with too little physical challenge. Playground planners have much to do to offer the crawler and beginning walker the physical activities they need to grow increasingly proficient and independent. The use of the Jolly Jumper shows how much an infant can propel himself with his feet to jump up and down by himself. Some form of this kind of activity might be incorporated into other items of playground equipment for the littlest ones who are eager to feel their "physical oats."

*An environment for standing and walking.* Sitting up by one-self and then standing are tremendous physical accomplishments. Once an infant is able to lift himself up to standing position, the amount of walking practice he can do is usually limited to the area of the crib or the somewhat larger playpen. He would benefit enormously from having low walking bars available for him for either hand to grab and hold onto, just as he needs undulating heights for mastering crawling, lifting himself up, and attempting to walk. Infants should have access to a low slide, moderately high platform, overhead tunnel, and adjustable ramp to satisfy their insatiable desire to practice their unfolding physical powers. They love to use their hands and legs to maneuver a walker about or practice jumping in a spring seat attached to an overhead door jamb. This is also the time to let them try differing heights by walking up and down a small set of stairs. We provide playgrounds and sports equipment for older children for competitive play, but for the stage when the urge to gain body control is at white heat, we do not provide well-designed tot playgrounds! Here is another open, challenging area for industrial designers. There is need for textured and sculptured play spaces where body positions can be experimented with and strengthened and a still uncertain sense of balance tested on indents and bumps.

Handling one's body and feeling sure of one's growing physical powers occupy the full time of six-to-eighteen-month-olds. The moment a baby discovers he can move by himself (by first turning himself over, then crawling, standing up, and walking), he begins a serious crash program of physical activity that leads to his complete body control. But he will not do any of this unless the environment challenges him to get up on his own two feet. In a study of infants in an orphanage in Iran it was found that many did not bother to stand up until late in their second year because they saw no reward in their standing or walking. There was no responsive adult to beckon them on nor exciting, tempting objects and vistas to explore.

By twelve months of age some children walk; others locomote across a room on one knee, two hands, and one "bottom." Some continue to crawl on hands and knees, while others use their hands and feet to move about. Whatever the mode of locomotion, they do get around, and with mobility comes greater physical prowess. Lifting anything and everything, pulling at table covers, touching everything, the toddler never seems to get enough to touch and explore. He has found his legs, and his ability to "go places" offers him a fur coat to fondle, books, bric-a-brac, and toys to handle, a soft rug to lie down on. A bed can become a trampoline. Light switches invite exploration (this is a warning to parents to tape all unused electrical outlets). Pots and pans are grand tools of play. The contents of the sewing box cry out to be emptied. While the world becomes "old hat" to most adults, to the beginning walker it is full of untold wonders. The toddler's adventuresome appetite is voracious, and it is important to give him free (albeit safe) rein. This period will tax adult patience and energy, but it builds ego and self-confidence in a young child and extends his investigative potency. Let the walking child wander! The responsibility of the parent is not to prohibit, but to be on hand while seeming to be somewhere else.

The novice walker is not tempted to venture forth unless he sees some justification for taking steps. The mother who encourages her child is his best reason for walking. A planned environment for the beginning walker can offer some of the encouragement and feedback that a mother usually provides, thus opening up broader vistas for her little one to conquer. To further motivate a child to walk, there may have to be a conspicuous display of commonly encountered objects that can be used in unusual ways. These can be spaced so that they require the child to take short steps to reach them. Then the objects can be placed in a sequence of more separated intervals, which will raise the child's tolerance for greater distance. The environment might require a larger playpen with inviting play projects in each corner and with hand holes and a safe, hard, walking surface that will give him a secure feeling. After reaching a set of playthings, the child could sit down for a spell of playing and then take off again on a "walking tour" to another play corner. The floor surface might be slightly inclined in some areas to provide opportunities to walk up and down, and there might be a hollowed-out area with a vibrating surface that would respond to little poking or kicking feet. Such an environment would be difficult for a parent to create, but it could be cast out of a single piece of foam to form a kind of rug by some toy manufacturer. Flexible bars and hand holes could be inserted into stanchions at intervals for the encouragement and convenience of the neophyte walker.

The living room usually serves best for the learning-to-locomote child because he can go from upholstered chair to chair without any fear of getting hurt. Unfortunately many parents keep their children away from the living room because of their fear of damage to their belongings. If the furniture were covered and breakable things put away for a while, this room could serve as a good environment. Of course, the parent would have to put some of the child's favorite toys about to get him to embark on attempts to walk.

Is the traditional baby walker the best aid? While they provide mobility, most commercial walkers are clumsy and encase the infant so rigidly that he cannot reach for or handle the object that attracted his attention in the first place and started his desire to walk. It might be better to give the beginning walker a heavy, broad-based push truck or a sturdy doll carriage that will respond easily to his pushing attempts and, at the same time, permit him to interact with the interesting things he sees. These have to be very stable so they will not topple. Most parents cannot afford the cost of the nursery school-type solid hardwood push truck or doll carriage that has the needed weight and balance engineered into it. A splinter-free, sanded wood crate on casters might serve as an excellent walking aid. The only problem is where to find a smooth crate? A plastic or fiber tote box or milk storage crate might serve as a mobile box car if put on free-wheeling casters. After a toddler graduates to a four-wheel kiddy car, his foot movements and steering ability begin to get co-ordinated in earnest.

Good equilibrium presupposes the ability to manage one's body smoothly. Devising an environment for developing skill in balancing would challenge even the most competent playground designer, let alone the parent, for when the twelve-to-twenty-four-month-old finds his locomotive skill, he has the impulse to put his power to use twelve hours a day. He goes up and down stairs and climbs up and down furniture. Like an exuberant puppy, he eagerly chases after any thrown object. The ease and speed with which he develops balance will depend on the number of suitable challenges that are provided. The home, with its many obstructions, steps, fireplace, et cetera, is not a good physical play center for the toddler. There is need for outdoor playgrounds brought down to toddler size.

*Designers should concentrate on playgrounds and play equipment for toddlers.* The toddler's playground should provide manageable areas for climbing, sliding, running, stepping stones, swinging, and so on. It should bring the toddler into encounters with varied heights, as in a toddler exerciser or tower. It should offer many and assorted physical manipulative challenges: foot pedaling, hand pumping, turning windmills, spinning pinwheels, et cetera. It should give the toddler a feeling of his newly acquired physical control—for example, a weighted, cantilevered walker-seat which would let him run and jump "high up in the sky" and then gently return him to earth. A toddler's playground needs sufficient space for numerous ride'em toys with or without trailers—jumbo trains, tractors, cars, planes, and so on—all with easy-rolling casters. Being able to make any such vehicle steer at the slightest push of the feet will give the toddler a sense of control over his world. Provisions need also to be made for large, weighted, rolling barrel-type toys with transparent plastic rollers, bells, bouncing balls, et cetera. If such rolling toys involve two toddlers in pushing activity, so much the better. Above all, a toddler playscape needs to be so safe that no inhibition of activity is ever required. No restrictions should be placed on a child's activity as long as it does not endanger the child or the children with whom he may be playing. Children of this age never play together as a group, and no attempt should be made to foster group play.

A good playground might be planned as a co-operative undertaking of the parents of toddlers or as a public facility. With today's massive plastic casting and extrusion techniques, it could be done in module forms and then assembled on site to form a total toddler play setting.

*After an infant finds his legs, he normally then finds his tongue.* When he was lying in his crib, the infant depended on his mother or other adults for the gratification of his every need. He did not have to talk to make his needs felt or satisfied. Mothers seem to understand each and every grunt of their babies. The mother knows when her child is hungry or wants to be bedded down. Early communication between mother and child is practically non-verbal. However, the walking child needs language in order to communicate with adults and his peers who are not members of his family. This necessitates the acquisition of words and then sentences. Every walking child knows that the time has come for him to learn words, and he gives his full attention to anyone who is willing to label his actions and the things in his world. For example, when he touches a rug, the mother or other adult can reinforce the process with the labels "soft," "fur," or "rug." When he picks up a ball, the mother can give him the words "ball," "round," and "smooth." On a trip through the park there are "birds," "squirrels," "leaves," "carriage," "little boy," "little girl," et cetera. He learns to meet a "dog" without fear. He loves to play with "water." Repeating each word and associating it with an action mark the beginning of a labeling process that starts earnestly at about twenty-two months and goes on throughout life.

When a child learns that a particular set of sounds refers to or represents an object, event, or feeling, he has found the single most valuable tool for understanding and predicting what is happening in his environment—language. Language serves two functions: it is a means by which one expresses thoughts and feelings; it is also a major tool with which one interprets, organizes, evaluates, and relates material perceived through the senses. Language does not unfold of its own accord; it must be learned and practiced, and nothing will incite the beginning talker more than encouragement, rewards, and the response and praise of adults who care. During the initial phase of language learning, the child's time is taken up with acquiring the names (labels) of objects and verbs. The child will see that many objects have similar attributes. "Ball" becomes the name of a whole class of things; "hot" applies to the stove, toaster, the sun, et cetera. Thus the child not only labels but also sorts various elements in his environment. First he must handle the ball, and his mother names it. Later on he will be able to visualize the ball without its being present. As this facility develops, the child can use language to free himself from things that are not actually present, and this expands enormously his ability to deal with the world. Now he can begin thinking about things that are not visible to him at the moment—which is the beginning of abstract thinking. When labeling is rewarded or tied up with agreeable experiences, language ability accelerates.

Government research (at the National Institute of Mental Health) shows that when adults intervene at the walking-talking stage, the greatest advance in language learning develops and IQ can be increased about twenty points. At no other age and stage can such a decisive change in oral language learning take place. For children from underprivileged homes, if we are to affect their language cognition when it counts the most, ways must be found to intervene, with home tutors and kits of common objects to name, as well as toys to play with and label. A child listens and learns when he hears, "Please pick up the ball," "Now say ball," "Say doll," "Give me the ball, dear," "Bring me your dolly, please," "Would you like to hear a story now?" Every child needs to be encouraged to listen, to make sound discriminations, to mimic sounds, to use sounds correctly, name objects and actions, and arrange words in meaningful sequence. Language-teaching tools should be the kind of materials that appeal equally to child and parent. The activity should be a game both can enjoy. Food, drink, eating utensils, body parts, articles of clothing, similarities and differences, relative position and placement, et cetera, comprise only a small segment of the hundreds of words needed for simple verbal communication.

*Two to three is the opportune age for ego building.* By the time a child walks and begins to talk, he takes great pride in his skills and wants to do everything by himself. If parents recognize their toddler's need to do all that he is capable of doing, at his own pace and in his own time, he will continue to strengthen his feelings of autonomy and self-worth. The mother has a difficult time with any two-year-old. He has no fear, no patience, great curiosity, and no sense of wrongdoing. Everything must be done at once for the toddler, and at his bidding. Warning him about danger means nothing to the two-year-old. It is no mean feat for the mother or nursery school teacher to find creative ways to help the toddler "feel big" while continuing to learn to manage his world. Activity is the toddler's way of learning and of developing his self-image. Every time a young child moves, and he is in motion all the time, he adds something to his store of knowledge of himself and the world in which he lives. Inner models of things, ideas, and events are created and then refined by every interaction he has with his environment. However, the interest span of the two-year-old is very short; results must come quickly for him. The three-year-old's attention span is somewhat longer. He will enjoy and benefit from play materials and equipment that entail lifting, handling, comparing, grouping, and ordering. Such activities help a child develop inventiveness as he devises his own ways of using the materials.

Free physical activity requires lots of space. Besides the public playground (imperfect as it is for toddlers) or back yard, basements can be converted into large, open play spaces. Ingenious fathers can build excitement into the area by constructing platforms of various heights. A child-sized log cabin, indoors or out, would provide endless play hours. A playhouse might incorporate peep holes with colored plastic windows and differing wide-angle lenses to promote other ways of viewing the world. Only with a sufficiency of space and appropriate equipment can young children learn to use their bodies smoothly in space.

Very important during this period is a parent or teacher whose relaxed attitude toward children and the equipment can free the children to be adventuresome and experimental in their physical play. The overanxious, fearful adult who finds it necessary to interfere with the play will inhibit the children and even make them timid in their approach to this basic means for attaining physical prowess, poise, and self-confidence.

Toddlers enjoy tricycles and wagons that permit them to develop mastery of two or more different physical skills at one time: foot pedaling, balancing, steering, and so on. Some wheel toys not popular at this time should still be included in the play yard or nursery school environment of young children. While most wheel toys provide only for pedaling, the Irish Mail is activated by hand pumping, a much-needed physical activity. Balancing and steering are promoted by single- or two-wheel wheelbarrows, a porter's hand truck, large hollow blocks, empty nail kegs, et cetera. The home and school might also provide a doorway gym (a bar which can be height-adjusted).

Through all the ages and stages of a child, adults have an important role to play. They have to know when to intervene in the child's play world, approving and rewarding each of his strides forward and supporting any transitory regressions. Positive interpersonal relations can prompt a child to play actively and to complete a project. Parents can help sustain their child's every effort by helping him master what he is capable of doing and distracting him from taking on any project that is not feasible at a given time. Parents need to enter into the play inobtrusively and sometimes redirect it into new areas that hold promise of greater learning, richer fantasy, less aggressions toward age-mates, and so forth. Therefore, in any home setting for children of preschool age, some place should be reserved for parents, whether as participants with the welcome of the child or as friendly observers.

*The fantasy and play world of four-to-six-year-olds.* These children are in greater control of their bodies and their tongues, and these achievements make a great deal of difference in the kinds of activities and environments parents and schools have to provide. Four-to-six-year-olds can initiate their own physical and other play activities. Because they now get around more, the things they see and hear during their interactions in home, school, and community arouse in them the desire to dramatize all their experiences. Since they also have more confidence with words and sentences, they verbalize as they re-enact in their play their varied adventures. Their fantasy is one way in which they experiment with feelings, ideas, and situations of all kinds. A child can play any number of roles, and as he dramatizes, he begins to comprehend complex social situations. As he builds community settings, he comes to apprehend environmental interdependence. If the toys are large and require play co-operation from his peers, he learns the social amenities, respect for different personalities, and the need of others. He can be a follower or a leader and change roles easily. This is the power of play in action.

The four-to-six-year-old needs as many play materials as one would find in a well-organized and supplied nursery school and kindergarten. The urge to be active in the adult world is so engrossing that children of this age group literally act out every family and community worker's role with whatever play materials are at hand. If they do not find the toys they need, they will create their world with paper boxes, cans, bricks, et cetera. But cans and bricks are not always conducive to play and paper boxes fall apart when roughly handled. Parents should provide in the home all the accouterments a child needs for his fantasy to go to work—a toy world in which everything is brought down to a child's scale so he can manipulate as he desires and that gives him full opportunity to be free and daring.

This period heralds much improved manipulative skill so that the child can undertake all kinds of constructions. Snap Blocks, Tinker Toys, Lego, Technik, Flexagons, and countless other put-together toys are available for the child to practice "engineering" techniques. These children also enjoy such simple expressive activities as painting, clay work, string sculpture, woodworking, and so on, which satisfy their urge to create and accomplish. They experiment with shape, line, color, pattern, distance, et cetera. But if a child is made to feel that his efforts are not up to adult standards, he may develop a sense of inferiority that will persist throughout his life. The four- to six-year-old stage is a prime time for developing initiative and daring. The child who has had positive experiences will be confident to tackle the new and the different in his ongoing years. He will have assurance that he can start anything from scratch, and he will not fear the possibility of making a mistake. Above all, he will not be afraid to play with ideas. The four-to-six-year-old is eager to try anything. However, he should not be overwhelmed with restrictive academic learning. It may make sense to postpone counting, reading, and other verbal learning in favor of countless opportunities for free, creative play. Language can sometimes get in the way of spontaneous play and serve as a substitute for doing. "Talk is cheap!"—doing is more difficult and usually more rewarding for ego and confidence building.

*Organizing the playroom for the release of fantasy.* It is more difficult to make provision for the rich fantasy play of four-to-six-year-olds in the average small home playroom. What is sad is that we hire architects and engineers to plan the classroom where some one thousand hours of schooling a year take place but do nothing to plan for the seven hundred and ninety-five hours of self-directed play each year in the home. What is even more distressing is how little money goes into the purchase of home play equipment and storage facilities for the basic materials of play. To play out the rich elements in the adult world, the child requires as much indoor space as he can possibly get. It may be a good idea for parents to give the master bedroom to their preschool children. Free floor space is needed for laying out a building block city or for a housekeeping play setting, and storage space must be available to hold all the attendant paraphernalia "ready for action."

Ideally, a playroom is divided into play corners, each one partitioned with a stationary or collapsible screen. In the housekeeping play corner there are a child-sized wooden stove or cupboard, toy dishes and utensils, rubber foods, pots and pans, a child-sized table and chair set, et cetera. The block-building corner has open shelves for storing a sufficient quantity and assortment of building blocks, play people, transportation toys in several scales, miniature farm and zoo animals, a small wooden train and tracks set, and other related community play materials. If the room is large enough, it might also accommodate an open box on casters to carry the play materials from shelves to where the play action is and later back to the storage shelves. There needs to be a place and materials for finger painting, working with clay, coloring with crayons, painting with poster paints, et cetera, as well as storage facilities for jigsaw puzzles, parquetry and design blocks, picture lotto games, and other manipulatives and musical rhythm band instruments. We believe the toy chest always invites a jumble and the destruction of toys.

Some technique should be developed to use height space for sleeping, thus freeing floor space for play in the home. Perhaps beds might be placed on raised platforms, using sturdy stilts for supporting storage shelves and dividers and for hanging appropriate physical activity equipment. On rainy days especially, the four-to-six-year-old wants to burn up his unused physical energy. From the under side of a raised platform could be hung a gym set, as well as a folding easel and blackboard.

Four-to-six-year-olds seek recognition from adults for their play and art creations. Their paintings and drawings should be hung on a bulletin board and should elicit recognition from parents, visiting relatives, and teachers. Building-block cities or other constructions might be kept intact a few days until Dad has had a chance to acknowledge his child's very real accomplishments. A child's stories or poetry should be set down on paper by the parent and then illustrated by the child, and the finished work read and enjoyed by all. Nature collections—shells, rocks, bark, pine cones, deserted hornets' nests, et cetera, can be placed in a special "wonder bowl," its fascinating contents to be handled and discussed whenever family members or visiting friends evince interest.

The play of the four-to-six-year-old can be creative or chaotic, depending on how his parents prepare his environment. The tools of play and fantasy for the preschooler are different than the gross motor playthings of the two-year-old, just as the play of older children grows more complicated. There is a tendency to plan the decor of a child's room only once and the furniture only twice—to change from a crib to a bed, from a table to a desk. A massive change of play equipment and the use of space is called for each time a child passes a landmark in his development. Skimping in this area shortchanges a child.

*The outdoor play environment for four-to-six-year-olds.* These children flirt with danger. They will climb over walls, up trees, and over each other, often managing to get into awkward and even difficult predicaments in the process. They use equipment in unorthodox ways; for instance, they will walk up a slide and not use it just for sliding down. Therefore, outdoor equipment for them needs to be challenging but relatively free from danger. One answer is a balanced supply of portable wood or metal equipment (which would include sawhorses in several heights, barrels, planks, wooden ladders in assorted heights, hollow blocks, packing crates, pails, et cetera), which poses physical challenges and fun and a wide margin of safe manageability by the children. When children are in control of the equipment, they are in control of themselves as well. When they want to test their balancing skill, for instance, they put a

plank on top of two low, hollow blocks and then gradually increase the height to that of the sawhorse or packing crate. They
learn from experience how to avoid hurting themselves—and
others. Means of mastering potential danger can be incorporated
into physical play equipment. Ladders and slides without handrails will teach a child co-ordination and competence. A cut-
down tree trunk with the bark stripped off and placed horizontally on or near the ground is a relatively safe challenge.
Courage mixed with good sense needs to be inculcated during
the early years. That is why the nursery school deliberately
provides this kind of "adventure" equipment. Portable outdoor
equipment can serve as well for imaginative play. The children
combine the pieces in ingenious ways to create a large boat, a
playhouse, and so on, thus making the environment work for
them.

*Most public playgrounds are a disaster area for young chil-
dren.* It would appear that they are designed by adults who do
not know the needs of these children. Usually they are bleak,
open spaces paved with asphalt, offering no protection from
wind or sun. There rarely is a toilet facility nearby. Often there
is no water in a drinking fountain. Some playgrounds boast
a few metal pipe structures for gymnastics, surrounded by a
forbidding wire fence. Dramatic play and appropriate physical
explorations do not flourish here. The movements of swings
and seesaws are unpredictable and dangerous. Walking by in
safety is a feat even for the most responsible four-to-six-year-old.
Boredom from doing the same thing repeatedly often leads a
child to try some dangerous variation. Instead of being environments for pleasant physical play and social interaction with
one's peers, such playgrounds usually become battlegrounds
where each child is on his own.

In the small town of yesterday a young child could go everywhere—to the blacksmith's, a milking barn, the town grocery,
or hardware store. As the adult worked at his trade, the child
would be there watching and sometimes even pitching in to
help. Children did not need a "special" place for playing; they
had woods and fields, the back yard, and safe pathways in

which to adventure. The arrangement of today's cities permits the young child very little direct contact with the dynamic adult world. Too little thought and effort have gone into the substitution of a proper play world in which a child can study and act out the adult roles he envies. There is great need for dramatic changes in our playgrounds. There have been some rumblings of new approaches to playground planning. Initiated in Sweden and introduced in the United States in 1959 by Creative Playthings, Incorporated, many new forms of play sculpture were designed that appeared in some major American cities and caught the fancy of forward-looking city planners. Play sculptures and playscapes are bold, amorphous, stationary forms that stimulate the fantasy of children while inviting them to adventure physically and socially. Just as no one has to tell children what to do with rocks, trees, or a stream, these dynamic, play environments encourage children to action. No small child can resist the sculptured tunnels, caves, tree climbers, oversized turtles, wavy walls, et cetera. At the same time, play sculptures aesthetically enhance any area in which they are situated, whether in a park, school yard, high-rise housing development, or outdoor community center. The forms provoke exploration and hold up under the constant use of exuberant, happy children.

*Creative play is at its high point for six-to-nine-year-olds*. It would be a mistake to think that because a child of six starts academic study that his play interests dwindle. On the contrary, play is at its apex at this time in content, variety, manipulative skills, and perseverance. Wherever sharp distinctions have been made between academic work and play, academic apathy ensues. Six-to-nine-year-olds are not ready to relinquish the play or physical manipulative approach to learning. Their verbal ability is not sufficiently advanced for them to rely entirely on words for tackling abstract ideas. Words must first have a physical dimension before the child can correctly use them in the world of academe. Therefore, whether in the classroom or at home, words and ideas have to be played out physically for them to take on meaningful dimensions. Children of this age group need countless handling and playing experiences in order to lay a foundation for building concepts.

Dr. Piaget, in his studies of four-to-eight-year-olds, found that there is a stage in between play and academic learning when children put together all their physical experiences into "schemata." Each schema then gets translated into words. It would appear that word learning puts man at an advantage over animals. As Dr. Bruner has pointed out, it is language that permits a child to internalize thought and develop concepts of the world about him. It is only after the age of nine that a child does not have to rely so much on physical activity or play to arrive at an abstract idea. There still is much controversy among the various schools of psychological thought as to whether children above nine require as much play and laboratory work as younger ones to master academics. But everyone is in agreement that words alone for six-to-nine-year-olds are unsafe.

*Play is still an important way of life and learning for six-to-nine-year-olds.* Their manipulative skills and exposure to all facets of community life make them competent players. They have great stamina and power of concentration and can play for hours by themselves or with other children. They are social animals who know how to give and take in their play, how to take leadership, and when to share responsibilities. For them, play is as powerful and meaningful a group life experience as their participation in family living.

Transportation and community play is more involved now. These children are no longer happy with just having small cars or trucks to dramatize their block constructions. They seek out cement mixers, cranes, derricks, and moon missiles and with them play out situations that are often even too complex for their parents. They beseech teachers and parents to read them stories about the heroes of the workaday world. They are always ready for trips to construction sites, docks, food markets, firehouses, et cetera, and from these they gain further information which they play out to attain complete mastery. Girls are avid doll house players and are able to handle the minutiae of a doll house. Boys and girls are more daring in their handling of the interplay between fathers, mothers, and their offspring, and they enact all kinds of family life situations. They will dress up at a moment's notice if provided the proper paraphernalia. Dressing up in the costumes of a cowboy, baseball or football player, a bride, a ballerina, a policeman, a fireman, and so on gives six-to-nine-year-olds an opportunity to experience new roles "in the flesh." If missed, this kind of play may be picked up in later years in what some adults term a "return to childhood." Our "hippie" subculture, with its great freedom and variety in dress, has been interpreted by some social scientists as such a reversion. With dressing up, goes the disguise kit, clown make-up, assorted dramatic hats and headgear, colorful scarves, feather and fur pieces, and so on ad infinitum. Smart mothers and recreation leaders collect accessories and props in a big trunk, discarded suitcase, or large corrugated cartons, set up a full-length mirror, and let the children role-play as they desire. Dramatic play places children in "tryouts for real life."

*Sex differentiations become more sharply delineated in the play of six-to-nine-year-olds.* Because parental attitudes and toys can be a means of stereotyping sex roles in children's play, we need to understand how parents, teachers, and society transmit cultural values that spell out sharp sex differences. Most psychologists indicate that "sex-typing" begins even before the birth of a baby. If the parents want a boy, the expectant mother will decorate the nursery in strong blue colors and select "boy-type" baby clothes. If they anticipate a baby girl, then soft pinks will be chosen. As soon as the neonate arrives on the scene, the mother treats a baby boy differently than she does a baby girl. It appears that mothers talk more to their girl babies, which may explain why girls have greater early language development than their male peers. Mothers usually touch and handle their girl babies more and breast feed them longer. By United States standards, boys have to learn early to "be on their own," and most are weaned sooner as part of their preparation for independence.

But it is largely in the selection of playthings and the kinds of play that the mother and father encourage or sanction that early sex-typing gets its greatest thrust. Mothers and fathers embolden their little sons to adventure and be daring more than they do their little daughters. Boys are given toy trucks, planes, construction sets, or popguns; girls are given dolls, plush animals, homemaking toys, or sewing sets. It is through her playing house and doll-baby tending that every girl comes to know the rituals, "myths," obligations, and attitudes of womankind. It is playing the pilot, truck driver, policeman, or cowboy that conveys to the boy the expected behavior and role of men.

There are those who believe that these early, rigid demarcations of standards and roles for boys and girls are set arbitrarily, and they see real reason for re-evaluating and rearranging them. Why can't a small boy play with dolls, set the table, and do some cooking and baking? Most of them become fathers later in their lives and some become outstanding chefs, dress designers, et cetera. Why can't girls play with chemical sets and electric trains and become scientists, architects, or anyone else they may choose to be in their adulthood? If we seek more freedom and choice for all people, parents shall have to guard against transmitting a sex difference in behavior, goals, and attainments to their small male and female children. That does not mean, of course, that a boy should not want to be a man or a girl a woman in adulthood!

Dolls should be freely played with by boys without adult snickering or criticism. Homemaking play in childhood and housekeeping in adulthood require interchangeable participation of both female and male members of the family. Today's homes require that a woman handle a hammer competently, maneuver a power lawn mower, or even fix a faulty electrical wire. A man may want to cook a meal and tend the plants in the home. Society does not have the right to limit the play and learning experiences of either girls and boys since life demands great flexibility and the ability to cope with all kinds of exigencies that are not necessarily "sex-coded." We believe girls should be encouraged to play football or baseball if they so desire and boys allowed to rock a doll baby to sleep or to knit. The time is upon us when our culture will have to remove all blocks in the way of women who have the competencies to perform in professions or vocations still reserved for the males of our species. The important point is that girls and boys should be given all those experiences that will qualify them to shape their own adult lives in a society that acknowledges both sexes as being entitled to equal opportunity for fulfillment.

*Attitudes toward study and work start with role playing at the six- to nine-year age level.* We are convinced that more vocational interests and careers are determined at ages six to nine than any other age. Young children are not able to master the skills needed for adult careers, but role playing can make children sensitive and alert and set them off on exciting adventures in their search for more information. This can also start children reading and collecting artifacts, pictures, clippings, and other interesting data. Research on some twenty "geniuses" of our time has indicated that many of them were an only child. They had to imagine and play out many different roles because they did not have a sibling with whom to act out adversary roles. Thus they created roles for their animals and other figures and acted these out in different imaginative settings of their own creation. This role playing apparently enabled some to write more sensitively or to create and invent effectively. The literary genius seems to have the capacity to take on different parts and interpret these with depth.

When they enter the academic world, six-to-nine-year-olds have drummed into them that they are now leaving the "play" stage and entering the "work" stage of their lives. For children who are not ready to give up their playing, this pronouncement can create a distaste for study that lives on and on. More children are lost to academics before nine years of age than at any other age level. We believe there is need to mix play and academic learning in this imporatnt period because otherwise we may be defeating our educational and development goals for children. Beginning schoolagers are physically not prepared for confinement to desks. They are not yet ready to completely give up their fantasy and role-playing activities. Therefore, astute teachers recognize that intellectual achievement during the first three grades of elementary school will come best by providing academic fun through game play and random lab experimentation. Many first- and second-grade teachers understand this and still maintain a doll corner, block-building area, play store, or a puppet stage. Using these as take-offs, they integrate mathematics and reading with these play situations and gradually get the children to switch voluntarily from "play" to "work," rather than turning their play off and work on. These children learn their math through running a store for the school and keeping records of items bought and sold. They are introduced to science by playing with air cars, doing sink and float experiments, observing the behavior of small animal pets, growing plants from seeds, et cetera. Projects must be very simple in the beginning, results must come fast, and the children must be allowed to enjoy what they have done. Six-to-nine-year-olds are not yet able to work on long-term laboratory research projects or to record involved findings.

Parents need to know that six-to-nine-year-olds are not ready to give up their playthings and playing simply because they have left the kindergarten for the elementary school. Many leading independent schools will permit even seven-year-olds to play with blocks and doll houses, but they correlate this play with social science concepts of community dependence and interdependence, or they develop the mathematics concepts of wholes and halves and positional arithmetic with blocks, colored beads, and sticks, et cetera.

*The play environment for eight-to-twelve-year-olds.* These "in-betweeners" are not yet ready to give up the play of an earlier age, nor are they yet able to attain all the skills needed to master the world of the adult. Not being ready, they resort to an intermediate stage of dramatization with puppets, dress-up, make-up, ballet dancing—to rehearse adult roles. They build and play with doll houses, sew curtains, paint or paper their walls, weave rugs, and so on. They dress up in a wide array of clothing to re-create adult functions and fun, from a ski party to a wedding. They are also addicted to games of skill and chance. Children of this age make involved layouts for electric trains and build and collect models of cars, planes, and boats. They collect stamps, trading cards, bottle caps, coins, international dolls, match covers, rocks, shells, and so on. These children enjoy having puppet stages for putting on shows and window boxes or shelves for displaying their models and collections. They need very large bulletin boards to hold their clippings, picture postal cards, and posters, and large mirrors for dress-up and disguise play. A closet to store costumes and other theatrical props will be much appreciated. A raised platform with draw curtains will work well for their play productions or magic presentations. They need, too, a workbench with good tools and supplies of lumber, balsawood, and nails for woodworking projects, as well as "organizers" for their sporting goods and musical instruments. Bookshelves are also a must at this time. Children this age are able to learn to use an adult sewing machine, the potter's wheel, and other simple motor-driven tools. How parents and teachers arrange and furnish the preteens' play and activity room can encourage or dishearten accomplishment in the many varied avocational interests of these children. After all, some of the activities initiated at this time may well become a lifetime vocation later on.

Making it possible and convenient for a child to read, write, do laboratory work, and research his ideas requires a good-sized desk (thirty by sixty inches), open shelves to hold reading and reference books, plus a large work table for model making and lab experiments. Pencils, crayons, small tools, and other materials should always be readily available. A sufficient supply of all kinds of paper, filing cards, loose-leaf notebooks, et cetera, are also needed.

The interests of eight-to-twelve-year-olds can best be furthered not by many "large" gifts on holidays or birthdays but by small "doing" projects presented as a monthly gift. Whether given science labs, hobby crafts, or model-building projects, these children will benefit from having stimulating materials on hand all year around. A "project-of-the-month" subscription might renew lagging interests and start a child on researching new interests. The young scholar needs wide experiences with numbers and quantity relations, biological and other phenomena, gravity and weights, the nature of matter, optics, and so on.

*"Ganging-up" is the life style of eight-to-twelve-year-olds.* They join groups and clubs for personal acceptance and desired activities. There is an irresistible pull to join a team and play more serious group games, whether physical or mental. These children seek always to "win." They will undertake a series of tasks that result in achievement awards, or "status symbols." Interest in joining the Scouts, Camp Fire Girls, Little Leagues, et cetera, begins at this age, and uniforms are an important part of the recognition they seem to seek. If an activity is not carefully planned and presented so that it will advance a particular avocational interest, it usually dies. Most children tire of any form of group life that has no discernible achievement or reward for participation.

*Eight-to-twelve-year-olds seek some affinity with adults.* The preteen years are awkward ones. These children mix work and play intermittently. They are beginning to be able to give up play with toys per se for play with ideas. They enjoy playing such games as anagrams, Scrabble, dominoes, checkers, Pickup Sticks, ringtoss, darts, jackstraws, tiddlywinks, Chinese checkers, et cetera. Their play still takes the form of dramatization, and they seek an audience with whom to communicate, as well as approbation. Acting is a form of play by means of which this age level "explores" life roles, or to temporarily "take a leave of absence from reality." These children have mastered many manipulative skills so that they do not rely so much on their parents. Model making, kite making, and collecting and trading are heightened now. This age is group-oriented and will form clubs of their own. They relish such standard team sports as baseball, hockey, and volley ball. Some girls and boys are ready for the physical discipline of tennis and golf. The nine-to-twelve-year-old has sufficient co-ordination and patience for handling the skills of music making and can begin to take formal piano, guitar, or violin lessons. They also enjoy playing the flute, a tonette, zither, autoharp, and harmonica and soon are able to advance from color or position note-following to the reading of actual musical notation.

*For the beginning teens, play takes on increasingly adult forms.* They might play in the school band. Some even earn money as performers in roving rock-and-roll groups. Many present puppet or magic shows at children's parties. They weave belts or string necklaces to wear themselves or give them as gifts. There appears to have to be some kind of "pay-off" for the "semi-adult," who "plays to win." Young teen-agers are not happy with toy versions of anything; both sexes now want "adult" things. They seek community recognition for their sports activities and hobbies. This group will seriously collect stamps, coins, stones and rocks, insects (butter-flies, for example), jokes, recordings, maps, calendars, old bottles, picture postal cards, buttons, sea shells, and so on. They become avid catalogue readers, looking for a bargain in a camera, tape recorder, ham radio, two-way speaker system, and so on ad infinitum. However, they will still put more energy into a play project than a work project. Young teen-agers derive great pleasure from folk dancing and group singing.

It is evident that the things we do voluntarily are given far more concentration and energy than the things we are made to do.

# CHAPTER SEVEN

# Play and the Creative Culture

In his fascinating book *Homo Ludens*, Johan Huizinga, innovative Dutch historian, assembled and interpreted one of the most fundamental elements of human culture, the instinct for play. He wrote: "When speaking of the play-element in culture, we do not mean that among the various activities of civilized life an important place is reserved for play, nor do we mean that civilization has arisen out of play by some evolutionary process, in the sense that something which was originally play passed into something which was no longer play and could henceforth be called culture. The view we take is that culture arises in the form of play, that it is played from the very beginning. Even those activities which aim at the immediate satisfaction of vital needs—hunting, for instance—tend, in archaic society, to take on the play-form. Social life is endued with suprabiological forms, in the shape of play, which enhance its value. It is through this playing that society expresses its interpretation of life and the world. By this we do not mean that play turns into culture, rather that in its earliest phases culture . . . proceeds in the shape and the mood of play. In the twin union of play and culture, play is primary."

When Dr. Huizinga explored how the world's poetry, dance, war, sports, theater, religion, customs, and festivals had their beginnings in early play, he set forth a profound proposition. Pity that he did not research the influence of play on the drive, creativity, will power, and self-image of a culture. An insightful historian and educator, he might have traced the influence of the early play of children on the creativity of nations —advantaged and disadvantaged.

A few years ago, we proposed to the commissioners of UNESCO and UNICEF the bold idea that if they wanted to help disadvantaged nations tackle their economic, health, education, and social problems, they might make more progress by first making it possible for these people to build their self-image and self-confidence through furthering the play life of their young children. Self-image and self-confidence come early in life through autonomous and imaginative play; they cannot be taught or communicated by words or formal education. Ego and confidence are acquired in early childhood through proper play and parental and societal support and reinforcement. We pointed out to the commissioners that those nations that had made the most progress in the twentieth century (Russia, Israel, and China) in the shortest periods of time took the important step of insisting that every child be guaranteed at least six early years of play. Their six-month-olds to six-year-olds go through extensive full-day play and self-discovery programs in crèches (day nurseries), kibbutzim, preschool centers, and kindergartens under carefully trained teachers. The results are evident in a generation of young people who appear to have developed drive, discipline, curiosity, and a strong desire for self-betterment. We propounded that early and effective play may yet be the answer for the world's underprivileged. It is to the credit of the commissioners of UNESCO and UNICEF that they granted us a full hearing. It was mutually agreed that after problems of health, food, and overpopulation were under control, they would seriously consider our proposal for the promulgation of more effective programs for early childhood play in the disadvantaged countries.

We will outline our analysis of the play life of the children of several nations to illustrate our theory of how it advances or holds back the progress of these nations. We will attempt to show how the nature of its early play "fashions" the personality of each nation and we would like to encourage discussion on this thesis from all interested parents, psychologists, educators, and scholars. We hope our readers will not too quickly set aside this line of thought as mere brainstorming on the part of the authors, who have devoted their adult lives to the subject of play in early childhood.

*Play in the United States.* Let us first consider the most advanced technological nation, the United States, and analyze its children's early play life. As a nation, the United States has drive, curiosity, invention, self-image, and confidence. As a people generally, we are permissive, playful, and daring, yet respectful of rules and regulations, our current socioeconomic and educational upheavals notwithstanding. The United States continues to lead in researching and developing new directions and new products. Are these traits of the United States as a nation the outcome of its children's play life? We venture to say that a careful study will indicate distinct patterns of relationship between national character and the play of its children.

Thanks to the early childhood educators of the 1920s in the United States, most of the toys used by American children in preschools and kindergartens are large. Whether of wood, plastic, or metal, usually the co-operation of two or three children is required if effective play is to go on. Large wheel toys have to be pushed by one or more children. Homemaking toys are also big and invite group use. In nursery schools, little children are encouraged to carry on their play in a gross motor fashion with large hollow blocks, giant crates, huge barrels, pulleys, swings, and walking boards. This play also evokes group participation and co-operation. Early interpersonal experiences are promoted by carefully structured large toys that further interaction with one's peers. Thus democracy is practiced early and often. Each child is afforded full opportunity to have his rightful share of the play or game, to respect the needs of others, and to be careful with the play constructions of his playmates. The proliferation of kindergartens, the post-World War II development of preschools, and the Head Start effort have provided American children with a type of play that instills regard for others.

Play life in the American preschool and kindergarten is informal and relaxed. Children can choose what they wish to do from several proffered activities and play materials. Even the toys and equipment come to the child without preconceived adult rules or demands. Large unit building blocks, paint, brushes, paper, clay, et cetera, are raw materials of play that foster a child's experimenting without his fear of failing; he is free to build up or tear down his own creations. Spontaneity and creativity are natural outcomes. Children's efforts are valued. Pictures are hung on the wall and block constructions are left up to be admired and played with. Clay work is fired in a kiln at the school and the child's finished products taken home. We believe that encouragement to work with unstructured play materials in creative ways shapes into our national character a sense of confidence and creativity, as well as a sense of playfulness and a willingness to try the impossible.

As a nation, we make it possible for even the youngest child to "speak his mind," to "fight back," and even to play a co-equal role in the democracy of the family. The environment of our nursery schools is child-sized, including its clothing cubbies, coat hangers, play stoves, sinks, furniture, storage shelves, et cetera. In this kind of world, a child gains a sense of control over his environment, and so his ego flourishes. We believe that other countries that have adopted our play approach in the nursery school and home are also developing greater drive and creativity in their national character.

Technology in the United States made a great advance from the 1960s to about 1970, when the nursery school-trained post-World War II generation reached adulthood. We are sure that a national survey of today's youth and business leaders would reveal that most of them had nursery school experience or came from homes in which play and fantasy were encouraged. American youth's outspoken demand for the protection of the environment, and for building a new sense of national values came not from the rank and file of workers, but from those middle-class graduates of nursery schools. They wanted as young adults to direct the destinies of the real world just as they had done in the constructive fantasy play world of their early childhood. Our survey of some of these leaders convinces us that there is a direct relationship between early childhood play and creative leadership in adulthood.

*Play life in the Scandinavian countries.* Exposed to the unstructured, unpainted, sturdy toys of Kay Bojesen in their preschools and homes, Danish children enjoy abstractions, free forms, and fantasy. Abstract toys stimulate all kinds of creative play. The same can be said of Swedish children, with their beautiful kindergarten toys fabricated by the Brio Manufacturing Company and other school suppliers in Sweden. In Finland, likewise, the Jussila Company's large, manipulative wooden toys have adapted the abstract designs that make for creativity in the play life of its children. All these countries may be called "permissive" in their attitudes toward children. Almost every child is obliged to go through a preschool program of shared active play. All the Scandinavian countries sponsor innovative parks and playgrounds and even children's amusement parks that indicate respect for childhood needs, desires, and play.

It is no surprise, therefore, that the adults of Scandinavia show almost the same drive, creativity, and democratic social responsibility as do we Americans. Relatively small countries, these nations contribute a disproportionate amount of good design in furniture, household goods, art glass, weaving, pottery, and jewelry. Where the early childhood play is more free and spontaneous, the creativity in adulthood is more pronounced, as in Denmark. Where the toys are less abstract and nursery education less evident, as in Norway, the creative contribution is reduced.

*Didactic toys pervade the play of Dutch children.* This may be because of the influence of the Italian educator Maria Montessori, who chose to live in Amsterdam after escaping Mussolini's ire. Much of the play of Dutch children is taken up with solving academic-oriented problems. Preschool materials are structured predominantly for playing with jigsaw puzzles and lotto games, matching colors as well as whole and fractional parts, putting pictures together, sequencing varied sizes, sorting slight differences, and discovering textures. A great deal of reading and arithmetic-readiness toys are made readily available to the Dutch child in home and school. Since achievement in academics is a prime requisite for success in Dutch culture, free play with unstructured toys suffers, and creativity as a national goal never seems to take off.

*German emphasis on miniature play.* A nation's people may have great drive, and even creativity, but at the same time can be too dogmatic in their political and cultural practices. Such would appear to be the case with West Germany. Germany has been considered the center of toymaking. Nuremberg's annual Toy Fair attracts representatives from every country of the world. Although it is an international event, what predominate are the miniature playthings of Germany. Each display booth attests to Germany's preoccupation with miniatures: diminutive pots, pans, and silverware, trains and railroad systems, people, lighting fixtures, soldiers, toy stores and toy foods, wooden houses and trees, Noah's arks, trucks, cars and horse-drawn wagons, farm animals, doll house furnishings, and so on. They are so very small that a tiny bag holds the complete setting of a village, a farm, or a train layout. In southern Germany the entire populations of farm villages are corralled in winter months for hand carving or forming these miniature sets. Children delight in them because in a matter of minutes their eager imaginations can make a whole scene unfold. When play with such miniatures goes on interminably, a child may be imbued with his power to manage "whole worlds" and "dictate" everything that can transpire.

Play with miniatures has positive and negative aspects for

the development of personality and influencing future behavior. It is purposeful because it can build confidence in one's own prowess, questionable because if exclusively used it may foster a dictatorial type of person. Although Friedrich Froebel, a German, was the father of the kindergarten movement, most German nursery school and kindergarten toys are unlike their American counterparts. German kindergarten suppliers sell toys by the kilo because they are too tiny to be counted one by one. With these minuscule playthings, a child needs no one but himself to be master of a play world of his design. We believe that too much absorption with miniatures restricts co-operative endeavor. In fact, it can fan the fantasy of pleasure in rigid domination over objects and, later, over people. Of course, miniature toys do include many unstructured design items, such as beads, village blocks, design cubes, et cetera, which further a measure of creativity. However, we think that unrestricted control of things and ideas may not be conducive to creativity and playfulness in adult life.

Also, German parents tend to demand strict obedience from their children. They do not tolerate outspoken children. Classroom environments are desk-oriented, and freedom of choice and activity is less apt to be practiced in Germany than in the early childhood center of the United States. So little gross motor play with child-sized housekeeping toys or giant hollow and unit building blocks exists in Germany that opportunities to play and work co-operatively in early childhood are at a minimum. More recently, U. S. Army-supported kindergartens have imported some of the gross motor toys to Europe, which have filtered into today's West German kindergarten system. What is missing is the proper mix of the miniatures that permit solo play and large toys that require democratic sharing.

*Play in Great Britain.* Constant play with miniature toys may contribute to a culture of colonialism. If one structures into the play life of children hundreds of toy soldiers, knights, generals, forts, and castles one may just be encouraging a sense of world domination in adulthood. It would be interesting to research whether the fantasy of complete control and personal manipulation that surrounds extensive layouts of small castles, knights, and soldiers may not have contributed to the build-up of the imperialist character of Great Britain. Early in the nineteenth century English children were surrounded by the miniature toys produced by the famous Britains Miniature Models Company: soldiers, forts, and farm and zoo animals. They collected these tiny toys avidly, and even today miniature transportation toys and figures are enjoying great sale in Great Britain.

At the same time, English toymakers have excelled in the making of fine baby dolls and rag dolls, as well as elegant doll houses, small toy shops, wagons, spades, wheelbarrows, skipping ropes, balls, tops, and boats. Other major toy products of Great Britain include toy theaters, construction toys, and model railways.

At the turn of this century, the intervention of British educators prompted the inclusion of gross motor play in English kindergartens, providing young children with big blocks, ride'em trucks, water play, sand, child-sized home-making and store play equipment—all of which added the dimension of democratic interpersonal activity to play. British national character even today seems to be a mixture of love of freedom and overseer of the emerging nations. Can the dichotomy of British national character have its roots in the duality of its children's playthings and play? Or is the early play style of today's English children changing the national character of the country?

*Miniature play on the European continent.* Miniature toy soldiers and war machines are not solely the property of Great Britain. The history of toys reveals that by the sixteenth century mock warfare was a popular pastime of European children. In continental Europe around 1500 a form of table tournament was enacted with sumptuous models of knights on horseback and string-pulled horses in jousting battles. German and French infants were presented with collections of miniature cavalry, infantry, and war machines and were taught the "art" of waging war. The first metal soldiers were patterned after Frederick the Great and his army and were made of molten tin and lead in Nuremberg, by Johann Gottfried Hilpert. These flat figures, three to six inches in height and hand painted were an instant success. They were used to decorate Christmas trees and became an important part of every household. Ultimately civilian, pastoral, and marching figures and animals were added. French firms, like Lucotte and Mignot of Paris, also exploited the demand. Military play was and still is a popular pursuit in Germany and France. The toys were exported to England for many years until William Britain in the early 1900s rivaled this flourishing monopoly with his own line of toy soldiers.

Whether due to the miniature size of the toys or their subject matter of mock war play, there seems to be too close a parallel between childhood play with metal soldiers and the real wars waged in Germany, France, and Britain. It evokes considerable uneasiness about the relationship between playing at war and the real thing. Whether wars come from economic causes or a desire to practice early childhood play fantasies, we leave to future historians. Suffice it to say, parents would do well to question overemphasis on miniatures and on war play.

*French and Italian toys emphasize good grooming and fashions.* At the Paris Toy Fair distinctive French toys do not appear to exist. Yet one cannot escape the fact that the French are impressed with their prowess in fashions and cosmetics, and much French childhood play revolves around dolls, their clothing, and beauty care. The Paris Toy Fair abounds with hundreds of stunning dolls of every kind, as well as miniature dolls lying in their own suitcases, each one fully equipped with a comb, hair brush, hair dryer, and so on. At this annual fair, French and Italian toymakers vie with each other over which one can produce the most beautiful dolls and garb them in the latest, most glamorous fashions. Hence most of their toys reflect their nations' preoccupation with fashion and smart grooming. In the nineteenth century, France's dolls were regarded as the finest in the world, and Paris led in the creation of dolls that could speak and close their eyes. For boys, all kinds of warlike toys are made in France: miniature soldiers, muskets, and sabers, and all kinds of ingenious clockwork war machines.

Never world-renowned for its toymaking, Italy did create splendid Christmas cribs which contained figures of the Nativity executed with reverence and skill out of wood, wax, or ceramics. Of course, these are not playthings, but they are of interest because they indicate the strong religious fantasy feelings of the people of Italy. Maria Montessori's didactic materials are not to be found on the Italian toy market; neither is there a public nursery school nor a kindergarten program available to Italian preschoolers. However, there is a new movement afoot today in both Italy and France to manufacture "educational" playthings for infants and preschoolers. It will be interesting to see how these new materials of play affect ongoing generations of French and Italian children.

*Child play in the Soviet Union is collective-oriented.* The early Russian revolutionists were profoundly influenced in their attitude toward earlier childhood education by the wife of Lenin, N. K. Krupskaya, who convinced the Bolsheviks that a complete reversal of capitalistic attitudes would come only from the special indoctrination and training of the very young child. She proposed the initiation of the crèche and preschool to cater to the needs of all children from six months to seven years of age. To permit mothers the freedom to work equally with their menfolk, she helped formulate early national plans for establishing crèches where working parents could leave their children early in the morning and then pick them up before going home at the end of the day's work. Whenever necessary, a parent could leave the child even over a weekend, for example, when their work or studies demanded their complete time and attention.

In 1965 more than 30 per cent of all Russian children from the age of two months through the seventh year were enrolled in their public *yasli-sad*, or crèche-kindergartens. For seven years, Soviet children learn via play and rigidly structured daily health, play, and "work" activities how to live in a collective society. From the very beginning these infants and preschoolers are exposed to each other in the most extensive program of child care and group education in human history. In their earliest months of life, up to six infants are placed in an oversized playpen to grow and learn together.

"Nothing is left to chance," explains Professor Urie Bronfenbrenner, writer and researcher in child development and professor of psychology at Cornell University in Ithaca, New York, in his introduction to *Soviet Preschool Education: Program of Instruction*. Dr. Bronfenbrenner has visited the Soviet Union several times to observe their nursery schools and kindergartens. "Dolls and toys are routinely passed around and shared . . . Not just interaction, but aggressive cooperation is taught and practiced." A large banner in each nursery declares: "Mine is ours, ours is mine." The Soviet equivalent of an "emergency" is a child playing or working by himself. The young children are not only taught to help one another; they even are responsible for disciplining each other.

Much of the collective attitude is accomplished through structuring the play and living environment according to their set standards and goals and by teachers who intervene and firmly direct the course of the play at all times. Group and role playing are emphasized. Eighteen-month-olds, for instance, are taught self-reliance, and they are able to dress themselves completely. Three-year-olds care for themselves at the dining table without adult supervision. As soon as the child learns to talk, games are introduced that involve role playing of various worker tasks and occupations, like farming, mining, steel working, et cetera. When the children are old enough, they are taken on trips to visit workers on their jobs in factories, on farms, and so on.

In the earliest years, infants are stimulated to practice their sensori-motor powers, and learn health habits in a disciplined way: to live according to a schedule, to develop the ability to fall asleep quickly, to strengthen motor skills, to locate the source of sounds with their eyes and follow objects visually, to grasp and hold objects, and to develop movements for crawling. By show-me and hide-and-seek games and the use of toys, the parent encourages the infant to locate items named, to imitate sounds, and to "take out" and "put in." At ten to twelve months, more complicated manipulations with objects are introduced to help perfect their physical co-ordination.

Throughout two to seven years, games, selected toys, and planned environmental conditions become the important ways for bringing the children close together and training them. The aim is to make each child concerned for the other's welfare, for adopting a code of behavior in their peer group, and ingraining self-discipline. Pretense and fantasy play is built around construction workers, workers on a kolkhoz (collective farm), running a store, sailing ships around the world, transporting passengers in buses, trolleys, and planes. With the increase of language, group games unite the children even more. Roles are shared and interchanged. Group games are introduced in the fourth through sixth years, and rigid rules are set down and adhered to.

With the exception of the United States, no country has such a vast child care, educational, and play program for its early childhood population. No nation uses play so much to inculcate the adult standards of behavior and social attitude that are sought by the Union of Soviet Socialist Republics. Soviet nurseries and preschools are directed by carefully trained educators, not just caretakers, who purposely intervene in the growth and the play life of the young children.

This drastic intervention of the state crèche and preschool in the life of the Russian family built a generation of resourceful young people in the 1940s who unfortunately had little chance to show their talents because they became actively engaged in a "holy war" against Hitlerism, which literally decimated this large, play-trained segment of the population. Those young people who survived were given positions of responsibility in the rebuilding of the devastated cities and villages of the U.S.S.R. Their gigantic tasks were sufficient challenge to keep this generation of "community players" satisfied about their power to control their environment.

However, in the late 1950s and early 1960s a new generation of nursery play-trained youth became so self-confident and so demanding of an active role in directing Russian society that Khrushchev found the group impossible to handle. The old-line Bolsheviks were not ready to relinquish their power to these young "upstarts" and "troublemakers." Whereupon Khrushchev ordered them sent to farms for two years of manual labor "to get close to the earth" and workers' standards. Thus the threat of rebellion from this generation was temporarily eased. No one in the government had the imagination to relate these unexpected demands of their youth to control their world to the ego-building power of their extensive program of structured play and learning, and no one was prepared to give them opportunities for leadership in the government.

*Play in other Communist countries.* With the U.S.S.R. as an example, it was only natural for the People's Republic of China, Hungary, and Czechoslovakia to follow the Soviet principles of infant care and preschool training. In their eagerness to give women equality with men, these nations established large networks of crèches and preschool centers, all with a structured curriculum of play. In the early 1960s, the play-way trained youth of the People's Republic of China, termed the "Red Guard," also became a self-confident group and they too demanded a prominent role in running their country. When this was not readily given to them, they literally ransacked the country and became pawns in a fight for leadership. Universities were closed for two years in an attempt to contain this assertive generation, and many were sent off to farms to do manual labor.

With the forced entrance of Czechoslovakia after World War II into the Communist fold came a repeat of extensive networks there of crèches and preschools for the children of working parents. Twenty years later, in the early 1960s, youthful Czech citizens sought to oust their Russian "masters" so they could run their country themselves.

The spirit and drive of this preschool educated sector were neither accidental nor coincidental. They reflect what play can do for the self-confidence, assertiveness, and power of generations of children. Although the revolts of these youths led to their repression, they indicate that there is a power in play that builds leadership qualities and national self-image.

(The same situation has been evolving in the United States these past few years. The leadership of an antiwar movement on college campuses, the equal rights movement for blacks and women, to name two, came not from academic public school trained youth, but from young people who had enjoyed long years of play and preschool education.)

*The kibbutzim of Israel.* Another emerging nation, Israel, also took the "play-and-learning" road to creating in children a viable adult personality wholly different from that of their parents in one single generation. Using the early kibbutz (collective) technique in child rearing, the Israelis devoted considerable resources, energy, and manpower to raising their children.

From birth, Israeli infants live in a cluster of children's houses (babies in the infant house, toddlers in the toddler house, preschoolers in a group nursery school, and so on) and pass through a series of "ages-and-stages" programs until they reach their compulsory military service age. Through early childhood, the Israeli child is cared for by a metapelet, the "other mother," while the biological mother works in the fields or at a job in the collective. The metapelets are highly trained and usually are mothers themselves. In the children's center, the play equipment is built by members of the collective.

In later years kibbutz-reared young people appear to do well. They do not show signs of delinquency, or drug addiction. They have courage and are resourceful. They perform well scholastically. Research shows that this has no bearing on the fact that their parents are or are not educated. Even children of deprived Oriental and Yemeni immigrants in Israel who are exposed to the child-rearing program of the kibbutz show the same IQ of other similarly trained children. The youthful, play-oriented generation of Israel is showing great drive and creativity, an achievement of no mean accomplishment since it was done with immigrants from the ghettos of the world.

*Mexican fantasy.* Fantasy can often be passive and so lose much of its play significance for children. To put it another way, a culture may be rich in fantasy yet offer a child little that he can manipulate. Such is the case with the cultures of Mexico and Japan.

The early folk toys developed by the various Mexican Indian groups were rich in fantasy, but they were fabricated out of materials that were so fragile—clay, straw, papier-mâché—that in the hands of little children they rarely lasted beyond a single play session. Thus they ended up as decorations for the home or festivals rather than as playthings for children. Children revered but never touched them. The earliest Mexican toys were ceramic whistles, bells, animals, flutes, and rattles. Archaeological excavations have revealed fired clay figures of all sorts. The Spanish Catholic infiltration in the Indian culture influenced the nature of these figures. Life, death, religion, and the Nativity of the Christ child began to be inculcated in the fantasy of the Mexican Indians' clay artifacts. The clay whistles, bells, figures, and animals began to take new shapes, and the painting became more playful. "Trees of life" were created which incorporated animal and human figures as well as birds and flowers. These unique assemblages, which are in fact brightly colored candelabra, were used for religious ceremonies. Fashioned out of clay and painted in brilliant colors, they could not be used as playthings. Death, in the form of skeletons, devils, and angels, began to show up in the fantasy of the Indians. Skeletons created out of clay or papier-mâché were given musical instruments to "play in the life hereafter." Angels, devils, Christmas crèches, and other items were hand fabricated in all types of material—tin, wood, clay, and paper. But these were not played with, as we understand play today; all set a scene which children were encouraged to admire but never to touch.

There also were wooden, tin, and papier-mâché toys that re-created busy market-place activity and the dress of the Indians. Crude carved wood figures of the Holy Family were made for sale. Clay, papier-mâché, and cloth representations of fruit, poultry, straw, and meat peddlers were also available. Even today in Mexico and Peru, sized cloth is shaped into market-place vendors. In Peru colorfully painted sculptured plaster and cloth figures, like the Three Kings at Christmas time, are too delicate for active play, but they are beautiful ornaments. One Christmas we found in Oaxaca, Mexico, oversized wood carvings of such Mexican heroes as Emiliano Zapata, Benito Juárez, et cetera. These are brightly painted and sturdy enough to be played with by children. In the main, however, Mexican Indian craftsmen are making miniature wooden furniture, tiny clay pots, straw sombreros, miniature tin and copper kitchen utensils, tiny hand-blown green glassware, and so on. There are minuscule settings of cafés, bullfights, and other familiar scenes encased in glass, tiny clay musicians and dancers, platters of food and bowls of fruit made of chicle and painted. Very few of these glass, clay, and papier-mâché miniature toys permit active manipulative play by children and they usually end up in decorative settings made by adults. One can say that the Mexican and Peruvian child lives in an environment rich in fantasy, but has little to play with. He sits and watches the world go by because he lacks toys with which to re-create it for himself. This may explain the lack of ego of the average Mexican.

However, a change is taking place in the play life of today's middle-class Mexican child. Blow-molded plastic is replacing tin, wood, clay, and papier-mâché. (Molds abandoned by American manufacturers seem to find their way to Mexico.) Plastic toys are cheaper than the craftsmen's handmade wares. Groupings of craftsmen are becoming "company towns" where plastic manufacturers are paying better wages for the machine casting and hand painting of plastic toy trucks, cars, and dolls than for handcrafting. Although less beautiful and less imaginative in concept and design, these new playthings are more durable.

They may have the desired result of improving the play life of small Mexican children. Stamped out of a mold, however, the rich fantasy settings initiated by the Mexican Indians are fast disappearing. It would be interesting to see if as the result of play with plastic toys, Mexican children develop greater drive, self-confidence, and ego because they now are in more active control of their play.

The playthings of modern Mexico show the effect of American technology on its culture. Mexican preoccupation with cars, trucks, planes, motorcycles, et cetera is reflected in the preponderance of wheel goods, especially in the cities of Mexico City and Veracruz. Bikes and trikes with sidecars and ride'em autos are desired by every child who watches privileged children in small cars careen around in circles in Mexico City's Alameda Park. Peru also seems to have discovered the inexpensive blow-mold process of forming plastic toys, and everywhere where toys are sold there are now displays of large plastic transportation toys, commandos, and guns. The fact that soccer is a national sport results in soccer board games, as well as numerous, colorful versions of the soccer ball. It is a recognition of maleness to give a boy such a ball.

One of the disturbing things about modern Mexican toys is their failure to build self-image. Dolls are white skinned and fair haired. It is almost impossible to find a doll to match the range of skin tones in Mexico (from the light Spanish to the dark brown Zapotec) that abounds in a vast country 94 per cent Indian in origin. The exciting daily life of the Mexican—the market place, the second-class bus, and farm life—is not revealed in today's Mexican toys. Representations of the fiesta, the mariachi band, and the circus are to be found only in tourist shops and figures of Mexican heroes—Benito Juárez, José Morelos, Father Hidalgo, to name a few—must now be hunted down in handicraft shops.

A few wooden reproductions of United States "educational toys" do exist, but are made flimsily and so cannot bear the brunt of hard use. Homemaking toys have recently appeared on the market in the form of child-sized cleaning sets, small stoves, cupboards, and refrigerators. Doll houses can be purchased, but miniature doll families are missing. Too few nursery-type play materials exist for the Mexican child to gain a sense of accomplishment. What nursery schools and kindergartens are available are privately operated and inadequately equipped.

What does involve the young child is the pageantry of the Catholic Church, with its fiestas, street parades, dress-up, religious plays, firecrackers, sparklers, and Christmas crèches. Children delight in the excitement of the many rituals and the decoration of the Nativity at Christmas time. Straw, tin, and wood are fashioned into angels, clay and wooden animals and the Madonna are colorfully painted, moss is gathered for bedding down the Christ child, and the entire panorama is a playful, albeit serious, religious project for the entire family. So powerful is the fantasy of their religious rites that soon they become inculated in the life of every Mexican child and adult. Mexicans appear, however, to be acquiring more personal drive and self-image. Whether this can be attributed to a decided change in the home play materials and play of today's Mexican children needs further investigation.

*The influence of folk toys on national character.* Most nations boast some playthings that are synonymous with their tradition, folklore, culture, or homage to king and queen or to a deity. In Thailand shadow-play figures of an ancient hero, King Rama, and related characters are handcrafted by skilled artisans out of donkey skin and used to re-enact the story from generation to generation. In Japan the March Girls' Doll Festival continues to stimulate the methodical collecting of dolls and detailed miniature furnishings and accessories reflecting life in the court of the Emperor and Empress of Japan. In Denmark the colorful King's Guards show up in decorative parades of miniature wooden soldiers in shop windows and homes across the land. In the Soviet Union the famed babushka (grandmother) is translated into wooden nesting dolls, cloth tea cozies, stuffed toys, and hand puppets. In Bavarian Germany colorful and intricate wood turnings are carefully put together in the form of merry-go-round music boxes, miniature horse-drawn wagons, windmills, et cetera.

Do these folk toys encourage or discourage the kind of early manipulative play required in today's technological world?

*Japanese folk toys instill respect for authority.* In many countries, the adoration of traditional folk toys encourages passive collecting and even religious veneration that are not conducive to the creative animated play of childhood. In Japan children and adults alike enjoy the legends and artistry that are part and parcel of its folk toys. No other country equals Japan in the variety and production of folk toys. They vary in design and material from village to village and district to district, each area contributing its own specialities—kites, tops, badminton paddles, masks, elegantly dressed kimono dolls, wooden kokeshi dolls, and papier-mâché and clay animals. There are the papier-mâché and origami products of Matsue, and jointed snakes of bamboo, fluffy suzuki grass owls, softwood birds with shaved tail feathers, crudely fashioned painted clay puppies, and rice-straw horses. Traditional patterns appear in endless, fascinating variety—paper birds, wooden creatures on pull-along wheels, embroidered balls, fish and bird whistles, et cetera. The East introduced the West to the Yo-yo, shuttlecock, kite, top, and dry paper flowers enclosed in miniature clam shells that unfold in water to become colorful blossoms. In Japan most of these items are for collectors, aggressively sought for decorative purposes, but rarely played with actively. There are also annual toys, papier-mâché animals and charms that the Japanese believe will ward off sickness, epidemics, or bad luck, or bring prosperity in business. For example, representations of cats are believed to be supportive of business success or a good harvest. Countless varieties of these exist, all of which have great meaning to the legends, ancient customs, history, and manners of the Japanese people.

Folk toys are also associated with their regional festivals. Twelve different toy animals (one for each "Day of the Dragon," et cetera) are collected, and a miniature animal is deposited each month at a shrine. Rows of paper dolls on mats are bought on the day of the Girls' Doll Festival in March. One set of the paper dolls is set afloat on a river; the other is carefully put away with the regular Doll Festival set as a charm to ward off bad luck in the coming year. The famous bobbing-head tiger of Shinno, made of papier-mâché, is sold to worshipers at the Shinno-san shrine during the November festival there and is supposed to ward off epidemics. The unique Miharu shrine horse is sold as a charm to insure the healthy growth of a child.

Beautiful wood-turned kokeshi dolls are found wherever one travels in Japan. They are avidly collected by Japanese school girls who adorn their desks with one or two of them. Originally related to a household god in the Tohuku region, kokeshi dolls are loved today for their simple artistry. Early Japanese dolls were believed to house ancestral spirits and deities empowered to ward off disaster or bring good luck. The origin of Japanese folk toys goes back to this nation's superstitious beliefs and practices.

At the beginning of every year Japanese department stores feature these folk toys from every region of the country. For the most part in wood, clay, or papier-mâché, they greet the New Year with a flood of new folk toy designs honoring some animal. For instance 1972 is the Year of the Rat; 1971 was the Year of the Boar. Every prefecture and district contributes animals in varied forms for the occasion. Even their regional dolls, an art in which the Japanese excel, are items to be collected and placed under glass to be seen but not played with. Doll making and dressing is practiced by most girls and women, as well as by commercial firms. They are made of cloth or paper and are intricately decorated. Girls who participate in the March Doll Festival customarily receive a new addition to their Emperor and Empress doll collection. This may be a new doll, a wheeled cart, a piece of inlaid doll-sized furniture, a miniature cherry tree, screens, a lantern, et cetera. Seven long shelves need to be filled in appropriately until a complete setting is established for their Imperial Majesties. Collecting and admiring such a set throughout childhood may instill unquestioning respect for royalty or authority. Whether the authority be an emperor or a business leader, paternalism and respect are an integral part of Japanese mores even now.

For Japanese boys, the collecting of artifacts of authority and respect are also encouraged in the Boys' Festival in May of each year. Each boy is given a ceremonial sword, a shield, and the many trappings of a warrior of old. All of these come with an ornately decorated trunk in which the artifacts are stored. These "playthings" are rarely used actively. They remain on shelves, behind glass, or in trunks. A child's ego, playfulness, and creativity are afforded very limited opportunity for growth in such passive adoration of decorative settings.

Japan's preoccupation with mechanical wind-up and now electronic motion toys also contributes to childhood (and adult) passivity. Although most of these toys are made for export, enough of them are sold in Japanese shops to make them an important element in a Japanese child's play life. Mechanical toys, amusing as they are, merely reinforce quiescence. A steady diet of mechanical toys and folk toys builds a passive kind of fantasy, we are sure. It fails to give a Japanese child the feeling that he is in control of his own world. Such toys are so made that they are for collecting and displaying and not for manipulating. The child is not able to construct a whole out of parts nor create a new environment. Playfulness and inventiveness never get activated.

Fresh research and new designing have not been a part of Japanese business efforts heretofore. Business organizations in Japan seemingly found it easier to adapt Western ideas than to pioneer their own. However, in 1960–70, a change began to take place in the nature of early childhood play in Japan. The mass production of plastic toys from 1960 on is providing Japanese children with a new assortment of transportation toys, dolls, and manipulative playthings. For the first time Japan's economy has become so stable that it is importing or licensing toys from the United States, Scandinavia, and Germany. Now Japanese children are constructing, playing house, using unstructured play materials, and creating toy cities and farms. They are enjoying moving toy cars and planes about and dressing and undressing dolls. They are playing actively.

We believe that as a "playing" generation grows up in Japan, feeling more confident in its ability to play with ideas, the world might be able to look to increasing Japanese originality and research leadership.

*Folk toys flourish in many nations.* They continue to link us to the past because old traditions and customs are mirrored in them. Many are marketed during religious or national holidays the world over. Nativity sets at Christmas time have always had strong appeal for devout children and adults. Crèches have been displayed in churches and homes from Christmas Eve to January 6 since the Middle Ages. In the past, whole families participated in making the figures out of wood or clay and arranging them to create a tableau of the Holy Family. This is a Christmas tradition in many homes in many lands even today. In Italy crèches are made of wood, ceramics, and wax. In Mexico hand-painted figures are lovingly hand-fashioned out of wood, clay, or plaster. In Peru they are made of clay or cloth hardened with glue and then hand-painted. Bavarian craftsmen and model-makers create elaborately carved crèches out of wood. However, folk toys, enchanting as they are, are not for playing; most are too flimsy and delicate to withstand the rough handling little hands would give them.

*The folk toys of India.* Indian folk toys may be said to be "the autobiography of the Indian people." Terra cotta figurines, modeled by hand by village craftsmen, were either sunbaked or fired symbolic representations that gradually changed into toys for children. How these clay human and animal objects got their start is not known. A terra cotta dog or horse placed at a shrine is a religious offering, but to a child at home, it is a toy. There is a close link between adult ritual and child's play, which contributes to the totality of tradition that has remained constant in India. A village mother makes a clay image of a household deity, at the same time explaining its significance to her children. Connected as they are with mythological themes and their use as votive offerings, these figures preserve the religious mysticism prevalent in Indian life. After clay, wood is the material most used in the making of folk toys in India. The makers of wood, pith, and bronze toys are guild artists, who usually are men and are known as *sutradhara* (carpenter), *malakara* (garland maker), and *karmakara* (metal worker). Metal toy making in India is limited to a small group of highly skilled men.

Indian folk toys are not intended to be exact copies of an object. Rather, the craftsmen strive for basic simplicity. Throughout the ages, Indian tradition has survived in Indian toys. The craftsmen have worked out age-old forms, and countless variations of these shapes perpetuated respect and reverence for tradition. Indian dolls and toys bear striking resemblance to certain types found in ancient Egypt, Crete, and even among the Mayans. The folk tales and mythology of India served as a continuous source of inspiration to rural artists and craftsmen.

Most of India's contemporary toys, made in the rural areas by hand and of fragile materials, are still steeped in tradition and have religious significance. They are not intended for active play use. Most children, therefore, appear bound to the mystical powers of these artifacts rather than free to express their own play inclinations. For a very limited number of privileged Indian children there are Montessori didactic materials and imported educational toys which permit unrestricted play possibilities. These children can now put their own fantasy into play with sturdier dolls, boats, occupational figures, and assorted animals. If more Indian children were exposed to active free play with sturdy playthings, it is our belief that India may be able to put itself into the twenty-first century.

*Play as a factor in building national drive.* If we would have the disadvantaged of the world overcome their "national autism" (their feelings that they, the people, can do nothing about their own destinies), we shall have to find ways to encourage more active worlds of play and fantasy in the lives of the very young children in these countries. If we can provide all young children with play worlds they can control with suitable playthings—and ample opportunity for play—it may well be that there can be developed in one generation the desire and drive to tackle the real world and its problems when they enter it in adulthood.

# CHAPTER EIGHT

# Pioneers in Play
## Pedagogues, Psychologists, Designers, Toymakers

Throughout recorded time there have been philosophers and educators who thought and wrote about the learning power of play and the importance of the beginning years of child life. There have been gifted, playful artists and craftsmen who have heightened the power of play with their toy designs. Then came child psychologists and education researchers who highlighted new findings in the stages of child development. Making their special contribution were those pioneering toy manufacturers who have helped make playthings and play a vital facet of the educational scene. In this chapter, therefore, we are presenting a cursory review of some of the major contributors to child development and learning through play.

Although the value of play was noted by many early pedagogues, only now is greater appreciation apparent, not only for deprived children, but for all children everywhere. The premise that a child's beginning years are the most crucial is not new. It has been expressed countless times in as many different ways. What is new and exciting is the increasing amount of research activity and evidence in its support.

The Ancient Greeks were the first exponents of play in education. In *Education by Plays and Games*, published in 1907, George Ellsworth Johnson wrote: "Plato urged state legislation in regard to the games of children and condescended to give good practical advice to mothers on nursery play that would be ideal for a modern mother's meeting. In the women's chamber, for both boys and girls, were the rattle, ball, hoop, swing, and top. The boys also had stilts and toy carts, and the girls, dolls. Children sometimes made their own toys. Aristophanes speaks of a child who made ships and even frogs of pomegranate peel. Plato . . . encouraged free play, those 'natural modes of amusement which children find out for themselves when they meet.'" In the following quotation from one of Plato's books of *The Laws*, he appears to be advocating the setting up of nursery schools—"At the stage reached by the age of three, and the after ages of four, five, six, play will be necessary. There are games which nature herself suggests at that age; children readily invent these for themselves when left in one another's company. All children of the specified age, that of three to six, should first be collected at the local sanctuary—all the children of each village being thus assembled at the same place. Further, the nurses are to have an eye to the decorum or indecorum of their behavior . . ." (The nursery school teachers in those days in Greece were often highly educated people.) In *The Republic* Plato wrote: "Our children from their earliest years must take part in all the more lawful forms of play, for if they are not surrounded with such an atmosphere they can never grow up to be well conducted and virtuous citizens." Plato also wanted to "let early education be a sort of amusement, for that will better enable you to find out their natural bent," which indicated that he understood that one can learn much about children by watching them play.

Although no definite system of education by play was followed until Froebel's time, many writers and teachers recognized its value in education, and some even made practical use of it. The teachings of Plato, Socrates, and Aristotle greatly influenced the philosophers, educational theorists, and teachers who were to follow them in other parts of the world.

*Marcus Tullius Cicero* (106–43 B.C.), outstanding Roman philosopher, orator, and politician, regarded education as the process by which the natural talents of man are perfected. He, too, believed that education should begin in earliest childhood. He was concerned about environmental and other influences on the "susceptible" infant. Unfortunately, he also stressed the training of memory and the cramming method of teaching, which have not yet been completely eradicated in many school systems in the United States and elsewhere.

*Marcus Fabius Quintilian* (A.D. c.35–c.95) rhetorician and teacher of the Christian era in Rome, had high regard for the inherent powers of children. He thought that children who could not learn were rare, and that children's play should be so arranged as to develop their intellects. He held that inferior teachers were not good enough because the children would then have to unlearn what had been taught them.

*John Amos Comenius*, the last bishop of the Bohemian Brothers, was born in Moravia in 1592. He contended that all children should be taught in school. In 1641 the English invited him to reform their schools according to his principles. Sweden asked him to do the same thing the following year. He aimed at the development of the whole human being. According to Comenius, first the senses were to be put to work, then memory, and, finally, understanding and judgment. He considered playgrounds to be essential to a well-ordered school. He set up a system of educational institutions consisting of a maternal school, vernacular school, Latin school, and an academy. The maternal school was under the mother's direction and lasted through the first six years of the child's life. The mother attended to the physical welfare of her child and offered him opportunities for "cheerful play." Comenius outlined an elementary course of object lessons and exercises in intuition, thinking, and speaking. His vernacular school, for children from six to twelve years of age, taught only the vernacular language, which was to be learned by the conversational method and stressed practical education. The curriculum included reading, writing, arithmetic, singing, history, religion, natural science, geography, and astronomy, all of which were intended to prepare the students for life as well as for the higher institutions of learning. Comenius encouraged the play interests of children by using objects, pictures, and puzzles in his lower schools. He worked for a universal system of education offering equal opportunities to women. Comenius died in 1670.

*Jean Jacques Rousseau*, the French philosopher whose writings greatly affected the world's thinking on freedom and progress, was born in 1712 in Geneva, Switzerland. For all its fuzziness, Rousseau's theory contained the germs of modern education. He believed that man is educated by nature, by other men, and by things. He was a theorist, not a practical educator, but his ideas, as presented in his pedagogical novel, *Émile*, which appeared in 1762, had tremendous impact on the course of education. To Rousseau, who died in 1778, the ultimate objective of education was to teach men to live.

Not until the eighteenth century was there the first of the prophetic geniuses to apply science to the education of the handicapped. *Jacob Rodrigue Pereire* (1715–80), a French physician whose sister was a deaf-mute, noted that a baby who is born deaf often understands speech and even uses it as long as he lies on the vibrating chest of his mother. Put down to crawl and walk, the child is a deaf-mute from then on. Pereire decided to teach speech by touch and sight. The pupil grasped the teacher's throat while watching the facial movements that produced the sound vibrations. His was the first attempt to base the training of the handicapped on the development of the senses.

*Johann Heinrich Pestalozzi*, whose theories laid the foundation of modern elementary education, was born in 1746 in Zurich, Switzerland. He was educated by his mother and a female servant, both of whom overprotected him after the death of his father in 1751, which may account for his lack of practical sense and excessive sentimentality. It may also explain his love of mankind and his assigning to the mother the most important role in the education of children. In 1775 he opened on his farm a school for fifty poor children. The children farmed in summer; in winter they were busy spinning and weaving. In their leisure hours, they were instructed in speaking, reading, and writing. The school failed in 1780, the year he published his first work, *The Evening Hours of a Hermit*, which contained his thoughts on education. His theory was based on the importance of a pedagogical method that corresponds to the natural order of individual development and to concrete experiences. "Everything the child learns is acquired by his own observation, by his own experience," Pestalozzi wrote. He believed that education calls for the development of all the faculties and capacities of the individual, that all instruction and practice must be adapted to each child's needs. In 1781 Pestalozzi published a novel, *Leonard and Gertrude: a Book for the People*, in which his heroine appears as a model for all mothers. He wrote: "The most important period in the child's development is that from birth to the end of his first year." He also published *How Gertrude Teaches Her Children* and, in 1803, *Book for Mothers*. Pestalozzi established his institute at Yverdon in 1805, where he continued until 1825. In 1826 he published his autobiography, *Swansong*, in which he tried to express all his ideas on education. He sought to help the lower classes improve their way of life by having their children understand what they were studying, by having them learn about the life around them, and by having them use their minds. He was against memorization without understanding, which was the educational procedure then in widespread use. He believed in the need to train the senses, in children's self-activity, and in contact with nature. Pestalozzi died in 1827. Although all his enterprises failed, he freed pedagogy from dogmatic limitations and kindled in others active enthusiasm for universal education.

*Robert Owen*, industrialist, philanthropist and socialist, was born in Newtown, Wales, in 1771. The son of a saddler, he had little formal education, but was an insatiable reader. He was working at the age of ten and by nineteen he became the manager of a cotton mill in Manchester. He purchased some cotton mills in Lanark, a drab factory town in Scotland, in 1800 and rebuilt the community into a model industrial town for that time. Owen's daring educational and social experiment in New Lanark was begun after the start of the Industrial Revolution, a period when every preschool child worked as an apprentice in the mills for twelve hours a day. He abolished child labor in New Lanark and introduced playgrounds (because he wanted small children out of doors as much as possible), a community system of education that included the preschool period, and Pestalozzian methods of teaching, all because he sought a better childhood for children of the working class. Robert Owen believed that learning came in response to each child's innate curiosity.

He established many co-operative communities in Great Britain and the United States, including one at New Harmony, Indiana (1825–28), all unsuccessful. In addition to founding the first infant school in Great Britain in 1816, he was responsible for the first one to be established in the United States, in 1826, at New Harmony. From 1834 until his death in Wales in 1858 Robert Owen spent his time preaching his advanced educational, moral, and other ideas.

*Friedrich Wilhelm August Froebel* was born in pious German Protestant surroundings in 1782. He had an unhappy childhood and little formal schooling, learning mainly from close observation of nature and extensive reading. Later, while studying architecture at Frankfurt-am-Main, Froebel was induced by Anton Gruner, master of the model school in Frankfurt, to become a teacher. Froebel visited Pestalozzi at the latter's institute at Yverdon, Switzerland, and became his most enthusiastic disciple. Froebel was endowed with more philosophical insight and more thorough knowledge than Pestalozzi. His voluntaristic philosophy led him to repudiate the emphasis

Pestalozzi laid on learning through object lessons rather than through play and experience. In 1816 Froebel founded the Universal Educational Institute at Griesheim in Thuringia, Germany, to which teachers came to study his methods. Froebel asserted, like Pestalozzi before him, that education must begin at birth. Froebel also believed that the child is attracted most by living things and by moving and movable objects. These observations led him to create several playthings, which he called "gifts"—balls, cylinders, variously dissected cubes, quadrilateral and triangular tablets, sticks, and mats for weaving. By playing with these, according to Froebel, the child would gain notions of color, shape, size, number, et cetera. He looked upon play as the cornerstone of his system and planned his materials for the "self-employment" of little children. Froebel believed that simple manipulative materials, games, stories, songs, group activities, and pleasant surroundings helped young children develop application and co-operation and made the transition from home to school easier. In 1826 he wrote his most important book, *The Education of Man*, translated into English in 1885, which pointed the way to independent, productive, and creative activity in early childhood.

Froebel opened his first kindergarten in Bad Blankenburg in 1837. He regarded little children as formative beings whose growth must be led and followed by the teacher just as the growth of plants is cared for by the gardener—hence the name "kindergarten"—garden of children. As the originator of the kindergarten, Froebel aroused widespread interest in child play. He fostered the development of physical vigor and skill through gymnastic exercises and the cultivation of power in language through spirited conversation and song. A salient feature of his kindergarten was the training of the social nature of the child, but without crushing individuality. Froebel wrote *Mother Play* in 1844, which Susan Blow, an American educator, translated into English in 1895. Froebel advocated self-activity on the part of the learner—the principle of learning to do by doing. Some time after his death in 1852, his ideas began to spread through Europe and the United States. Froebel was responsible, too, for the eventual employment of female teachers in kindergartens and elementary schools. The original interest of Froebel and his followers in play, in self-expression, and creativity as the basis of early education were forgotten until they were restored during the last decade of the nineteenth century by the reconstructive movement in kindergarten education.

*Édouard Séguin* (1812–80), French physician and educator, was instrumental in formulating a scientific method for the education of mentally retarded children. He was one of the most brilliant students of Jean Marc Itard, who also based his work with the feeble-minded on developing the senses. Séguin opened a school for retarded children in Paris in 1839, the first of its kind. Like Pereire, Séguin regarded touch as the most important sense. He came to the United States in 1848 to further his pioneering work. Progress in educational methods with young children has come in large part from Séguin's study of the severely retarded. In 1861 he received a medical degree from the University of the City of New York (now known as New York University). Séguin assisted in setting up the first three state institutions for the mentally deficient in Massachusetts, New York, and Pennsylvania. Although the use of his educational principles failed to cure one case of retardation, Séguin did spearhead a movement toward the improved, more humane treatment of the mentally deficient.

Dr. Séguin, on whose educational system and apparatus for deficient children that of the Montessori method is based, was once head of the school for the mentally deficient in Waverley, Massachusetts. His aim was "to lead the child, as it were, by the hand, from the education of the muscular system to that of the nervous system, and of the senses." He became president of what is known today as the American Association on Mental Deficiency. He called his teaching "the physiological method—the whole training of the whole child." As an example of his approach to the mind through the body, he might have a child follow, step by step, footprints painted on the classroom floor, some close together, some far apart, some pointed in, others out, and all going in unexpected pathways. Séguin's influence was enormous. He lectured widely and wrote many books. In one of them he wrote: "We must teach every day the nearest thing to that which the child knows or can know. We must not forget to create gaiety and mirth several times a day; happiness is our object as much, nay more, than progress, and children will not be sick if they laugh."

*William James*, American philosopher-educator-scientist, was born in New York City in 1842. After studying at the Lawrence Scientific School at Harvard, he attended Harvard Medical School where he earned his M.D. in 1869. However, he did not practice medicine; instead he joined the Harvard faculty in 1872 as lecturer on anatomy and physiology, subjects he taught until 1876. As an intuitive philosopher, he began to explore and evaluate the relatively untried area of human beliefs and emotions. From 1880 to 1907 Dr. James taught philosophy and psychology at Harvard and lectured in many parts of the world. Speculation and discovery were more meaningful to James than a set philosophic system for evaluating man's ideas and emotions. He wrote many books, including *Talks to Teachers on Psychology*, in which he stated: "Whatever appears in the mind must be introduced; and when introduced, it is as the associate of something already there . . . Your pupils . . . are . . . little pieces of associating machinery. Their education consists in the organizing within them of determinate tendencies to associate one thing with another . . . The more copious the associative systems, the completer the individual's adaptations to the world . . . You may take a child to the schoolroom, but you cannot make him learn the new things you wish to impart, except by soliciting him in the first instance by something which natively makes him react. He must take the first step himself." He also wrote: "During the first seven or eight years of childhood, the mind is most interested in the sensible properties of material things . . . The more different kinds of things a child gets to know by treating and handling them, the more confident grows his sense of kinship with the world in which he lives."

The ideas of William James profoundly affected American pedagogical methods and institutions and greatly influenced John Dewey, who was seventeen years his junior. The most authoritative philosopher of his time, Dr. James died in 1910.

*Elizabeth Palmer Peabody* was born in Massachusetts in 1804. She founded a school for girls with her sister Mary, which failed because of poor business management. She was a publisher and bookseller for a time also. She and Mary wrote *Moral Culture of Infancy and Kindergarten Guide* in 1866. During 1867 and 1868 Elizabeth Peabody studied Froebel's methods in Germany. Upon her return, she established the first kindergarten training school in the United States. Until her death in 1894 she traveled extensively in the cause of kindergarten training.

*Milton Bradley* was born in Vienna, Maine, in 1836. He was educated in the grammer and high schools of Lowell, Massachusetts, and Harvard's Lawrence Scientific School, specializing in engineering studies. Although he started out as a civil and mechanical engineer, he became interested in lithography and through that in the publishing of games for home amusement. In 1863 he organized the Milton Bradley Company at Springfield, Massachusetts, which still exists, for the manufacture and publication of school material. Perhaps his most important contribution was his strong support of the then new kindergarten movement in the United States. He favored the concept of teaching young children through play. One of the difficulties that faced the early schools was that of finding suitable equipment: blocks, paint, beads, weaving sets, and so on. Milton Bradley produced the required play materials and equipment, working closely with Miss Peabody and others, even though he knew that their sales would be limited at first because there were very few kindergartens at that time. He also developed the Bradley system of color instruction, which he based on standard spectrum colors. He wrote and published several books on the use of color in kindergarten and school, as well as *The Kindergarten Review*. He died in Springfield, Massachusetts, in 1911.

*Susan Elizabeth Blow* was born in 1843 in St. Louis, Missouri. She studied in New York with a disciple of Froebel. When she returned to St. Louis in 1873, she opened the first successful public kindergarten and, the following year, a training school for kindergarten teachers. In addition to translating Froebel's book *Mother Play*, mentioned previously, she wrote *Symbolic Education* in 1894 and *Educational Issues in the Kindergarten* in 1908. This outstanding American early childhood educator died in 1916.

In the United States today, kindergartens are generally a part of public school systems. The first kindergarten in America was founded in New York by Mrs. Carl Schurz. It was followed by Elizabeth Peabody's private kindergarten in Boston in 1861 and by a public kindergarten set up by Susan Blow in St. Louis in 1873, as indicated above.

*John Dewey*, American educator and philosopher, was born in 1859 in Burlington, Vermont. Graduating from the University of Vermont in 1879, he taught high school for a few years and then went on to Johns Hopkins University, where he got his Ph.D. in 1884. After teaching at the Universities of Minnesota, Michigan, and Chicago, he became director of the new School of Education at the latter university. In 1897 Dewey published a compact statement called *My Pedagogic Creed*, which became the "emancipation proclamation of childhood." Dewey wanted children to live and learn happily and well according to their own needs and interests. In 1904 he went to Columbia University as professor of philosophy and remained there until his retirement in 1930. Active for over sixty years, Dewey became the most authoritative single academic figure in America's educational history.

Dr. Dewey and his associate at Columbia Dr. William Heard Kilpatrick believed that children learn best when the material meets a recognized need, not by the memorization of extraneous information; that children require contacts with people, places, and things in addition to books; that the school must be concerned with each child's physical, emotional, mental, and social development; and that meaningful activity is more purposeful than imposed routine. Traditional schooling allowed little leeway to initiative and individual creativity, both educators maintained. Even today too many children study the same lessons from the same books and feed back to the teacher the same dry facts. Dewey believed that education must be interwoven with practical experience. The best known of his ideas about method is his principle of "learning by doing." John Dewey, who died in 1952, lived to see his ideas on education and psychology transform the American public school system.

*Margaret McMillan*, British educational reformer, was born in New York in 1860, but was brought up near Inverness in Scotland. Wishing to improve the physical health and general well-being of little slum children in London, she opened the first school clinic there with her sister Rachel in 1908 and the first open-air, play-oriented nursery school in 1914. They organized several nursery schools, each of which cared for eighty to one hundred of the children of working mothers in London. In 1917 Margaret McMillan was successful in getting permissive legislation and state grants for nursery education in England. Although nursery schools were not a part of state education in England until passage of the Education Act of 1918, their influence on the English infant school (the British infant school corresponds to the American primary school) went back to 1816, when Robert Owen established the first such school in New Lanark, Scotland. Both Robert Owen and Margaret McMillan espoused the idea of small children developing in a natural way in a garden. Margaret McMillan, who worked unceasingly for compulsory medical inspection of preschool children and open-air nursery schools, was honored for her great contribution in 1917, when she was made a Commander of the Order of the British Empire. She died in 1931, having also influenced the nursery school movement in the United States.

*Karl Groos* (1861–1946), German philosopher and writer

on aesthetics, saw the growth of thought and activity in play and presented a penetrating analysis of play in his book *The Play of Man*. He was the first to wonder why the various forms of play exist. Groos was interested in the mechanism of the imagination employed by children in their play. His "rehearsal" theory, derived from his study of animals, defined play as the means of attaining growth and development. He noted that the higher animals have longer periods of infancy and, associated with that, extended periods of more intensive play, on which he placed great value. The originality of his thinking lies in his interpretation of make believe as "preexercise." According to Groos, play is pre-exercise because it contributes to the development of many functions that reach maturity only at the end of childhood—general functions, such as intelligence, to which games of trial and error are related, and specific instincts. An instinct comes into play at its own time, he believed, and the preparatory exercise necessary for its maturation is the specific occupation of childhood—and that is play. Groos also saw play as a safety valve for the release of children's negative and destructive feelings. Far from being purposeless activity, therefore, play in infancy and childhood can only be conceived of as the pursuit of pleasure and important specific ends.

We believe one of the great preschool educators and educational toymakers was *Caroline Pratt*, founder and first director of the City and Country School in New York City. She was born in 1867 in Fayetteville, New York. She taught her first class at seventeen, without any teacher training, in a one-room school in the country. For five years she taught in the Fayetteville primary school, which led to her getting a scholarship at Teachers College in New York City in 1892. Miss Pratt did not complete the kindergarten course because she rebelled against the sterile methods being taught. She transferred instead to an arts and crafts course, where she learned how to saw and hammer. After two years, she got her diploma and went on to teach manual training in the Normal School for Girls in Philadelphia. Dissatisfied with the system she had been taught, she took a summer course in manual training at the Slöjd School in Sweden. After seven years at the Normal School, she returned to New York City, where she took three part-time jobs: one in a small private school; the other two in settlement houses. In all of them she had a free hand in conducting manual training activities for children. She had them make boxes, stools, and toys. She believed that learning came to children not only by doing, but also by thinking and planning the doing.

At about this time, a friend's inventive six-year-old son affected her subsequent thinking about education. One day she saw him playing on the floor of his room with a miniature railroad system which he had created with blocks, toys, odd paper boxes, and other handy material. She was so impressed by the intensity of his play that she decided that play activity might be developed into an ideal way to teach young children. She began to make toys that were related in size and function and would reproduce a child's experience with his environment. Her toys were simple in design and construction so they could be used as models if children wished to make others along the same line. She called her toys "Do-withs," and got a Mr. Castleman to produce them commercially. The venture failed because parents did not understand the abstractness of her toys and so did not purchase them.

In 1913 Miss Pratt opened a play school for little children in New York City. May Matthews, then the head of Hartley House, offered her the use of the assembly room of the settlement house for a two-month trial period. Miss Pratt started her experiment with six five-year-olds. She provided building blocks and other toys she had designed and made herself, as well as crayons and paper. She had seen children playing with blocks designed by Patty Smith Hill when the latter was in charge of the kindergarten at Teachers College. Miss Hill had the children use her blocks only during their free periods; they were not used as a part of her regular teaching program. The Patty Hill blocks consisted of a series of large wooden blocks, pillars, wheels, and rods designed to give children unstructured material for building a wide variety of child-sized houses, stores, boats, and even wagons the children could get into. Her blocks were the outgrowth of children's insistent demands for material with which they could build structures in which they could actually play. The blocks ranged in size from three inches to thirty-six inches long. They were made of finely sanded, natural maple wood. The thirty-six-inch blocks had deep grooves on each side into which other blocks could be slipped, thus holding them together at both ends. For added stability, heavy wire rods were provided, to be slipped into the holes at the top and bottom of each long block. However, the Patty Hill blocks were for older kindergarten children. There existed few educational toys for the very young at that time.

Miss Pratt's finest accomplishment is her set of Caroline Pratt blocks. These floor play blocks consisted of many integrated units: the unit block is $5\frac{1}{2}\times3\frac{3}{4}\times1\frac{3}{8}$ inches, the square is $2\frac{3}{4}$ inches long, the double unit is 11 inches long; and the quadruple unit measures 22 inches long. Also included were curves, cylinders, and pillars. She eliminated the long rods and bolts of the Patty Hill blocks. The smooth, accurately engineered blocks of natural finished hardwood are easily handled by children and can be put to an infinite variety of uses. Miss Pratt thought that blocks were suited perfectly to children's play purposes because a simple geometrical shape could become any number of things to a child—a house, truck, plane, boat, railroad car, barn, or skyscraper. Building with blocks starts out as an individual play activity. Co-operative block play begins at about five years of age when plans and constructions grow increasingly more complicated.

More than most toy designers, Miss Pratt grasped the concept of embodying in play material physical activity and learning opportunities about shape, size, scale, community interdependence, and aesthetics. She knew that the secret of good toys is multiple usage, freedom from frustrating details, and ease in manipulation. She created wedge people—six-inch-high wood cutouts of everyday community workers and family figures, wide at the bottom and thin at the top so that they stood without toppling. She experimented with trucks and cars that were free of wheels for easy maneuvering. She developed long, interlocking floor trains with extra flat cars for carrying freight. She also designed playground equipment for physical and dramatic play: the now-famous hollow blocks, so large ($5\frac{1}{2}\times 11\times 22$ inches) that they required the use of a child's back muscles and full physical energy to carry about and build with; the three-way wood ladder; ladder box; wood barrels; the walking plank; wooden sawhorse; platform truck; oversized wood packing crate—all of which were exciting, movable playground items that called for co-operative action on the part of the children. She also provided unstructured art materials. Each playroom had a double easel, long-handled bristle brushes, and large sheets of newsprint paper. There were covered tubs of moist clay, as well as blocks of soft wood and real hammers and nails. The homemaking corners included child-sized equipment: a stove, cupboard, wash tub, ironing board, brooms, dust pans, table and chairs—all of which invited intergroup co-operation. Miss Pratt introduced rhythm band instruments, as well as areas for quiet play with jigsaw puzzles, design blocks, picture lotto games, et cetera. All the foregoing materials and equipment have become the basis of the play equipment in general use in all of today's nursery schools and kindergartens.

Caroline Pratt believed in teaching children to "manage danger." To this end, she removed guard rails on climbers, slides, and platforms (four feet from the ground). She increased the "danger" with each grade. The tens pedaled an automatic jigsaw machine; the elevens operated a printing press; the twelves worked on a motorized wood lathe. A child graduating from the City and Country School usually developed manipulative skills, regard for safety, and self-control that served him well throughout his lifetime.

Every new toy that appeared on the market was evaluated by Miss Pratt and her staff before it became acceptable material in her school. "What could it do for the self-image, confidence, and creativity of the children?" "Was it manageable?" "How much learning was inherent in the material?" One of the authors attended a student-teacher meeting of hers at which finger paints were being reviewed. "Was it a smearing activity only, or would the children use the material to express color, shape and form?" "Were not sand and water or a paint brush and water a better smearing activity for the four- and five-year-olds?" "Was water color painting a better means of personal expression for six-year-olds than finger painting?" And so it went for every play and learning item that came to her attention.

Miss Pratt may have been the first progressive educator to take children on trips to get them to study their world directly. This practice eventually became part of the curriculum in most public schools through the United States. "What I had in mind," said Miss Pratt, "was to provide city children the kind of opportunity to learn through firsthand observation what country children find in nature study. So we followed the coal trucks to the river and saw them being filled from barges. We raised questions about the meaning of all the traffic we saw on our streets and answered their questions by our own observations and by talk with the workers we met. What I discovered was that this kind of study of familiar work activities fitted in with the children's spontaneous play interests and enriched their play in a way that nature study has rarely been able to do. These children were able in their play to make actual use of the information and new interests they had acquired on the streets."

With the help of Edna Smith, then active in the Women's Trade Union League, Miss Pratt opened an experimental school in a three-room apartment on Twelfth Street in New York City. At the end of the first year, Miss Pratt, Miss Smith, and Helen Marot rented a small house on Thirteenth Street, using a portion for their living quarters and the ground floor and part of the second for the school. The school was enlarged to include four-, five-, and six-year-olds. The first recognition of her school in educational circles came from its mention by Evelyn Dewey and her father, John Dewey, in their book *Schools of Tomorrow*.

Harriet Johnson, then a visiting teacher in the program set up by the Public Education Association for the public schools, paid Miss Pratt's school a visit with Lucy Sprague Mitchell. Mrs. Mitchell saw there "a miracle; that schools could be places in which the spirit and the mind of the child could be nourished and helped to unfold." Enthusiastically Mrs. Mitchell offered a larger home for the school, a converted garage in MacDougal Alley behind her own Washington Square home, and became a teacher of the fives. Mrs. Mitchell made a noteworthy contribution to the school's language work and, later on, in geography.

Miss Pratt's curriculum objectives included play experiences (block building, dramatic play, art); practical experiences (shop work, cooking, the care of materials); skills or techniques (sense training, number work, the language arts, music techniques); and enrichment of experience (later called organization of information, which included trips, discussions, the use of books and stories—in short, all the ways of seeking and pooling information). The rooms had no fixed desks or chairs, and the wide floor space was furnished only with movable tables and chairs; open shelves and other materials lined the walls. By the fall of 1921 the school had again outgrown its quarters and moved into its present buildings on West Twelfth Street in New York City.

While play with blocks and assorted play materials dominated the community-oriented curriculum of the three- through seven-year-olds, the curriculum for the older children was built around school community work projects. Miss Pratt's innovating "job group program" for the eight-to-twelve-year-olds began with a store for the eights, which they ran themselves. The children bought school supplies from wholesalers, sold them to their fellow students, and did all the accounting. As Miss Pratt put it: "I know only that children cannot escape practical arithmetic if it is taught in connection with a job." The store was open for half an hour every morning, with a rotating committee of children in charge, and the experiment was a huge success. The following year the nines set up a school post office. The children were paid fifteen cents an hour for their work as postal workers and storekeepers. The tens did hand lettering of reading charts, flash cards, et cetera, as ordered by the teachers, for which they were paid fifteen cents an hour. The tens found time to undertake a second job, that of helping out in the school lunchroom. The elevens did printing of books and other school graphics with a hand press (subsequently an electric press was installed). The twelves used an automatic lathe to make toys for the preschool levels. All the children were proving that they thrive on freedom to work and the discipline of work, both as individuals and in groups.

Very early, Caroline Pratt accepted as student teachers a few volunteers who wanted to work in her school. This seemed to her to be a good way to train the new kind of teacher her experimental school required. It was as the first male nursery school student teacher at the City and Country School in 1932 that one of the authors got his basic orientation and feeling for the power of play in early childhood. Every year Miss Pratt trained eight student teachers at her school. The student teachers received invaluable background in the power of play and the nature of children. Some went on to teach, others became directors of teacher-training institutions. A few, including the late Paul Kelly (Washington, D.C.) and the authors (New York City) went on to set up educational toy shops and to manufacture toys. Still others published children's books, and some became directors of leading experimental elementary school centers. Miss Pratt convinced them all that a child's urge to play must never be set aside nor treated as something apart from serious work.

*Harriet M. Johnson* (1867–1934) was one of the pioneers of nursery school development in our country. Her outstanding contribution was in the area of child study. Unlike the other educators, she recorded daily the play behavior of the children, analyzed their records as an integral part of teacher training, and carried on truly empirical efforts. Miss Johnson founded and directed the nursery school of the Bureau of Educational Experiments in New York City. The bureau itself, later called the Bank Street College of Education, was established in 1916 by Harriet Johnson and Lucy Sprague Mitchell and underwritten by Elizabeth Sprague Coolidge. The nursery school, subsequently named the Harriet Johnson Nursery School, was a laboratory for the experimental education of preschool children, as well as a center for child research. Miss Johnson worked closely with the City and Country School, which she regarded as the original inspiration of her pedagogic thinking.

*Johan Huizinga,* historian and educator, was born in 1872 in the Netherlands. His father was a professor of medicine at the University of Groningen in the Netherlands, and Johan Huizinga was educated at this institution, where he studied philology and history. He also spent a semester at the University of Leipzig, Germany, where he studied Indo-Germanic linguistics. In 1897 he received his Ph.D. at Groningen and taught history at a high school in Haarlem, the Netherlands. From 1905 to 1915 he was professor of history at Groningen, and after that he was professor of general history at the University of Leiden.

His first publications were in the field of Indian literature and cultural history, but his interest soon shifted to Dutch and European history. He never became a specialist in one period or one country, although his main historiographical work deals with the Late Middle Ages and the Renaissance. In his later years Dr. Huizinga's research was devoted mostly to general themes of cultural history, and his most important work in this regard (though not so evocative as his *The Waning of the Middle Ages*) is *Homo Ludens: A Study of the Play-Element in Culture,* first published in Dutch in 1938. Huizinga died near Arnhem in 1945, shortly after having translated *Homo Ludens* into English.

For many years Huizinga had the conviction that civilization arises and unfolds in and as play, that play has left a timeless imprint on world civilization and adult culture. According to Huizinga, "It has not been difficult to show that a certain play-factor was extremely active all through the cultural process and that it produces many of the fundamental forms of social life. The spirit of playful competition is, as a social impulse, older than culture itself . . . Ritual grew up in sacred play; poetry was born in play and nourished on play; music and dancing were pure play . . . We have to conclude, therefore, that civilization is, in its earliest phases, played."

The late *Lucy Sprague Mitchell*, educator, author, geographer, and one of the founders and the first president of the Bank Street College of Education in New York City, was born in Chicago in 1878. In 1930 the Bureau of Educational Experiments (as the Bank Street College was then called) added to its other activities the development of an experimental program for the education of teachers. Nearly fourteen years later the Bank Street College entered into a collaborative program with some of the public schools in New York City. Thus, in June of 1943, Mrs. Mitchell brought her long, valuable experience in independent schools to enrich the public schools in which she deeply believed. Like all sensitive educators, she held that to teach, one must watch and listen to children, that experience is most meaningful when the child can connect the new with what he already knows. Mrs. Mitchell wanted "all human beings to develop a zest for living that comes from taking in the world with all five senses alert; lively intellectual curiosities that keep one ever a learner; flexibility when confronted with change; courage to work in a world of new needs, new problems, new ideas; a striving to live democratically in and out of schools as the best way to advance our concept of democracy." She created new, fresh literature for children and their teachers—and parents. Her most famous book, *The Here and Now Story Book*, was first published in 1921. It is still being reprinted today. Mrs. Mitchell believed that stories for children should help them make some sense and order out of the unpredictable, not always stable, world in which we all live.

*Some notes about the nursery school movement.* It had its beginnings as an educational movement in the United States in 1914. The earliest American "laboratory" nursery schools, where preschool children were cared for and observed professionally, were those established by Harriet Johnson of New York's Bureau of Educational Experiments (later the Harriet Johnson Nursery School of the Bank Street College of Education); the children studied by Arnold Gesell at the Yale Clinic of Child Development beginning in 1920; and the Ruggles Street Nursery School (later becoming the Nursery Training School of Boston), which opened in 1922 under the direction of Dr. Abigail A. Eliot. (Dr. Eliot had gone to England to study the open-air nursery schools established and operated by Margaret and Rachel McMillan.) Also the nursery school of the Merrill-Palmer School in Detroit, which was opened in January, 1922 with Dr. Edna Noble White as its director. These nursery schools cared for children from more or less privileged homes and stressed the educational guidance of the children and their parents. This was a sharp departure from the custodial care programs that formerly had been considered adequate for the preschool children of working mothers.

In 1923 the Laura Spelman Rockefeller Memorial, with Lawrence K. Frank as administrator, began paying large grants to enable child development centers to get under way in the United States. Through these grants, the Universities of Iowa, Minnesota, California, and Teachers College, Columbia University, were enabled to make major contributions to the understanding of child development.

During 1920 to 1930 the number of nursery schools reported to the United States Office of Education increased from three to two hundred and sixty-five, which increase may have been due to the needs of only children, too limited play space, women seeking work outside the home, and parents seeking the best possible environment for their preschool children.

During the Depression of the 1930s three thousand nursery schools, serving sixty-five thousand needy preschoolers, were organized under the Federal Emergency Education Program.

About fifteen hundred of these nursery schools were continued under the Works Projects Administration, with one hundred and fifty thousand families enrolled in a Family Life Education Program. In 1933 American nursery schools became for the first time an integral part of a federally supported program.

The employment of women in industry during World War II created conditions for children similar to those at the beginning of the Industrial Revolution, when Robert Owen established infant schools in Scotland. Thousands of emergency child care centers and nursery schools were formed hastily by our government and industry to meet another socioeconomic exigency. Many of the early government nursery schools were maintained and continued beyond the war period by co-operative parent groups. In a few instances, on the east and west coasts (in the state of California and the city of Philadelphia), they were made part of the public school program.

In England separate nursery schools had been established by voluntary efforts long before its Education Act of 1918 gave local education authorities the power to aid and supply them. In 1944 nursery education in schools or classes was set up as a statutory part of the English educational system. Since 1944 the overwhelming numbers of English children between five and eleven had made it impossible in many places to spare accommodations or teachers for the children under five, and many nursery classes had to close. Fortunately the nursery schools in England did not decline in numbers.

Since their onset, nursery schools have had a tremendous impact on infant education. Out of preliminary concern for the physical well-being of very young children came real interest in understanding more about their growth and development in all ways. The upsurge of interest in the Montessori method is due in large part to the sponsoring by the federal government, in the early 1960s, of its Operation Head Start and other educational programs to enrich the backgrounds of culturally deprived preschool children and the mentally retarded, as well as the demands of modern education reformers for curriculum revision in mathematics and science. Over a half-million children attended Head Start in the summer of 1965 in classes whose size was fixed at fifteen. To this writing funding for Head Start is still on an uncertain year-to-year basis and the program has not become an accepted part of regular school business and planning. The New York *Times*, on October 23, 1966, cited studies indicating that the educational advantages of the Head Start program tended to disappear as a child moved on through the later grades and that "either because of poor teaching or because of an uninspired curriculum in the public school, the preschool child's thirst for knowledge went largely unquenched and the other advantages of preschooling rapidly dissipated."

We believe the time is close at hand when nursery schools and child care centers in the United States will be included in its general education program. It is the nursery school that aims to help young children attain their potential and, at the same time, helps them to accept the limits (and rewards) of life in a democratic society.

*Maria Montessori*, world-renowned Italian physician and education innovator, was born in Chiaravalle in the province of Ancona, Italy, in 1870, the only child of cultivated, adoring parents. She attended the usual state day school there, but when she was almost twelve years old her parents moved to Rome in order to make better educational opportunities available to her. She showed mathematical aptitude as a child and had intended to become an engineer. Instead she became the first woman in Italy to take the degree of Doctor of Medicine at the University of Rome in 1896. Dr. Montessori practiced medicine for a few years. In 1899 she became the first director of the new state orthophrenic school at Rome, an institution for defective children. She left this post in 1901 to enroll as a graduate student in psychology and philosophy at the University of Rome. Her postgraduate work in psychiatry and her study of abnormal children led her to conclude that their nervous disorders could be treated best by education, which idea had in fact been initiated earlier by Édouard Séguin. As assistant doctor at the Psychiatric Clinic of the University of

Rome, Dr. Montessori visited insane asylums to select subjects for the clinic because at that time mentally deficient children were housed in the general insane asylums!

Inspired by the pioneering work of Itard and Séguin, Dr. Montessori designed a series of didactic materials that she had manufactured in the workshops of the Humanitarian Society in Milan. Her educational methods and "hardware" prepared mentally retarded children to perform reasonably well on school problems that previously had been considered far beyond their capacity. Her first real success came when she presented children from mental institutions at the public examinations for primary certificates, which was as far as the average Italian went in formal education in those days, and her children passed the test. Thereafter she was an educator, not a medical doctor. Dr. Montessori lectured on pedagogy at the University of Rome from 1900 to 1907. She was invited to organize normal infant schools in the tenements of the Roman Association for Good Building, of which Edoardo Talamo was the director. Olga Lodi, a mutual friend, christened this new kind of school *Casa dei Bambini* (*Children's House*). The first Casa dei Bambini was opened in a Roman slum tenement on January 6, 1907, and followed by others elsewhere in Rome and in Milan. Her association with these schools terminated in 1917 as the result of a misunderstanding she had with Mr. Talamo.

In *The Montessori Method,* Dr. Montessori wrote: "If a parallel between the deficient and the normal child is possible, this will be during the period of early infancy when the child who has not the force to develop and he who is not yet developed are in some ways alike. The very young child has not yet acquired a secure coordination of muscular movements and, therefore, walks imperfectly and is not able to perform the ordinary acts of life, such as fastening and unfastening its garments. The sense organs . . . are not completely developed; the language . . . shows those defects common to the speech of the very young child. The difficulty of fixing the attention, the general instability, etc. are characteristics which the normal infant and the deficient child have in common. Many defects which become permanent . . . the child acquires through being neglected during the most important period . . . the period between three and six, at which time he forms and establishes his principal functions."

The main features of the Montessori method are the development of a child's initiative through freedom of action (however, the Montessori concept of liberty is based in Catholic tradition wherein there is freedom to do "what is right," but authority—in this case, the teacher—always retains the power to decide what is wrong; hence the freedom is not unalloyed); improvement of sense perception through training; and the cultivation of co-ordination through exercises and games. The teacher provides the material and acts as the children's guide.

In the schoolroom of the Casa dei Bambini a series of low cupboards are provided for the storage of the didactic materials to which the children have ready access. Potted plants, small aquariums, and some commercial toys are kept on the tops of the cupboards, also within easy reach of the children. Blackboards are hung low. Child-sized tables and chairs are light in weight and movable. The physical environment is planned to help each child "learn to command his movements." Among the Montessori apparatus are wood frames, each mounted with two pieces of cloth or leather, to be fastened and unfastened by means of buttons and buttonholes, hooks and eyes, lacings, zippers, and so on. Each of the ten frames represents a different dressing procedure. To help train the tactile sense, Dr. Montessori devised a wood board divided into two equal rectangles, one covered with very smooth paper, the other with sandpaper. She provided a set of little metal bowls filled with water at varying degrees of temperature for developing the thermic sense in young children. For the baric sense, she used wooden tablets smoothly finished with clear varnish and differing in weight. A child takes tablets in his hands and balances them to gauge their weight. The first didactic material Dr. Montessori used for sharpening a child's sense of touch were Froebel's cubes and bricks. With regard to taste and smell she wrote, "This phase of sense education is most difficult, and I have not as yet had any satisfactory results to record . . . The olfactory sense in children is not developed to any great extent." For sight training, there are three different sets of solid insets. Each varnished pine block holds ten wooden cylinders set in corresponding holes, with each cylinder to be handled by the tiny knob on top. The first set has cylinders of equal height but differing diameter. In the second, the cylinders differ in both height and diameter. The child removes the cylinders, mixes them up, and then puts each one back into its proper opening. To help children learn the concept of length, Montessori provided a set of ten four-sided rods in differing lengths, but with the same width and height and painted alternately red and blue. When the rods are placed in sequence, with the longest rod at the base and the shortest rod at the top, the completed set has the appearance of a right angle triangle. A child can also count from one to ten with this set and construct addition and other arithmetic tables. Well known is her set of plane geometric insets of wood for developing the visual-tactile perception of form. There are sixty-four small, flat tablets that are wound with colored wool or silk in assorted colors for sharpening color perception. Each classroom is given two sets. For the beginning exercise, red, blue, and yellow are used in pairs, all six tablets being placed upon the table in front of the child. He is shown one of the colors, asked to find its duplicate among the mixed tablets and then to arrange the tablets in a column, pairing them according to color. A series of little whistles are used for training sound discrimination, and small boxes filled with different substances (sand or pebbles, for example) are employed for work in gradation of sounds. Exercises with a clock and a lowered or whispered voice were found successful for developing hearing acuity.

For use with blind children, Dr. Montessori prepared a little chest of drawers filled with rectangular pieces of assorted fabrics.

The director has the child touch each piece and teaches its appropriate name as it is handled. For teaching reading and writing, she made cards on each of which one letter of the alphabet was mounted in sandpaper. The child traces the sandpaper letters with his fingertips before attempting to reproduce them on paper. There are unmounted cardboard letters for composing words. Numbers are treated the same way. Some commercial toys are also used to teach reading: doll house furniture, balls, small dolls, miniature trees, assorted animals, tin soldiers, railways, and a variety of simple figures. Each toy has a corresponding card with its name written on it. The children who know how to read are allowed to take turns in drawing the cards from a basket. If the child pronounces the word clearly and indicates the correct object, he is permitted to take the toy and play with it.

Maria Montessori's insights and methods are contained in four of her basic texts, originally written in Italian and translated into English in the year noted after each title: *The Montessori Method* (1912); *Spontaneous Activity in Education* (1917); *The Montessori Elementary Material* (1917); and *Dr. Montessori's Own Handbook* (1914). These have all been published in new editions in the United States in 1965. She also wrote *Pedagogical Anthropology* (1913) and *The Secret of Childhood* (1936).

Opposed to her country's participation in World War I and to fascism later, Dr. Montessori lived most of her later years in voluntary and involuntary exile. She opened Montessori Schools in England, the United States, Spain, Denmark, India, and the Netherlands. Maria Montessori died in 1952.

Dr. Montessori's materials and their use are prime examples of how structured playthings can further the practice of sensory powers and academic skills by young children. What was unique was that she engineered into her didactic materials self-corrective devices so the children could themselves ascertain whether they were mastering a given concept. Dr. Montessori was the first educator to incorporate in her manipulatives concepts of place value in arithmetic and the first to prove that kindergarten children could handle computations involving large numbers. It took American educators fifty years to catch up with Dr. Montessori.

Although she veered away from spontaneous play, Dr. Montessori's development of materials that could communicate academic ideas to young children remains valid today. Her medical background gave her the ability to create the most effective programed learning materials ever developed. They are matched by no one to this day.

Her influence on the educational toy business was also profound. Many American toy manufacturers, including the Holgate Brothers Company, the Playskool Manufacturing Company, the Educational Equipment Company, Judy Company, Sifo Company, and Creative Playthings, Incorporated, translated some of Montessori's materials into self-directed wooden toys. To attract parent purchasing, they took the basic Montessori shape-fitting items and "dressed them up" into the House That Jack Built, the Postal Station, the Form Block Cart, et cetera. Shape and size recognition boards became the Color Cone, Block Stack, and jigsaw puzzles for manipulation and enjoyment by the preschool child. Few toy manufacturers dared credit Montessori's influence on their toys because her rigidly structured program conflicted with Dewey's philosophy of free choice, which was always more popular in the United States in the 1920s, 1930s, and 1940s.

In 1958, when president of Creative Playthings, Incorporated, one of the authors imported a complete set of Montessori materials from Amsterdam. Over two hundred didactic items were put on public exhibit in the company's display rooms on University Place in New York City. Four Saturday morning sessions for educators were held there, and it became evident to many educators that Montessori's method and materials, albeit an *incomplete* system for early childhood education, represented the considered work of a gifted, competent, original, dedicated woman who had sought greater personal involvement of preschool children in their own learning.

*Research contributions of child psychoanalysts and psychologists.* In the 1930s psychoanalysts and psychologists began reporting on interpersonal relations in early childhood, physical growth and behavior, and parent-child relationships. Among them were Dr. Anna Freud, youngest daughter of Dr. Sigmund Freud and outstanding child psychoanalyst, writer, teacher, and lecturer; Dr. Susan Isaacs, English psychologist-educator; Lawrence Kelso Frank, American social scientist, psychologist, and author (who died in 1968); and others in both the United States and England, who advanced the theory of the development of personality through play.

Psychiatrists, psychoanalysts, and psychologists began to use play to ascertain the inner needs and emotional disturbances of children. Some began to use play therapeutically so that children could confront their difficulties on the conscious level. Sigmund Freud was the first psychiatrist to recognize that a child's play is not merely a casual activity; rather, it is a means by which the child strengthens his mastery of self and environment, for which he persistently strives. From their psychoanalytic work with adults, psychiatrists built up a body of knowledge about how the adults had felt as children; how their early play was a way of expressing their unconscious wants, feelings, and drives; that children mirror their satisfactions, problems, strengths, and weaknesses in their play. Out of these findings came the awareness that play is the poignant language of childhood; that fears, jealousies, hurts, and hatreds could be ascertained through play sequences; and that many emotional problems could be resolved by means of imaginative, sensitive intervention in play therapy sessions.

It was *Dr. Anna Freud* who, more than any other child psychoanalyst, alerted psychiatrists to the behavior mechanisms used by children to defend themselves against harsh reality. She was one of the first to apply psychoanalysis to the treatment of neurotic children. By measuring the demands on the child's ego and the degree of defense, she was able to assess the boundaries between normality and pathology in children. It is to her credit that she studied the nature of these defenses not only in terms of their conflicts but also of their constructiveness; that is to say, how these made children stronger and healthier. She demonstrated how the fantasies of children could be a road to constructive play and to imaginative storytelling and intellectualizing.

Early in her career Anna Freud established in Vienna the first day nursery as well as the first primary school, based on the knowledge she had gained from psychoanalysis about the educational needs of normal and abnormal children. Anna Freud and her father emigrated to London in 1938. In 1940 she organized a residential war nursery for homeless children in London, which was in operation to 1945. After World War II, she founded and has been the ongoing director of the Hampstead Child Course and Clinic in England, the largest center in the world for the treatment of disturbed children and the training of child analysts. Anna Freud has greatly influenced many child psychoanalysts. Always with the aim to protect the "natural rights" of children, she has lectured widely to teachers, social workers, nurses, pediatricians, and hospital authorities. Now over seventy-six years old, she is continuing to make a tremendous contribution in the field of "ego" psychology. Anna Freud has been a staunch advocate of the power of play in and out of the therapeutic setting. She was made a Commander of the Order of the British Empire in 1967 in recognition of her tireless work for the well-being of children.

*Arnold L. Gesell,* well-known child specialist, merits attention for his pioneering research in the stages of development and the play of infants and preschool children. A graduate of the University of Wisconsin, Gesell received his Ph.D. in psychology from Clark University in 1906. In 1911 he became an assistant professor of education in the Graduate School at Yale University, at which time he also established the Yale Clinic of Child Development. In further preparation for his clinical and research work in child development, he studied medicine at Yale, receiving his M.D. in 1915, and was appointed professor of child hygiene at the Yale School of Medicine. From 1928 on, Dr. Gesell was attending pediatrician at the New

Haven Hospital in Connecticut. In 1932 Dr. Frances L. Ilg, a graduate of the Cornell Medical School, joined Dr. Gesell's staff at the Yale Clinic in New Haven. Dr. Gesell supervised the years of systematic research at the Clinic concerned primarily with the growth characteristics of infants and very young children through their universal stages of development. In his laboratory and nursery school, he and his staff made a full and detailed study of the development of movement and skill, from birth onward, among a great many children. Scientific devices were used for observing, recording, and photographing the behavior of the subjects in their spontaneous play, as well as their responses to actual tests.

Dr. Gesell found that if children are aware of being watched, they behave differently, so he devised an observation screen that was opaque in one direction and transparent in another. Hence the children could be viewed without their seeing the observers. When he founded the Clinic, Dr. Gesell's chief interest was in the study of backward children. For several summers he was assistant professor at New York University, concerned with special training in psychology and pedagogy for defective children. By 1919 he had shifted his attention to normal children whose complex behavior he deemed important to clinical medicine. He developed methods for the early diagnosis of defects and deviations in the mental growth of infants and preschoolers. Dr. Gesell used cinematography as a main research tool in charting the growth and analyzing the characteristics of early behavior and, in 1930, set up the Photographic Research Library for Yale Clinic films of child development. Dr. Gesell wrote many books, of which three of the best known, written with Dr. Ilg and others on the staff of the Yale Clinic, are *Infant and Child in the Culture of Today*, *The First Five Years of Life*, and *The Child from Five to Ten*.

*Jean Piaget*, world-renowned Swiss child psychologist who changed the education world's way of thinking about human intelligence, was born in Neuchâtel in 1896. Very early he became absorbed with the biological explanation of knowledge, but he also drew upon the disciplines of psychology and logic to further his investigations of the development of intelligence in children. Dr. Piaget believes that automatic patterns of behavior play a minor role in the development of human intelligence, that it is only in the first few days of an infant's life that his behavior depends upon reflexive reactions. He maintains that each adult is the product of the interactions between his heredity and environment and that it is not possible to draw a sharp demarcation between inborn and acquired patterns of behavior.

Dr. Piaget is a professor of child psychology and the history of scientific thought at the University of Geneva, where he teaches, conducts seminars, and supervises doctoral candidates. He also is co-director of the Institute for Educational Sciences and the International Center for Genetic Epistemology. He founded the latter in 1955 with a grant from the Rockefeller Foundation. He is a prolific writer who has produced over thirty books and countless articles. However, it is only within the past decade or so that his writings have come to be appreciated by American psychologists and educators. It is unfortunate that while his thinking is significant and clear, more often than not his writing is obtuse and hard to follow.

Dr. Piaget tested many of his ideas on his own three children as he watched them grow through infancy and childhood. He and his associates have worked with young children more extensively than have other investigators in studying the process of developing intelligence. Some forty years have passed since he reported his first observations of the way in which the growing child adjusts himself to the world in which he lives. The increasing complexity and adaptability of the child's action patterns are dependent not only on growth but also on his opportunities to act on something, and what each child assimilates depends in part on the patterns he already has available. The baby practices everything he learns as he plays in his crib, his bath, or his playpen. From 1922 to 1929 Jean Piaget explored the depth of children's spontaneous ideas about the physical world and their own mental processes. He came upon this line of inquiry while working in Alfred Binet's Laboratory School in Paris, where he went a year after receiving his doctorate in biological science at the University of Neuchâtel. In the course of some routine IQ testing, he became interested in what lay behind the children's answers. To clarify the origins of their answers, he began to interview the children in the open-ended manner he had learned while serving a brief internship at a psychiatric clinic in Zurich. This semi-clinical interview procedure, aimed at revealing the processes by which a child arrives at a particular answer to a test question, has become a trademark of Piagetian research investigation. What he found was that children reason differently from adults and that they have a completely different view of the world.

The second phase of Piaget's investigations began in 1929, when he sought to trace the origins of a child's spontaneous mental growth to the behavior of infants. Some of his most significant observations at that time had to do with what he called the "conservation of the object," using the word "conservation" to convey the idea of permanence. To the older child and the adult, the existence of objects and persons who are not immediately present is taken for granted. On the other hand, to the baby, out of sight is literally out of mind. It is only during the second year of life, when children begin to represent objects mentally, that they seek after toys that have disappeared from view. Only then do they seem to be able to attribute an independent existence to objects that are not present to their senses.

Children are bombarded with constant change. Dr. Piaget's investigations since 1940 have focused upon how the child copes with change, how he comes to distinguish between the permanent and the transient and between appearance and reality. He found that the young child has difficulty in dealing with the results of transformations, whether they are brought about by a change in the object itself or by the child's movement with respect to the object. His methods have to do with testing the child's abilities to learn that a quantity remains the same despite an alteration in its appearance; in other words, *the quantity is conserved.* In a now-classical example, a child is shown two identical drinking glasses filled with equal amounts of juice, and he is asked to say whether there is the same amount to drink in the two glasses. After the child says that this is so, the juice from one glass is poured into a taller, thinner glass so that the juice now reaches a higher level. Then the child is asked to say whether there is the same amount to drink in the two differently shaped glasses. Before the age of six or seven, most children say that the tall, narrow glass has more juice. The young child cannot deal with the transformation and bases his judgment on the static features of the juice, namely, the levels. Age six thinks a tall glass has "more to drink" in it than a squat glass. When he figures otherwise, he is reaching the "age of reason." If the child judges only on the basis of appearance, he cannot solve the problem. When the child is able to deduce that there was the same amount in the two glasses before and that nothing was added or taken away during the pouring, he concludes that both glasses have the same amount of juice— even though this does not appear to be the case. The five-year-old has no concept of the conservation of substance. For the same reason, the child who does not understand the conservation of length will maintain that a belt laid out in a straight line is longer than an identical belt that lies in a circle. The average child has both these concepts by the time he is eight. Piaget devised five conservation tasks covering quantity and length, as discussed above, as well as distance, number, and area.

Another important finding by Piaget has to do with the nature of the elementary school child's reasoning ability. Seven has long been recognized as the "age of reason." It had been assumed that once the child reached this plateau, there were no longer any substantial differences between his reasoning power and that of the adolescent and adult. Piaget discovered that this is not so. While the elementary school child can reason, his reasoning ability is limited in an important regard;

unlike the adult, he can reason only about things and not about verbal propositions. Piaget found that the roots of logic in a small child are in actions, not in words. Young children are able to carry out activities that require thinking without using language. Piaget's early insight was that language often is a misleading indicator of the level of a child's understanding, that there is much logic in children's actions that their verbal formulations do not reveal.

According to Piaget, a child passes through four major periods in a sequence of stages related to age: (1) *Sensori-motor* (birth to two years), when the infant develops patterns for dealing with external objects and events. Toward the end of this period, he begins to indicate things by gesture or word. (2) *Pre-operational* (usually two to seven years), which covers those abilities that have to do with representing things, that is, the acquisition of language, the beginning of symbolic play, the first attempts at drawing, and so on. Actually this is the period of greatest language growth. (3) *Concrete operational* (usually seven to eleven years), when the child acquires internalized actions that permit him to do "in his head" what before he would have had to accomplish through real actions. This is the period he acquires fine motor skills. His ways of thinking begin to get progressively more like those of the adult. (4) *Formal operational* (above eleven years), when the adolescent is able to think about his thoughts and to reason realistically about the future. In each period, there is achievement of new mental skills that determine what can be learned. Piaget believes that the order in which the stages appear holds true for all children, but the ages at which the stages evolve depend on the native endowment of each child and the quality of the physical and social environment in which he is reared. He has said repeatedly, "You cannot teach concepts verbally; you must use a method founded on activity." In short, he also concurs with John Dewey's dictum of learning by doing.

Some of the books resulting from Piaget's investigations are *The Origins of Intelligence in Children, Play, Dreams and*

*Imitation in Childhood* (which deals with the development of the child's representational ability), *The Construction of Reality in the Child,* and *The Child's Conception of Number* —all of which may well be behind the research in infant behavior now current in the United States and abroad. Although *The Language and Thought of the Child* was published in English in 1926, it was not until the early 1950s that Piaget's ideas made any impact in our country. In *Play, Dreams and Imitation in Childhood,* Piaget wrote, "Everything during the first months of life, except feeding and emotions like fear and anger, is play. When the child looks for the sake of looking, handles for the sake of handling, moves his arms and hands, and in the next stage shakes hanging objects and his toys, he is doing actions which are an end in themselves . . . and which do not form . . . actions imposed by someone else or from the outside." It may well be that each child uses every past learning and reproduces new experiences in his play. All child psychologists are not agreed that the development of an abstract idea cannot be influenced by a very careful sequence of experiences, that each of Piaget's four stages of intellectual development is as rigidly fixed as Piaget seems to imply. However, in spite of some premature and erroneous applications of his thinking to education, Jean Piaget has had a more positive than negative effect, and his tests are being used more extensively to evaluate educational outcomes.

A "critical period" philosophy of child development has also been promulgated by *Dr. Bruno Bettelheim,* head of the University of Chicago's orthogenic school for the rehabilitation of disturbed children and also professor of educational psychology in the university's Departments of Education, Psychology, and Psychiatry. In his book *The Empty Fortress,* an exhaustive study of autism in children (a shutting out of the world before two years of age), he points out that children who for various reasons feel they cannot affect their interpersonal or material worlds give up and withdraw emotionally into themselves. Dr. Bettelheim terms eight months a critical period for infants for interpersonal relations with one or two adults and eighteen to twenty-four months a critical period for language development as well as ego and self-image building. He says that "love is not enough" for establishing security in children. They need to feel that they can control the world of things also, and play is one of the best ways for children to manipulate their physical world. Dr. Bettelheim, one of the world's outstanding authorities on childhood emotional development and disorder, was born in Vienna in 1903. He received his first training in psychoanalysis in that city. He came to the United States in 1939 after a year in the concentration camps at Dachau and Buchenwald. His book *The Children of the Dream*, published in 1969, offers a sympathetic appraisal of communal child rearing in an Israeli kibbutz (Hebrew for "group"). Dr. Bettelheim concludes that such a comprehensive environmental approach is considerably more effective in preparing children for school and society than any of the supplemental teaching programs now used in the United States.

*The contributions of toy designers.* Interestingly, pedagogues and researchers are not the only pioneers in play. Play has been considerably advanced by the creativity and skill of designers and craftsmen who have aesthetically structured into playthings many ways of seeing relationships, of making discoveries, and of learning. They provided the wherewithal for children to manipulate and control the fantasy world of early childhood. In recent years designers and craftsmen have worked closely with educators to bring forth toys with unlimited play value and built-in pleasure. Among these are major designers and artists like the late Kay Bojesen of Denmark, Antonio Vitali of Switzerland, and Jarvis Rockwell of the United States, to name a few. Rockwell initially supervised the design of the Holgate line of toys.

*Kay Bojesen*, who was born in Copenhagen in 1886, was the son of a publisher and the founder of the Danish equivalent of *Punch*. The elder Bojesen was full of bright ideas and was reputed to have been one of the biggest jokers of his day. His children grew up in a home where imagination, ingenuity, and humor were encouraged and fostered. It came as no surprise that Kay Bojesen early manifested a creative, fertile imagination. He became a silversmith in 1910, and the stamp of originality in everything he created sprang from his imagination and experience.

Kay Bojesen believed that combining the aesthetic with the practical should be the aim of every designer. "Lines must smile," he said. "The things one releases must have life and warmth; one must enjoy handling them." His interest in woodenware began in 1922, when he made his first toy, which won a prize in a competition at Dansk Arbejde's large exhibition. It was a brightly painted beechwood toy steam roller with an attached seated wood figure with movable arms. Several years went by, however, before he started to try and instill a sense of quality into children through their toys.

In Denmark, kindergartens were the first to back him up and to understand the pedagogical value of his playthings. They are so well made and well designed, so strong and simple that they can stand really rough treatment, and they satisfy a child's need to use his own imagination. Bojesen considered himself the special friend of four- and five-year-olds. He especially responded to children who could imagine that a stick was an airplane or a mottled stone, a brindled cow. In the thirties he made his unpainted beechwood blocks in many shapes and the fine train series that won him much recognition. He created a natural maple double rattle for infants in 1932 and a plump, natural beechwood horse in 1935.

In his toy production, as elsewhere in his work, Bojesen had good collaborators. At one time, architect Ole Wanscher designed excellent toys for him, for example, the amusing bricks in the form of Copenhagen houses and steeples. The painter Laurits Larsen's tug and barges of natural beechwood date from roughly the same period. In 1949 R. Wengler, basketmaker by royal appointment, designed several items that Bojesen produced, for example, a doll's pram of varnished cane with rubber-tired wheels and a doll bed and stool of varnished cane. But by far the greatest number of his many models are Bojesen's own designs, including unpainted and painted wooden toys: the king's guardsmen in gala uniform, the convertible car, the skittles cart, the counting frame, and the Danish farmyard series, all perceived with his lively humor. He considered wood handsomest without paint. Since 1951 a winsome group of jointed animals appeared: a teakwood chimpanzee, an oak and maple bear, an oak elephant, and a jointed teakwood rabbit. (It is interesting to note that Ernest Bojesen, his father, had often amused himself and his children by carving fabulous animals. This may be one reason for the son's deep interest in good wooden toys.)

Kay Bojesen remained a great individualist all his life. In 1953 we went to his retail shop in Copenhagen, where we saw a crowded and fascinating display of his toys, woodenware, silverware, and cutlery. We especially liked his simple, sturdy natural finished hobbyhorse, jointed wood monkey (so much so, that we carried the largest model home under an arm), good, chunky wooden elephant, and colorful parade soldiers. Before going to see Mr. Bojesen, we had explored the largest toy shop in Copenhagen, where we were told: "Bojesen doesn't sell any more; too costly; not realistic enough for adults." "More's the pity," we thought then, and still believe. We had a stimulating chat with the playful, silver-haired, pink-cheeked Kay Bojesen. He said, "A ball is timeless; so is a block and an egg." Bojesen thought that the best play materials are sand, water, and small animals. In 1954 he created a boy and girl doll of natural beechwood with movable arms and heads, a dog of the same material, and a puffin of painted alderwood with a movable head. Kay Bojesen's sense of artistic harmony, his high spirits, and his sound aesthetic judgment live on in his enchanting, sturdy playthings for children and in the designs of toymakers who have copied him profusely.

*Antonio Vitali*, sculptor-toymaker from Zurich, was born in Sondrio, Italy, on the Swiss border in 1909. His father was Italian and his mother, Italian-German Swiss. He studied art in St. Gall, Switzerland (where he became intrigued with woodcarving), and in Paris. He began to create simple, modern wooden toys for his own children, but did not at first consider mass-producing them. For several years he was a designer of modern furniture for a company in Zurich. He began actually to produce toys commercially in 1943, designing handsome, simple wooden animals, people, and jigsaw puzzles. Like Bojesen, Vitali believes that toys should be "things of beauty." To this end, he works tirelessly to attain and maintain high standards of aesthetics and imaginative play use in every toy he produces. Unlike the Bojesen toys, which are machine-turned and then hand-painted, Vitali's playthings are machine-carved out of solid blocks of beautiful hardwoods and then carefully hand-sanded and lacquered or stained in soft colors. Influenced by Swiss hand-carving techniques, Vitali modernized them for commercial purposes by using loose sand-papering machines to finish his playthings. The results are lovely pieces of "abstract sculpture" which parents sometimes forget to give their children. His "mother and father on a string" is a perfect infant toy, as are his wood teether, animal-shaped water toys, sailboat, small transportation vehicles with peg drivers and passengers, family and community play people, and his artfully formed wooden animals. His unbreakable "solid block" natural hardwood doll house furniture is already a toy classic favored in home and school for its beauty and sturdiness.

In the late 1950s one of the authors brought Antonio Vitali to the United States to design a special line of wooden toys for Creative Playthings, for its school and home market. The beautiful, abstract shapes and fine finish of Vitali's "play forms" have had great influence on the design efforts of other toy manufacturers here and abroad. When we saw him at the International Toy Fair in Nuremberg, West Germany, in February of 1972, he told us that he was currently devoting his design efforts to translating into manipulative playthings for preschool children some of the conservation theories of his compatriot Jean Piaget.

Many others have contributed to the design and content of the playthings and play of early childhood. Most of them have been associated with large and small toy manufacturers. Their designs usually are the result of the efforts of various people on design staffs or in production centers. Considerable creativity has come out of the factory of Décor, near Basel in Switzerland, where hand-carvers have taken old folk toys and given them more modern playfulness. Their Noah's Ark, with sculptured Mr. and Mrs. Noah and paired animals, their carved wood doll house with carved play people and furniture, among other items, are beautiful and sturdy playthings. The Décor jigsaw puzzles are so beautifully conceived and hand-painted that few American manufacturers have been able to match them.

In Germany, companies like Dusyma, Lorenz, Baufix, Habermaass, and others produce lovely miniature wooden toys—beads, people, cars, trucks, village sets, parquetry blocks, et cetera. Larger wooden toys made in Germany—trains, trucks, cars, horse-drawn carriages, dolls, doll houses, and so on—reflect the here-and-now of European life and have made a substantial contribution to the preschool play life of children in European homes and kindergartens. More recently East Germany has contributed exciting toys made of molded plywood which are setting new design standards. Froebelhaus, a commercial company in East Berlin, is producing large, heavy wooden trucks, planes, trains, and other play materials that excel many made in the United States.

In Czechoslovakia, old companies like J. Schowanek still produce wood-turned toys with a coloring process unexcelled in all the world.

Brio is the most important educational toy producer and kindergarten supplier in Sweden. No innovative designs have been forthcoming from this source, but the quality of their home and school playthings have made their products acceptable for purchase by toy stores and school suppliers all over Europe and the United States.

In Finland, Jussila, a fine, small company, continues to win design awards for its unpainted, simplified wooden trucks, pull-and-push toys, boats, animals, and trains.

In England, the Educational Supply Association and the James Galt Company produce fine, school-type toys that are an integral part of the equipment of every nursery school and kindergarten there. Independent toy retailers, like Paul and Marjorie Abbatt, in London, designed some of their own play materials. Both the Abbatts also took leadership in international movements to improve the quality and content of playthings and play. One such movement, *Gutes Spielzeug*, initiated in Germany by Lilli Pée of Ulm, has had vast influence on the character and scope of German toys shown each year at the International Toy Show in Nuremberg. Competitions sponsored by the Design Centre of London have greatly affected the aesthetic quality of English toys.

In the United States, several toy companies deserve to be cited for their contributions, including the Playskool Manufacturing Company (now a division of the Milton Bradley Company), Creative Playthings, Incorporated (now a division of the Columbia Broadcasting System), the Fisher-Price Company (now a division of the Quaker Oats Company), and Skaneateles Handicrafters, to mention a few. The Educational Equipment Company (Edco), no longer in existence, in the early 1930s was a prodigious manufacturer and supplier to schools and homes of tested and approved play materials, in addition to carefully chosen toys made by other toy companies. In 1939 Murray Shapiro, its owner and operator, printed a catalogue of one hundred and thirty-six pages which described and illustrated the fine items he offered to nursery schools, kindergartens, the primary grades, camps, and homes. At that time, its offices and showrooms were located in the building that then housed the Harriet Johnson Nursery School and the Bureau of Educational Experiments at 69 Bank Street in New York City. The new ideas developed there were given tangible and practical form in Mr. Shapiro's workshop. His advisory board read like a "Who's Who" of outstanding progressive educators. The board members recommended new items and suggested improvements for equipment already being used. Wrote Mr. Shapiro in his catalogue: "A child wants above all else something he can play with—something he can enjoy. He is superbly indifferent to the fact that this toy will develop his co-ordination or that the other one will build his muscles." Edco further developed and extended Caroline Pratt's building blocks until there were twenty-two different types, all related to one another in size and shape, which were made of splinterless poplar. Among the items of outdoor equipment were the Castle Gym (later called a Fireman's Gym), climbing and portable ladders, hollow building blocks and play boards, slides, kegs, walking boards and sawhorses, a ladder box, push truck, wagons, wheelbarrows, and sandboxes. The company also made tables and chairs which were child-sized, as well as rest cots, block cabinets, and toy cubbies. There were sturdy toys for infants, toddlers, kindergartners, and first-graders. Edco's all-wood doll carriage was sturdy enough to hold the child who wished to play the baby. Edco manufactured jigsaw puzzles cut in seven to fourteen pieces for children two to five years of age. Reviewing this 1939 catalogue in 1972 was quite a jolt to us because it revealed the shocking advance in the cost of educational toys and equipment and how few new designs in school play materials and equipment have been introduced since that time.

With regard to the Playskool Manufacturing Company, it was officially founded in 1938 by Robert J. Meythaler and Manuel J. Fink, who as early as 1928 saw possibilities in educational playthings as opposed to small-scale toy copies of the adult world. Mr. Meythaler was an insurance accountant whose hobby was woodworking. Mr. Fink was a department store buyer. Bob Meythaler created many of the first original wooden Playskool preschool educational toys in his basement workshop. In those days few toy shops would make place on their shelves for the abstract, shape-fitting toys and toddler-geared push-and-pull toys of this pioneering company. It took years of patient cajoling and hard selling to get retailer support for "educational toys." Playskool offered the toy market thirty-five toys in 1938; today its line comprises some three hundred toys, twenty-two of which are from the original line. World War II decimated the metal toy industry in the United States, and the wooden toys of companies like Holgate, Playskool, Fisher-Price, and Childhood Interests were in great demand. For the first time, Americans discovered the play value inherent in a carefully designed and manufactured educational toy. Playskool and Fisher-Price grew tremendously. In time, Playskool acquired such companies as the Appleton Juvenile Furniture Company (makers of musical rockers, pegboard desks, et cetera), the South Bend Toy Manufacturing Company (makers of doll carriages, croquet sets, and recreational sports equipment), the Halsam Products Company, Holgate, et cetera. In 1959 Playskool purchased the Holgate Company, adopting many of its best designs. The Holgate Brothers Company erected its first woodworking factory in 1789, but it was not until about 1929 that it began to make wooden educational toys for preschool children. At that time, the daughter of the treasurer of the company married Lawrence K. Frank, one of the leaders of the movement in the 1920s to establish child study institutes in the United States, and both convinced her father to start Holgate on the manufacture of educational play materials. Its 1930 catalogue offered Little Craftsman blocks, Holgate blocks, Junior blocks, Jerry blocks (with which children could form railroad cars), Holgate bricks (for forming houses), and a peg porcupine. When Jarvis W. Rockwell joined Holgate in March of 1931, he added nested blocks, color cubes, pegboards, beads, the stacking cone, counting frame, hammer toy (later called Bingo Bed), rolly toys, Noah's Arks, cutout animals, dramatic play figures, log cabin sets, bungalow blocks, and a fishing game with wooden fish. When Playskool acquired Holgate, Mr. Rockwell became director of Playskool's design staff. He had become a toy designer almost by chance. While he was in the investment banking business, he designed educational toys as a hobby. He showed some of his toys to buyers for Macy's in New York City, who referred him to Holgate in 1930 when they were seeking a toy designer. Mr. Rockwell's first commercially successful toy was a simple pegboard with pegs and wheels which converted it into a pull toy. He also put holes in a wood box into which small blocks of various shapes could be dropped and turned the box into a small house, the House That Jack Built. Said Mr. Rockwell: "You can't make the educational toy perfect. You've got to leave something for the child's imagination to work."

Playskool has been producing Lincoln Logs for many years. This now-classic wood construction toy was created and named by John Lloyd Wright, son of America's late, innovative architect. Some of Playskool's toys that remain popular with today's young children include the postal station, Nok-Out bench, Caterpillar pull toy, puzzle plaques, pegboards, Rattle Push, Color Stack, Col-O-Rol Wagon, pounding bench, parquetry blocks, hammer-nail set, and lacing boot. Unfortunately, Playskool sometimes features comic-character art work in their playthings in order to catch the fancy of the buying adult. In the main, however, the company has served the play needs of small children well. In 1968 the Milton Bradley Company purchased Playskool.

Fisher-Price Toys of East Aurora, New York, was founded in 1930. It has made a real contribution with its line of inexpensive, action-and-sound, lithographed paper-on-wood push-and-pull toys for toddlers and, more recently, with its "community worker" settings. Their appealing toys roll along making funny noises or musical sounds, accompanied by amusing, erratic motions. Fisher-Price also uses comic-character art work to beguile adult toy buyers, which tends to dampen the enthusiasm of nursery schools. However, children and their parents love the humor and playfulness of the toys and buy them in tremendous quantities. Favorites continue to be Snoopy Sniffer (a low-slung dog pull toy), the Quacky Duck Family, et cetera. All heighten a young child's color sense and help sharpen his sound perception. Only in the late 1960s has Fisher-Price begun to incorporate community activity play in some of its products—its barn, firehouse, and doll house, for instance, replete with family figures, at prices even families with limited incomes can afford. Only when this company met the real demand for educational toys at a proper price did their volume of business double.

Skaneateles Handicrafters, a very small company in upstate New York, is distinguished for its superior designing and ongoing maintenance of high quality. Although the company makes only a miniature wood train and track set (including switch tracks, signals, bridges, and other related accessories) out of natural-finish, smoothly sanded, hard rock maple, its beauty, sturdiness, and playfulness have made it a household toy name with countless small children and adults alike. The founder of Skaneateles Handicrafters, Marshall Larabee, recognized that no mechanical or electric train could give the very young child the same sense of power and delight that he experiences while *pushing* a train on a track. Mr. Larabee's original toy idea has been extensively copied in wood and plastic here and abroad, but no one can truly compete with his excellence. Since its introduction in the early 1940s, Skaneateles has never compromised on quality. It is one of the few toy companies that has continued a fair price level throughout the ups and downs of the inflationary 1960s and early 1970s.

Some other companies have designed and manufactured toys solely to meet the play and learning requirements of children at home and in school. Throughout its phenomenal growth, Creative Playthings has maintained the fine sense of abstraction, quality, aesthetics, and playability that count. It has contributed new designs in toys for infants, furniture for school and home use, innovative sculptured playground equipment in concrete, steel, and wood, as well as beautiful, sturdy playthings. It has embodied in a special line of learning materials a sense of understanding and appreciation for mathematics, science, art and design, et cetera, which has won the accolades of school authorities everywhere. Creative Playthings, which had its modest beginnings as a tiny educational toy shop at 102 West Ninety-fifth Street in New York City, was established by the authors in 1944. With a five-hundred-dollar investment in building-block lumber, Frank Caplan cut and hand-sanded Caroline Pratt unit building blocks in the rear of the shop while customers waited good-naturedly out in front. Soon auxiliary materials for block play were added: trucks, cars, planes, trains, and play people and animals to provide a total block play environment. Aided especially by the sales efforts of Theresa Caplan and the unsolicited publicity of the newspaper *PM* (now defunct) and other publications that delighted in discovering the unique toy shop with its sincere play and education philosophy, the numbers of its customers grew, as did the variety of its play materials.

As the result of a chance encounter at a New York toy fair, where one of the authors had an exhibit of educational toys, a loose association of co-operation was formed by Frank Caplan and Bernard M. Barenholtz, who at that time was operating a toy shop with his wife Edith in Clayton, Missouri. Common catalogues were produced for both shops. In 1950 Caplan and Barenholtz left the retail toy field to specialize in the custom manufacturing of play materials and equipment for schools and other educational institutions. Within ten years, Creative Playthings, Incorporated, offered preschools and kindergartens some eight hundred items of educational toys and equipment. The company popularized through the four million catalogues it sent yearly to parents the concept of play and good toys.

In July of 1966 the Columbia Broadcasting System purchased Creative Playthings as part of its move to enter the education industry. After two years with CBS, Frank Caplan left to start pioneering designing once again in a new company he formed, Edcom Systems, Incorporated, of Princeton, New Jersey. Edcom has been researching and designing, among other things, an "ages and stages" line of toys for infants and toddlers as well as innovative sleep-and-play cribs and corrals.

The field of good toys has also been advanced by the Society of Brothers at Rifton, New York which, under the trade name of Community Playthings, produces school-type toys of such high quality that few can compete with them in the United States and England. The Childcraft Equipment Corporation of New York City not only makes sturdy playthings for school and home use, but scouts the markets of Europe for good design toys for its popular parent catalogues.

The play life of every child requires four-way communication and co-operation between the educator, child psychologist, industrial designer, and toy manufacturer. The pedagogues set guidelines for play and learning, spelling out directions and needs. The psychologists test and evaluate the ego-building and learning power of play materials and play. The designers bring aesthetics, usefulness, and fun to the final prototypes. Ideally, manufacturers incorporate high quality and safety in all their toys, maintain fair prices, and keep communication flowing between their ideas and products and the ultimate consumer market.

# Projecting the
# Future of Play

*Play at home and nursery education will expand.* Attitudes toward play in the United States are already changing. The parents of today's preschool children are indicating greater appreciation of the power of play and are beginning to rear their children in ways that were not understood by older generations. Because young adults are learning to play themselves, they can encourage their children's play and fantasy naturally and intervene sensitively. We believe we can look to more provisions for children's play in the next decades—a vast increase in the nursery school movement, reducing the age level of participation in the preschool to two years, and improving the playroom in the home. With the demands of the Women's Liberation Movement for more freedom for women and mothers, many of whom wish to practice in their professional fields, there will be more day-care centers attached to factories, offices, schools, and even hospitals—wherever mothers work. More lay people will be given paraprofessional training as day-care workers serving the needs of infants and toddlers alike. New multiple housing, whether public or private, will make provision for play centers for preschool children on roofs or in basements.

*An infant education system will be initiated in the United*

*States*. We believe that education will begin with the newborn. Efforts will be undertaken to train mothers and paraprofessionals in techniques for stimulating infants in the home. There will be developed a detailed program for mothers to follow and play and learning materials will be developed that take advantage of the sensitive maturation periods in the first three years of life. Mothers of exceptional or disadvantaged infants will be paid adequate sums to take the semiprofessional training. More toymakers will research and develop an extensive sequence of "ages and stages" play materials that will build meaningful interaction between infants and parents. There will be visual and perceptual kits, oral stimulation units, crawling, standing, and walking equipment, verbal interaction play kits, and so on. Each will have information on pertinent child developmental ages and stages of growth. The federal government will not only set safety standards for infants' (and other) toys, but on their cognitive values as well. Pediatricians will take a more active role in educating new parents in crib play enrichment programs.

A *revolution will take place in early primary education.* We believe that the same factors that motivate intense learning in preschool play situations will be transferred to the environment and curriculums of grades one to six in the elementary school. Self-choice will be introduced and rigid state-imposed curriculums will be set aside. Classrooms will be doubled in size by taking down walls between two of the same or differing age groups. Classrooms of the future will become organized much like today's preschool centers, with self-discovery corners for experimenting or playing with mathematical and science materials, quiet reading corners, theater stages, music and art areas, and so on. The materials and equipment, not the teacher, will serve as the stimulation for exploring. The teacher will extend the learning by intervening with information or specific help as needed. Relations between child, peers, and teacher will be completely informal. It may be that new centers of primary education in the United States will be patterned after the open prepared learning environment now in operation in British infant schools.

*Playthings will improve in content and safety.* The imposition of safety standards by the government and the industry will drive out those toy manufacturers and toy importers who will not abide by minimum quality and safety standards. This should lessen the excessive search for low-cost labor overseas on the part of American toymakers and bring back concentration on new design and high standards in this country as a competitive alternative. We believe there will be dramatic improvement in the content and quality of our children's playthings. With the take-over of smaller toy companies by large food processors (Quaker Oats, General Foods, General Mills, and so forth) there should be more money for long-term research and design.

*We can look forward to more research on play.* There has been general neglect of play as a subject for research or study. Scientists seem to have difficulty taking the subject of play seriously. While some biologists, anthropologists, and psychologists have studied play, in all cases it has been concerned with animals. While some funds have been available to study the therapeutic aspects of play or recreation as a healthful activity for humans, little if any funds have been on hand to study the cognitive aspect of play, the proper balance between structured and spontaneous play, or what constitutes a responsive play environment for each age level. As more understanding of play as a powerful learning tool develops, there will be more government funds appropriated for delineating the processes of play in which academic learning results. We believe that in the years ahead play will be given the recognition now given to education.

*The power of play will attain the consideration and support it should have.* Look to UNICEF to tackle the problem of play in the underdeveloped nations. Look to an increase in museums of play and fantasy. Look to the appearance of a magazine on the subject of play. Look to the explosion of play power in all walks of life in the United States and elsewhere!

# *Appendix*

*What does a toy mean to me?*

In an artists' competition sponsored jointly by the London Institute of Contemporary Arts and the Welsh Arts Council in 1969, participants were asked to create a toy and define what a toy and play means to them. So many interesting definitions were offered that we have digested the best of them in order to share them with our readers. We are indebted to all concerned with the competition and the publishers of *Play Orbit*, a fascinating book published in 1969 by Studio International of New York and London. The quotations that follow are from that book:

> *"Play is the imposition of the imagination on the fabric of the real world; and can be achieved in terms of activity and manipulation of object and people or through imaginary solutions which can be shared with others."*

> "A toy is an escape to another reality!" *Anthea Alley*

> "Toys are part of playing. Playing involves the creative or fanciful participation in isolated real-life processes or skills without regard to scale, time, place, or consequence . . ." *Kenneth Armitage*

> ". . . Toys are useless except to the imagination. To children, play is natural, stimulating their curiosity and sense of adventure . . ." *Lise Bayer*

> ". . . Playing seems to be both disinterested and passionate at the same time; disinterested in that it is not for real, and passionate in the absorption it requires . . . A good toy must balance the toy-maker's inventiveness against the player's inventiveness. If a toy is too well defined by its maker, it becomes inflexible to play with and consequently boring. If, on the other hand, it is too

loosely defined, it will fail to provide the stimulus necessary to make it worth playing with . . ." *Oliver Bevan*

". . . The real quality that makes a toy a toy is an unreal one, and is derived from the quality of play itself. All toys . . . become 'make-believe' objects as soon as they are picked off the shelf . . ." *Tony Bindloss*

"Toys may extend a child in terms of his sensuous experiences, manipulative and tactile skills, sociability and communicativeness, fantasies, logical and deductive abilities. Toys should have a 'resistance' quality in the sense that they pull the player along—gradually extending his inventive powers . . . Where necessary, they should provide avenues of escape from the pressures of imposed adult values and structures—there should always be the opportunity to create private and unique environments . . ." *Michael Bull*

"A toy is a situation which enables the participator/ operator to grasp hold of a mental/physical state, which makes him larger than life." *Ron Dutton*

"My interpretation of the toy is not necessarily anything you can touch. When I was a child, my greatest treat was to look at a glass cabinet with fascinating snuff boxes, fans, coins, etc. The game was to conjure up the people who had used the snuff boxes, waved the fans, or clinked the coins. So they became real toys to me . . ." *H. Eastwood*

"Anything is a toy if I choose to describe what I am doing with it as play . . ." *Garth Evans*

"Object plus attitude equals toy." *Tom Frame*

"The toy is a screen on which a child's imagination is projected. It is a basic element in the development by the child of meaningful relations with people . . ." *Jacqueline Garratt*

"The particular aspects of 'Toy' that interest me are:
1. The parallel reality (action or decision without consequence=escape value).

2. The imitation of the real=a change of time scale.
3. Involvement value=thought provoker: decision-making stimulant: manipulation value: excitement value . . ." *Roy Grayson*

"A toy to me is a physical projection of my own fantasies about other people . . ." *David Grice*

"A toy is an enjoyable means of extending one's knowledge and experience of the world . . ." *James and Joanne Griffiths*

"A toy can be an object which the child utilizes for the extension of his or her own inventiveness/imagination/ pleasure." *Michael Harvey*

"A toy is a 'pretend' object—it imitates a real thing in the adult world and allows the inexperienced and the vulnerable to explore the idea of, and feeling of things— painlessly—without risk—without danger—and without responsibility . . ." *Dennis Hawkins*

"A toy is something to play with.
A toy is usually for a child.
A toy is often given by an adult to a child.
A toy is thus often the expression of adult fantasy, rather than the child's . . ." *Adrian Henri*

"I attempted to make a toy as open ended as a pile of bricks, where the stimulation that one gets is of a personal nature, because the experience depends on what you bring to the toy and in this way this object can have a thousand possibilities . . ." *John Jackson*

"A toy amuses, but a more interesting possibility is that you muse over a toy . . . Toys are to trigger *dreams*. Children move easily into a world of their own where string becomes snakes and rivers, a box a rocket to the moon . . ." *Liliane Lijn*

"A toy is itself unaffected by time and often appreciates hard use. It is quite willing to serve any master regardless of age, colour or creed . . ." *Jeffrey Lloyd*

"Play is the investigation, the involvement of externals in one's fantasy life. Toys must be ambiguous, thus becoming satisfying only if they can be involved in many games or fantasies . . ." *Mike Moore*

"It is not possible to say what a toy is, as positively distinct from a real thing. There is a constant merging between toyness and realness . . ." *Victor Newsome*

"A true toy extends the participator from within. If its usage is rigidly dictated, the evolution of the personality is stunted, but if through play one can select what is essential for the moment, then creative growth and self-knowledge can follow . . ." *John Phillips*

"A toy is a highly translatable object requiring participation . . ." *Michael Punt*

"An object designed to nourish a child's fantasy . . ." *John Reynolds*

"Toys seem to fall into many categories, those that are puzzles, those with which the child can imitate adults, . . . and those which are companions into the child's world of fantasy . . . the companion toy asks no questions; it wants what the owner wants . . ." *Gillian Southgate*

# Bibliography

ASSOCIATION FOR CHILDHOOD EDUCATION INTERNATIONAL: *Children and Oral Language*. Washington, D.C.: Association for Supervision and Curriculum Development, International Reading Association, and National Council of Teachers of English, 1964.

AXLINE, VIRGINIA MAE: *Play Therapy: The Inner Dynamics of Childhood*. Boston: Houghton Mifflin Company, 1947.

BETTELHEIM, BRUNO: *Love Is Not Enough: The Treatment of Emotionally Disturbed Children*. New York: The Free Press, 1950.

————: *The Children of the Dream*. New York: The Macmillan Company, 1969.

BLAND, JANE COOPER: *Art of the Young Child: 3 to 5 Years*. New York: The Museum of Modern Art, 1957.

BLOOM, BENJAMIN S.: *Stability and Change in Human Characteristics*. New York: John Wiley & Sons, 1964.

BOSTON CHILDREN'S MEDICAL CENTER AND ELIZABETH M. GREGG: *What to Do When "There's Nothing to Do."* New York: Delacorte Press, 1968.

BRAZELTON, T. BERRY: *Infants and Mothers: Differences in Development*. New York: Delacorte Press, 1970.

BRILL, ALICE C., AND MAY PARDEE YOUTZ: *Your Child and His Parents: A Textbook for Child Study Groups*. New York: D. Appleton & Company, 1932.

BRUNER, JEROME S., AND ROSE R. OLIVER, ET AL.: *Studies in Cognitive Growth*. New York: John Wiley & Sons, 1966.

CARLSON, BERNICE WELLS, AND DAVID R. GINGLEND: *Play Activities for the Retarded Child*. New York: Abingdon Press, 1961.

CHAUNCEY, HENRY, EDITOR: *Soviet Preschool Education*. New York: Holt, Rinehart and Winston, 1969.

CHESS, STELLA, ALEXANDER THOMAS, AND HERBERG G. BIRCH: *Your Child Is a Person: A Psychological Approach to Parenthood*

*Without Guilt.* New York: The Viking Press, 1965.

COMMITTEE OF THE ASSOCIATION FOR SUPERVISION AND CURRICULUM DEVELOPMENT: *The Three R's in the Elementary School.* Washington, D.C.: National Education Association, 1952.

CRUICKSHANK, WILLIAM M.: *The Brain-Injured Child in Home, School and Community.* Syracuse, N.Y.: Syracuse University Press, 1967.

DEANS, EDWINA: *Arithmetic—Children Use It!* Washington, D.C.: Association for Childhood Educational International, 1954.

DE GRAZIA, ALFRED, AND DAVID A. SOHN, EDITORS: *Revolution in Teaching: New Theory, Technology, and Curricula.* New York: Bantam Books, 1964.

DEWEY, JOHN: *Democracy and Education.* New York: The Macmillan Company, 1916.

————: *My Pedagogic Creed.* Washington, D.C.: The Progressive Education Association, 1929.

DONOVAN, FRANK R.: *Raising Your Children: What Behavioral Scientists Have Discovered.* New York: Thomas Y. Crowell Company, 1968.

EGG, DR. MARIA: *Educating the Child Who Is Different.* New York: The John Day Company, 1968.

ERIKSON, ERIK H.: *Childhood and Society.* New York: W. W. Norton & Company, 1950.

FISHER, DOROTHY CANFIELD: *A Montessori Mother.* New York: Henry Holt & Company, 1912.

FRANK, LAWRENCE K.: "Play Is Valid," in *Childhood Education* magazine, March 1968.

FRANK, MARY AND LAWRENCE: *How to Help Your Child in School.* New York: The Viking Press, 1950.

FRENCH, EDWARD L., AND J. CLIFFORD SCOTT: *How You Can Help Your Retarded Child: A Manual for Parents.* Philadelphia: J. B. Lippincott Company, 1960.

FROEBEL, FRIEDRICH: *Education of Man* (translated by W. N. Hailmann). London: D. Appleton & Company, 1906.

GARRISON, CHARLOTTE G.: *Permanent Play Materials for Young Children.* New York: Charles Scribner's Sons, 1926.

GESELL, ARNOLD, AND FRANCES L. ILG: *Infant and Child in the Culture of Today.* New York: Harper & Brothers, 1943.

————: *The Child from Five to Ten.* New York: Harper & Brothers, 1946.

GESELL, ARNOLD, HENRY M. HALVERSON, HELEN THOMPSON, ET AL.: *The First Five Years of Life: A Guide to the Study of the Preschool Child.* New York: Harper & Brothers, 1940.

GORDON, IRA J.: *Baby Learning Through Baby Play: A Parent's Guide for the First Two Years.* New York: St. Martin's Press, 1970.

GROOS, KARL: *The Play of Man* (translated by E. L. Baldwin). New York: D. Appleton & Company, 1901.

GROVES, ERNEST R., AND PHYLLIS BLANCHARD: *Introduction to Mental Hygiene.* New York: Henry Holt & Company, 1930.

HARTLEY, RUTH E., LAWRENCE K. FRANK, AND ROBERT M. GOLDENSON: *Understanding Children's Play.* New York: Columbia University Press, 1952.

————: *New Play Experiences for Children: Planned Play Groups, Miniature Life Toys, and Puppets.* New York: Columbia University Press, 1952.

HARTLEY, RUTH E., AND ROBERT M. GOLDENSON: *The Complete Book of Children's Play.* New York: Thomas Y. Crowell Company, 1963.

HECHINGER, FRED M., EDITOR: *Pre-School Education Today: New Approaches to Teaching Three-, Four-, and Five-Year-Olds.* Garden City, N.Y.: Doubleday & Company, 1966.

HOFFMAN, MARTIN L., AND LOIS W. HOFFMAN, EDITORS: *Review of Child Development Research,* Vol. I. New York: Russell Sage Foundation, 1964.

HOOVER, F. LOUIS: *Art Activities for the Very Young: From 3 to 6 Years.* Worcester, Mass.: L. Davis Publications, 1961.

HUIZINGA, JOHAN: *Homo Ludens: A Study of the Play-Element in Culture.* Boston: The Beacon Press, 1964.

HYMES, JAMES L., JR.: *The Child Under Six.* Washington, D.C.: Educational Services, 1961.

ISAACS, SUSAN: *Intellectual Growth in Young Children.* New York: Harcourt, Brace & Company, 1930.

————: *The Nursery Years.* New York: The Vanguard Press, 1936.

JACKSON, LYDIA, AND KATHLEEN M. TODD: *Child Treatment and the Therapy of Play.* London: Methuen & Company, 1948.

JAMES, WILLIAM: *Talks to Teachers on Psychology: And to Students on Some of Life's Ideals.* New York: Henry Holt & Company, 1915.

JERSILD, ARTHUR T.: *Child Psychology.* Englewood Cliffs, N.J.: Prentice-Hall, 1965.

JOHNSON, GEORGE ELLSWORTH: *Education by Plays and Games.* Boston: Ginn & Company, 1907.

KAWIN, ETHEL: *The Wise Choice of Toys.* Chicago: University of Chicago Press, 1934.

KILPATRICK, WILLIAM HEARD: *A Reconstructed Theory of the Educative Process.* New York: Bureau of Publications, Teachers College, Columbia University, 1935.

——: *Source Book in the Philosophy of Education.* New York: The Macmillan Company, 1936.

KIRKPATRICK, EDWIN A.: *Fundamentals of Child Study.* New York: The Macmillan Company, 1904.

LAMBERT, CLARA: *Play: A Yardstick of Growth.* New York: Summer Play Schools Association, 1938.

LANDECK, BEATRICE: *Children and Music.* New York: William Sloane Associates, 1952.

LANGDON, GRACE: *Your Child's Play.* Chicago: The National Society for Crippled Children and Adults, 1957.

LEE, JOSEPH: *Play in Education.* New York: The Macmillan Company, 1919.

LOWENFELD, MARGARET: *Play in Childhood.* New York: John Wiley & Sons, 1967.

MACKENZIE, CATHERINE: *Parent and Child.* New York: William Sloane Associates, 1949.

MATTERSON, ELIZABETH M.: *Play and Playthings for the Preschool Child.* Baltimore: Penguin Books, 1967.

MEAD, MARGARET, AND KEN HEYMAN: *Family.* New York: The Macmillan Company, 1965.

MONTESSORI, MARIA: *Dr. Montessori's Own Handbook.* New York: Schocken Books, 1965.

——: *The Montessori Method.* New York: Frederick A. Stokes Company, 1912.

——: *Spontaneous Activity in Education.* Cambridge, Mass.: Robert Bentley, 1965.

MOOKERJEE, AJIT: *Folk Toys of India.* Calcutta: Oxford Book & Stationery Company, 1956.

NEILL, A. S.: *Summerhill: A Radical Approach to Child Rearing.* New York: Hart Publishing Company, 1960.

NEW YORK STATE EDUCATION DEPARTMENT: *Child Development*

*Guides for Teachers of Three-, Four- and Five-Year-Old Children.*
Albany: New York State Education Department, 1957.

PETERSON, HELEN THOMAS: *Kindergarten: The Key to Child
Growth.* New York: Exposition Press, 1958.

PIAGET, JEAN: *Play, Dreams and Imitation in Childhood.* New
York: W. W. Norton & Company, 1962.

———: *The Child's Conception of Number.* London: Routledge
& Kegan Paul, 1952.

———: *The Construction of Reality in the Child.* New York:
Basic Books, 1954.

PRATT, CAROLINE: *I Learn from Children: An Adventure in
Progressive Education.* New York: Simon & Schuster, 1948.

ROBBINS, FLORENCE GREENHOE: *Educational Sociology: A Study
in Child, Youth, School and Community.* New York: Henry Holt &
Company, 1953.

ROWEN, BETTY: *Learning Through Movement.* New York: Bureau
of Publications, Teachers College, Columbia University, 1963.

RUDOLPH, MARGUERITA: *Living and Learning in Nursery School.*
New York: Harper & Brothers, 1954.

RUSSELL, BERTRAND: *Education and the Good Life.* New York:
Boni & Liveright, 1926.

SCHWARZ, BERTHOLD ERIC, AND BARTHOLOMEW A. RUGGIERI:
*Parent-Child Tensions.* Philadelphia: J. B. Lippincott Company,
1958.

SILBER, KATE: *Pestalozzi: The Man and His Work.* London:
Routledge & Kegan Paul, 1960.

STRANG, RUTH: *Helping Your Gifted Child.* New York: E. P.
Dutton & Company, 1960.

STRICKLAND, RUTH G.: *The Language Arts in the Elementary
School.* Boston: D. C. Heath & Company, 1951.

WALSH, JAMES J., AND JOHN A. FOOTE: *Safeguarding Children's
Nerves: A Handbook of Mental Hygiene.* Philadelphia: J. B.
Lippincott Company, 1924.

WANN, KENNETH D., MIRIAM S. DORN, AND ELIZABETH A. LIDDLE:
*Fostering Intellectual Development in Young Children.* New
York: Bureau of Publications, Teachers College, Columbia University, 1962.

WINN, MARIE, AND MARY ANN PORCHER: *The Playgroup Book.*
New York: The Macmillan Company, 1967.

# Index